Virtually Embedded:
The Librarian in an Online Environment

Edited by
Elizabeth Leonard
and Erin McCaffrey

Association of College and Research Libraries
A division of the American Library Association
Chicago, 2014

The paper used in this publication meets the minimum requirements of American National Standard for Information Sciences–Permanence of Paper for Printed Library Materials, ANSI Z39.48-1992. ∞

Library of Congress Cataloging-in-Publication Data

Virtually embedded : the librarian in an online environment / edited by Elizabeth Leonard and Erin McCaffrey.
   pages cm
Includes bibliographical references.
 ISBN 978-0-8389-8684-4 (pbk. : alk. paper) 1. Academic libraries--Relations with faculty and curriculum. 2. Academic librarians--Effect of technological innovations on. 3. Libraries and distance education. 4. Electronic reference services (Libraries) 5. Information literacy--Web-based instruction. I. Leonard, Elizabeth, 1971- editor of compilation. II. McCaffrey, Erin, editor of compilation.
 Z675.U5V465 2014
 025.1'977--dc23
               2013050001

Printed in the United States of America.

18 17 16 15 14   1 2 3 4 5

Table of Contents

part four: embedded in the bigger picture—scaling online embedded librarianship

Foreword

David Shumaker

Judging by the cover of this book, you might think that it's about embedded librarianship. But, as the old saying admonishes us, "Don't judge a book by its cover." For, in fact, this book is about something much bigger than embedded librarianship. It's about educating the next generation of students for success as professionals and citizens in the 21st century.

That may sound like a grandiose claim, but there are two reasons why I believe it to be true. The first is that we are living in a period of accelerating technological and social change. The second is that traditional higher education is being dramatically reshaped by the same forces—especially technological ones—that are transforming our entire society before our eyes.

Change is the only constant. We are educating students for jobs that don't yet exist and for a society that we cannot imagine. In this situation, we have rightly identified "learning how to learn" as a critical skill. Our students—our future citizens and leaders—cannot possibly enter adulthood with all the information and knowledge they will need. Their lives, if they are to be successful, will require the continual mastery of new information and knowledge.

Another name for "learning how to learn" is "information literacy." And who better to teach this skill than we librarians, specialists in information and knowledge. Yet, if we are to grasp this opportunity, we must do two things especially.

The first is to embrace the full meaning of information literacy. Information literacy is more than avoiding plagiarism. It's more than using the right keywords to formulate a search. It's more than properly formatting bibliographic references. The Association of College and Research Libraries has it right: It's the full range of skills—

recognizing a need for information, acquiring it, evaluating it critically, incorporating it into one's thinking, using it effectively for one's purpose, and adhering to legal and ethical imperatives while doing so. Our job is to help students master these skills.

That brings us to the second thing we need to do to grasp the opportunity awaiting us. That is to redefine our relationship to the institutions in which we work. For too long, many librarians have remained isolated within their libraries, more or less oblivious to the institutional life swirling around them. They were able to do that, more or less successfully, because students and faculty had to come to us when they needed information. Now, of course, we've put the information within reach of our faculty and students' fingers and thumbs, wherever they are. Our role has shifted dramatically away from "reference" and toward instruction. As we gain experience and sophistication, we're learning that our lessons are best taught in context. That is, we need to become embedded in the mainstream instructional work of our institutions, where we can teach information literacy as an integrated element of the academic program.

So the role we envision is that of partners in the educational process, working with faculty who are subject matter experts and taking responsibility for student success in the information-related learning that they need to master their fields of interest.

For the past decade, there has been a growing trend towards embedded librarianship in higher education. Following the 2004 publication of Barbara Dewey's seminal article, "The Embedded Librarian: Strategic Campus Collaborations," librarians have developed partnerships with subject faculty, attended classes, taught class sessions, counseled students, and graded assignments. For many, the results have been gratifying in terms of student success as well as professional satisfaction.

But while we've been busily pursuing this vision, higher education itself has begun to experience fundamental change.

Marc Andreessen, venture capitalist and creator of the first graphical web browser—later known as Netscape, has marked education as ripe for disruption—it's expensive and its effectiveness is disputed. Technology has offered attractive alternatives to traditional education, disrupting centuries of practice. First there was the disruption to the traditional residential college experience posed by all-online programs, followed more recently by the advent of massively open online courses, or MOOCs—a kind of online instruction on steroids.

We don't know where the current ferment in education will lead. What we do know is that educators—faculty and administrators everywhere—are revisiting the traditions and assumptions of the past. They are making decisions about pilot projects and experiments, ranging from blended learning to all-online courses to MOOCs to competency-based programs that eschew structured courses altogether, in favor of individualized learning that emphasizes evidence of mastery of a body of knowledge—not completion of a certain number of instructional hours and so many tests and term papers.

In the midst of this upheaval, it's clear that librarians cannot and should not stop by integrating our work into the educational process as we find it today. Instead, we must assume the role of partners with administrators and subject faculty in our institutions. Together we must identify better ways to prepare our students for the society they will shape and test the diverse educational innovations that promise to make our instruction more effective. What we know is that regardless of the forms education will take, the ability to practice lifelong learning will be vital, learning how to learn will be a primary goal of education, and, as the information literacy experts in our institutions, our colleagues will need us to contribute our best work to the r/evolution taking place in academia.

That brings us back to this book. The contributors represent some of the best of the innovative programs in our profession. They present a diverse range of approaches to embedded librarianship as it contributes to innovative modes of delivery, including computer-based courseware as a supplement to face-to-face class sessions, blended and fully online courses, and MOOCs. Their experiences and observations can serve as guideposts for all of us as we help chart the way forward for our institutions. Each of them has made an important contribution to our profession, and by compiling this collection, the editors, Elizabeth Leonard and Erin McCaffrey, have given us a vitally important resource.

Introduction

Erin McCaffrey and Elizabeth Leonard

Due to the growing presence of online education courses at both at nonprofit and for-profit institutions of higher learning and the increasing cost of higher education, some suggest that online (or distance) education will eventually become the dominant form of higher learning. The Internet has changed the way academia provides education to its students. Perhaps the most drastic of these changes is the transition to providing higher education in a virtual environment with technology as mediator. Because of the structure of online learning, librarians have greater, and possibly easier, opportunities to provide embedded services to students.

The only constant is change, and librarians must keep up with these trends. This casebook introduces librarians to 12 ways in which academic libraries have embedded themselves virtually in online environments, considering the evolution of the embedded librarian from physical to virtual classrooms and the development and implementation of unique programs both in and out of the classroom as well as how to scale embedded programs.

Part one, "The Evolution of Embedded Librarianship," discusses the development of embedded librarianship and defining characteristics of a virtually embedded librarian. The two chapters in this section examine how the position of an online embedded librarian differs from a physical embedded librarian and address the transition within academic libraries from the distance learning librarian to the virtually embedded librarian. In the first chapter, "Online Embedded Librarians: A Review and Overview," Linda Frederiksen and Sue F. Phelps review the literature and provide an overview of online embedded librarianship's history and development. The transition from distance learning librarian to virtually embedded librarian is presented by Audrey Donaldson and Alyssa M. Valenti in the following chapter, "Embedded Librarians: Evolving and Expanding in Higher Education," in which they examine challenges and considerations for the virtually embedded librarian.

Many libraries are successfully providing virtually embedded programs, and part two, "Developing Programs in the Online Embedded Environment," provides four case studies of embedded librarian projects targeted to students in the online environment. These studies address library instruction, reference, outreach, and collaboration, and they reflect a range of tools and technologies, including learning management systems, LibGuides, instant messaging, blogs, and wikis. Beginning with "Sustainable Embedded Librarianship to Foster Research Skills in an Online Graduate Program," Swapna Kumar, Kristin Heathcock, and Marilyn N. Ochoa describe the design, implementation, and assessment of an embedded librarian project in an online doctoral program. Programs where embedded librarians become a key part of the virtual academic landscape are showcased in Catrina Whited, Bridget A. Powell, and Gail Nicula's "Embedded Librarian in a Military Distance Education Program" and Alison Fields and Philip Clarke's "From the Antipodes: Embedded Librarians at the Open Polytechnic of New Zealand." In the fourth case study, "Web 2.0 Toolkit: A Guide for Virtually Embedded Librarians," Chanitra Bishop and Christina Sheley detail embedding in an online business course and successfully employing Web 2.0 tools in a library research component.

Part three, "Online Embedded Librarians—Outside the Classroom," presents two case studies focused on collaboration with faculty—librarians proactively reaching out to identify institutional allies, creating learning communities for faculty, and partnering in the instructional design process. In "Avoiding Curricular Combat Fatigue: Embedding Librarians in E-learning to Teach the Teacher," Kathleen A. Langan describes librarians using e-learning to "teach the teacher," providing information literacy education to faculty through an embedded teach-the-teacher program. Alex Mudd, Terri Pedersen Summey, and Matt Upson outline models for instructional design and describe the role of librarians on an instructional design team in "Not Just an Afterthought: Involving Librarians in the Instructional Design Process."

Once virtually embedded programs are established, how do libraries sustain their offerings? Part four, "Embedded in the Bigger Picture—Scaling Online Embedded Librarianship," presents three unique case studies from authors looking to expand virtually embedded library services at their institutions without adding greatly to the workload of their already busy librarians. In "Win-Win: Embedding Future Librarians to Extend Service to Online Classes," Timothy Peters and Julie LaDell-Thomas describe Central Michigan University's Global Campus Library Services' collaboration with San Jose State University School of Library and Information Sciences to embed student librarians to provide library support in selected courses. Next, Amy R. Hofer and Karen Munro, in "Embedding in the LMS: Faculty Evaluation of a Low-Touch Widget," examine use of a library widget as an embedding strategy in Portland State University's learning management system. Lastly, in "Linking to Course-Specific and Subject-Specific LibGuides from Blackboard," Pru Morris and Deirdre R. McDonald show how librarians with help from institutional colleagues can automatically link to LibGuides from their learning management system, enhancing student access to research help.

Finally, in the book's last chapter, "MOOCs: Getting Involved," Elizabeth Leonard and Erin McCaffrey present a review of the literature on MOOCs and academic libraries and the new opportunities MOOCs present for collaboration. While there are still many questions as to how MOOCs will evolve, one certainty is that they are being discussed across all levels within the spectrum of higher education. Will the strategies for virtually embedding in the online environment that are presented here work for academic libraries trying to integrate into MOOCs? We may not be able to answer that question just yet, but academic librarians are exploring new technologies and pedagogies as they consider outreach and service to this massive student population.

We hope the case studies presented here highlight the many different methods by which librarians working in online learning environments have developed successful programs and a library presence to become a key part of the virtual academic landscape.

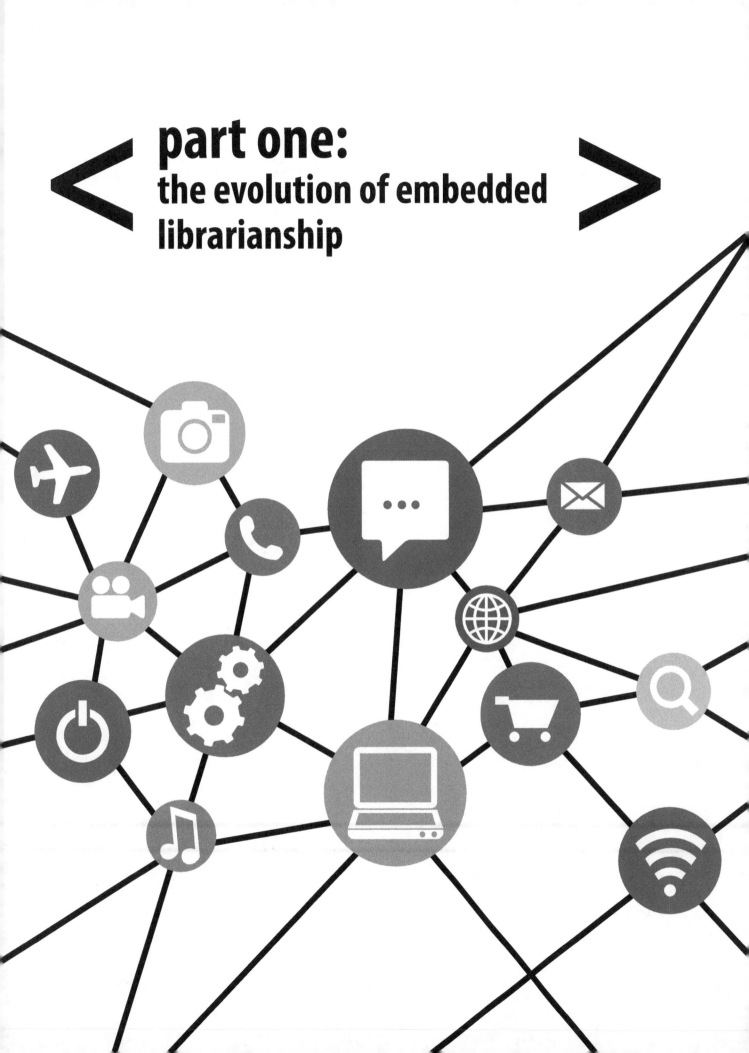

part one:
the evolution of embedded librarianship

Online Embedded Librarians: A Review and Overview

Linda Frederiksen and Sue F. Phelps

The rapid increase of educational offerings available online is a topic of critical importance to institutions of higher education in the United States and abroad. The number of students taking classes via an Internet connection has grown more than four-fold over the past 10 years with nearly seven million students currently taking at least one online course (Allen & Seaman, 2013). These impressive numbers have a significant impact on colleges and universities across the country and around the world as college administrators and faculty strive to put into place classes, courses, and programs that will attract, engage, and retain students in this rapidly growing environment.

Similarly, academic librarians are increasingly entering this landscape. As early as 2003, Shank and Dewald warned that failure to establish a library presence in student- and faculty-occupied virtual spaces would have significant negative consequences. Fortunately, as both the number of online courses and the number of students expanded over the past decade, libraries have found fresh and innovative ways to embed resources and much more into these spaces. What has emerged is a new model of librarianship that encompasses a variety of settings and a wide range of services. For many, being online and embedded is the future of the profession (Edwards, 2011). What that means exactly is less clear. "Online embedded librarianship" is a term that is still evolving.

Lack of consensus on the meaning of the term "online embedded librarianship" is not surprising considering its recent background and develop-

ment. Some information professionals see the roots of online embedded activities in online instruction (Francis, 2012), virtual reference services (Matos, Matsuoka-Motley, & Mayer, 2010), branch libraries (Drewes & Hoffman, 2010), or liaison work (Rudasill, 2010). Others look to the literature of library instruction (Pickens-French & McDonald, 2013) and online learning (DeBonis, Miller, & Pomea, 2013) for its historical beginnings. And, for a large number, online embedded librarianship grew out of both distance education and information literacy movements (Bonnand & Hansen, 2012; Edwards & Black, 2012; Tumbleson & Burke, 2010).

The current understanding of the phrase "online embedded librarianship" diverges slightly from the broader definition of embedding as a comprehensive, overt, and focused integration into the daily life of a primary group (Dewey, 2004). Instead, an online embedded librarian is identified as someone who establishes a library presence in a virtual learning space. Within this definition, the levels, scope, and degree of involvement or engagement by the librarian vary considerably. An ask-a-librarian chat widget in a class guide, for example, may be the level at which a librarian is embedded (Dennie, 2011). For those who participate in an online course by logging into a learning management system (LMS) to co-teach, interact with students, and grade assignments, the degree of integration is much greater (DeBonis et al., 2013). And, while much of current literature related to online embedding concerns itself with course-level integration by librarians in a LMS, proprietary software systems are not the only spaces or places where embedding occurs. All cases included in this review share some degree of "online-ness" that sets them apart from librarians working in face-to-face and in-person environments.

A review of the literature over the past decade illustrates that online embedded librarianship includes what has been called a "cascading array of services" (Hawes, 2011, p.58), ranging from the micro-level insertion of a hyperlink onto a class page or subject guide to macro-level involvement in the design and co-teaching of an entire online course. Similarly, those working in a variety of virtual and digital environments have been characterized as "lurking librarians" (Corinth, 2003), "personal librarians" (Ismail, 2011; Kadavy & Chuppa-Cornell, 2011) and "ebrarians" (Hemming & Montet, 2010), with job titles ranging from Informationist (Konieczny, 2010) to Distance Learning Librarian (Guillot, Stahr, & Meeker, 2010) to Blackboard Librarian (Kvenild & Calkins, 2011). There is some frustration expressed in the literature regarding the term "online embedded librarian;" however, no other term has yet gained wide acceptance (Hoffman, 2011). To provide a manageable overview of the current literature, discussions related to the physical presence of a librarian in an academic department or as part of a research team where face-to-face interactions and in-person activities are the principal models for involvement have been excluded. Likewise, articles that emphasized blended or hybrid librarianship are omitted from this review.

Although a great deal has been written about the topic over the past several years, we were interested in taking a new look at the field as it has developed, looking for patterns and trends as well as identifying emerging best practices. In the course of this review, the authors examined more than 60 relevant articles, three books, one dissertation as well as conference proceedings, blogs, and discussion forums. The majority of the sources reviewed relate to institutions of higher education in the United States; however,

there is also an important body of literature from corporate and health science libraries as well as a number of recent case studies of online embedded librarianship in public and school environments. The authors searched relevant databases for the keyword term "online embedded librar*" and included in this review materials that focus primarily on an online presence.

The sources reviewed are organized under these broad topic areas: current environment, emerging best practices, assessment, and what's ahead.

Current Environment

Over the past decade, new and improved technologies have provided additional opportunities for librarians to engage with students in both synchronous and asynchronous environments. As this has occurred, the work of academic librarians has also shifted in some significant ways.

In 2001, Machovec (2001) asked the question: Where is the library in course management software? Two years later, Shank and Dewald again raised the issue of a library presence in courseware (2003). It was not until 2004, however, that the term "embedded librarian" entered the common vocabulary. Dewey (2004) discussed collaboration and integration in both physical and virtual academic spaces, where a presence in a LMS was only one example of adaptation. By mid-decade, articles on individual projects and initiatives, some in LMS spaces and others not, began to appear in the literature. Although Appleton (2005) discussed embedding in terms of links to electronic textbooks, Drumm and Havens (2005), Hearn (2005), Matthew and Schroeder (2006), and Bozeman and Owens (2008) all described it as a collaboration with faculty that places a librarian in an undergraduate online course space.

Beginning in 2009, as more librarians begin to experiment with a virtual presence in student and research spaces and encounter the challenges that "online-ness" can often bring, the pace of publication in this area increased significantly. Davis and Smith (2009) described a project that positioned two librarian avatars in undergraduate classes taught within the Internet-based virtual world of Second Life. Another initiative placed library school graduate students in online nursing courses (Lillard, Norwood, Wise, Brooks, & Kitts, 2009). At Athens State University, when a librarian was designated as a teaching assistant in a LMS, a full assortment of options for electronically embedded library services opened up, extending from introductory e-mails to monitoring discussion forums (Herring, Burkhardt, & Wolfe, 2009). It was at this point that articles summarizing other efforts and best practices also began to emerge (Kesselman & Watstein, 2009; York & Vance, 2009).

By 2010, the assortment of services offered under the online embedded banner now included development and deployment of web tutorials (Held, 2010; Hemming & Montet, 2010), LibGuides (Daly, 2010), and web conferencing software (Montgomery, 2010). There was also a growing discussion surrounding workload (Edwards & Black, 2010), best practices (Hoffman & Ramin, 2010; Tumbleson & Burke, 2010), and assessment (Edwards, Kumar, & Ochoa, 2010) along with an early citation analysis study (Clark & Chinburg, 2010). At the same time, Hoffman (2011) defined an online embedded librarian specifically as someone who "participates in a particular online course by logging into the course management system (CMS)" (p. 453). Others argued that this was only one incarnation of online embedded librarianship and that it was a mistake to try to label it as the most common or valid form of embedding (Edwards, 2011).

Over the past two years, there has been an increase in the literature on online embedded librarianship. Hawes (2011) discussed a variety of technologies including chat, e-mail, web conferencing, and discussion boards used in multiple online courses over a five-year period at Saint Leo University. In addition to embedding in traditionally high-enrollment undergraduate classes such as English 101 (Kadavy & Chuppa-Cornell, 2011), articles describing the ability to meet students where they were, such as on Facebook (Haycock & Howe, 2011) and Twitter (Filgo, 2011) as well as in graduate-level courses (Bonnard & Hansen, 2012; Ismail, 2011), were published. Kvenild and Calkins' 2011 Association of College and Research Libraries' publication, *Embedded Librarians: Moving Beyond One-Shot Instruction,* provided further examples of the inroads made by librarians into virtual spaces.

During the same period, discourse around embedding took place in schools, corporations, and health sciences environments in the United States and abroad. For example, Midler (2012) and Cordell (2012) reported on different types of technologies used in school environments, including Google Docs, LibGuides, and Skype. Likewise, Shumaker and Talley (2009) reported on successful and less successful models for embedded programs amongst information professionals and customers based on a Special Library Association research study. Shumaker's 2012 publication titled *The Embedded Librarian: Innovative Strategies for Taking Knowledge Where It's Needed,* along with his popular blog—*The Embedded Librarian* (www.embeddedlibrarian. com), explored the development of embedded library and information services in organizations of all types. Similarly, online embedded librarians often provided assistance to students, physicians, and staff in hospital libraries via mobile devices (Kenefick, 2011) as well as through course management systems (Kealey, 2011). Programs and projects in China (Si, Xing, Zhou, & Liu, 2012), England (Robertson, McMurray, Ingram, & Roberts, 2012), and New Zealand (Chisholm & Lamond, 2012) also appeared.

If the expanding number of publications related to online embedded librarianship published within the last two years is any indication, case studies related to various projects, initiatives, and programs will continue to increase in the next several years, describing a wide range of services, technologies, populations, and practices. At the same time, as the sub-field of online embedded librarianship continues to mature, discussion surrounding best practices and assessment will further develop and evolve.

Best Practices

Librarians who have provided online embedded services have also been studied, and researchers have identified best practices in this area. Dewey's (2004) early publication provided one of the first comprehensive definitions of the field, discussed potential venues for embedding, and provided guidelines that have since become part of the best practices literature. Some librarians have written from their own embedded experience (Bozeman & Owens, 2008; Pickens-French & McDonald, 2013; Shell, Crawford, & Harris, 2013; Wright & Williams, 2011) and others have surveyed librarians in multiple library settings (Hoffman, 2011; Sullo, Harrod, Butera, & Gomes, 2012; York & Vance, 2009). The bulk of the recent literature on best practices reviewed here is related to student learning followed by faculty relationships, administrative support, technology, and librarian workflow.

When librarians are added to the LMS "classroom" as teaching assistants, they also gain access to the students and their work. It has been recommended that librarians begin by setting up a discussion board in the LMS, making it available from the first day of class for questions as well as providing contact information for more in-depth consultations (Bozeman & Owens, 2008). Additionally, librarians can proactively contribute to student learning through regularly posting tips (Knight & Loftis, 2012), grading a library assignment (Bozeman & Owens, 2008), writing and administering quizzes (York & Vance, 2009), and tying learning outcomes to the course research assignment (Wright & Williams, 2011). Further, the online embedded librarian can post links to specific resources via the LMS or through e-mail (York & Vance, 2009). It is helpful to plot a course outline of assignment due dates to anticipate

times when students may seek more assistance as well as when to post resources, tutorials, and tips (Hoffman, 2011).

In any instructional setting, advanced preparation and detailed organization is the first step, whether face-to-face or online. Collaboration with teaching faculty is described as essential. In the online environment, librarians should ask the instructor for details about the course assignments and log in to the class before it begins to read the syllabus and get an idea of due dates for assignments (Hoffman, 2011). Likewise, it is best to prepare learning materials in collaboration with the course instructor (Wright & Williams, 2011) and have the instructor introduce the library services to the class, emphasizing the librarian's area of expertise and encouraging the students to ask questions (Sullo et al., 2012). Another best practice is the suggestion that faculty set limits for students in advance so they understand the librarian is there to help them learn to do research, not to do their research for them (Herring et al., 2009). Particular to the environment of the LMS, the librarian should discuss expectations of involvement in advance with the course instructor and make clear the level of access needed in the LMS to fulfill those expectations (Bozeman & Owens, 2008).

Because of the technical nature of an online class it is also recommended that librarians become familiar with the campus LMS (Bozeman & Owens, 2008) and develop a relationship with the instructional designers (Shell et al., 2013) and administrators who support it (York & Vance, 2009). To avoid technical problems when providing synchronous instruction or consultation, web conferencing software should be tested in advance and troubleshooting tips should be posted for students and instructors who will be attending. It is also advisable to have a "Plan B" in place in the event of technology failure. For example, when presenting a slideshow that backs up live, desktop sharing can be used to ensure that instruction time is not wasted if the technology fails (Hoffman, 2011). Leveraging all available technology, whether it is the telephone, Skype, Elluminate Live, or Adobe Connect, to provide services at a distance and adding links to tutorials within the LMS are other best practices (Bonnand & Hansen, 2012; Sullo et al., 2012).

As the literature shows, being embedded in a course requires a time commitment. Often, embedded services begin as the experiment of one librarian and expand as services become popular. For this reason, library administrators need to be aware of potential staffing issues and more than one librarian needs to be onboard before services begin (Bonnand & Hansen, 2012; Hoffman, 2011). Librarians who wish to be embedded in a course are cautioned to be strategic with the course selection for embedding as one can easily become overextended (York & Vance, 2009). Lorenzetti (2012) asserts that "the embedded librarian will be of the most use in courses that are writing-intensive" and "introductory courses in which a good first experience with a librarian can change the way the student views this resource person" (p. 2). Because a single librarian can only be embedded in a limited number of classes at one time, libraries need to consider a variety of ways to reach online students (Bozeman & Owens, 2008). One way to reach out to students is to have a link to the library homepage embedded in the LMS as a matter of procedure (York & Vance, 2009). Another is to have a library-specific course shell that is open to all distance students. This strategy enables students to find all library information in a single location and allows the librarian to post frequently asked questions in a discussion forum. This discussion board can also be marketed with other library services when meeting with students face to face (Hoffman, 2011).

As with any new library service, online embedded librarians need to market the concept to faculty (York & Vance, 2009). Hoffman and Ramin (2010) suggest that a best practice in marketing is to send a concise e-mail to online instructors that explains the services; this e-mail should be sent personally by the librarian who wishes to be embedded in their course. If that librarian is not the instructor's usual contact in the library, it is further suggested that an introductory e-mail be sent from the subject liaison to introduce the new service in advance.

Since higher education institutions and the libraries that support them vary widely, the development of online embedded librarianship programs have also evolved to meet specific needs rather than a prescribed set of standards or criteria. Implementation of these activities and programs depends on a range of factors such as organizational environment, available technology and staffing, and budget. At the same time, librarians interested in becoming embedded must look to best practices to assist in planning, implementation, delivery, outreach, and assessment of their own projects.

Fortunately, a growing body of best practice literature offers some general characteristics of successful online embedded library programs:

a. Be proactive (Knight & Loftis, 2012).
b. Collaborate and partner with faculty and other campus departments (Hoffman & Ramin, 2010).
c. Set clear expectations and guidelines for students in terms of assignments, communication and feedback, and evaluation (Hawes, 2011; Hoffman & Ramin, 2010; Konieczny, 2010).
d. Develop technical and instructional design skills needed to create a quality online learning experience for students (Bonnand & Hansen, 2012; Pickens-French & McDonald, 2013).
e. Offer a variety of authentic learning activities (DeBonis et al., 2013), using different types of tools (Herring et al., 2009).
f. Reduce or recycle or reuse learning objects and tools (Kvenild, 2012).
g. Consider workload, budget, and sustainability (Tumbleson & Burke, 2010).
h. Market the service (York & Vance, 2009).
i. Build in assessment (Edwards, 2011; Edwards, Kumar & Ochoa, 2010).

Assessment

In a recent review of online embedded librarianship, one author observed that "Very few quality research studies using the conceptual phrase 'embedded librarian' exist" (Schulte, 2012, p. 128). Similar to other forms of academic evaluation, librarians seek to assess the needs and preferences of their patrons, the effectiveness of their services, and the impact on student learning as a result of bibliographic instruction. Evidence-based decision making by administration depends on program assessment as well. Because online embedding is a relatively new area of librarianship, the professional literature currently contains more component-based assessments than larger program or conceptual evaluations.

Student Satisfaction

When the library offers a new service, it is important to know how the service has been received by the intended audience. A fairly simple way that online embedded librarians have assessed student satisfaction in the past has been to add questions about library services to the course evaluations routinely administered at the conclusion of most college courses. In other cases, librarians have administered their own end-of-course evaluation survey. These surveys generally have asked if students used the resources provided, if tutorials were helpful, and about student perception of librarian presence. Very practical questions can help librarians decide where to put links to library resources as well as preferred methods of contacting the online embedded librarian (Tumbleson & Burke, 2010).

Usage statistics of library guides and tutorials help evaluate student interest in these services. Other quantitative data could be collected by counting participants in LMS discussion forums, e-mails to the librarian, or individual consultation appointments made with students from the course. Monitoring student conversations in the LMS discussion forums and consultation with the course instructor may also provide insights into the student attitudes towards the presence of an embedded online librarian.

Faculty Satisfaction

After collaborating with faculty in an online course, the literature indicates that faculty satisfaction is assessed informally through conversations with the course instructor and formally through administration of surveys. Survey questions may focus on specific elements of the embedded services such as the tutorial modules used to teach the information literacy components (Kealey, 2011) or more generally. Targeted questions might include if the faculty were satisfied with the experience, what their impression was of the collaboration, would they have a librarian embedded in another of their courses, and would they recommend this service to colleagues (Tumbleson & Burke, 2010).

Assessing Student Learning

Student learning is at the heart of the academic mission, and information literacy is one of the stated goals of many institutions of higher learning. For this reason, assessing learning as a result of bibliographic instruction and other library services is a growing concern for librarians seeking to demonstrate the value of the academic library. Assessment of learning via the virtual librarian is no different in that regard. In fact, learning is assessed in a virtual classroom very much like it is assessed in a face-to-face environment. Assessment ranges from pre- and post- tests (Hearn, 2005; Kadavy & Chuppa-Cornell, 2011) to graded assignments and tests (Bozeman & Owens, 2008; Hoffman, 2011) to citation analysis (Clark & Chinburg, 2010; Kadavy & Chuppa-Cornell, 2011) to assessment of e-portfolios (Robertson et al., 2012). In addition to demonstrating the value of library instruction and support for students, assessment results are used by librarians to improve learning objects, adjust the focus of lessons, and strategically locate resources in the LMS or virtual classroom.

Technology Assessment

The development and growth of technology in education has made the online classroom possible. Assessment of the online tools used to teach is important. Ismail (2011) explored the comfort level of adult learners in a master's degree in social work program. Students were surveyed to assess their comfort level with the technology applications used in their online course, including resources offered by the library. Twelve of the 13 respondents indicated they were aware of the library forum in their LMS and of having a "personal librarian" available to them for their course. A majority also reported that they were aware that they could contact the librarian in a variety of ways besides the LMS library discussion forum. However, most of the respondents did not use the forums and indicated in the survey that it was their least favorite way to seek assistance, though they did read the posts of the other students and the librarian; e-mail ranked as the favorite. Knowing in advance the preferred technological approaches of student groups allows the online embedded librarian to focus time and resources toward the services that students are more likely to use. In this case, it may mean having to anticipate questions over the course of student projects and putting information in the discussion forum at the appropriate time.

When meeting students in an online learning environment, it is important for students to know there are resources for technical support. Technical problems are one of the main challenges online learners experience, and they can greatly affect student satisfaction with the course. Lee (2011) and colleagues studied the relationship between students' perceived support and learning outcomes in an online course. They found that students wanted more technical support and contact with faculty or peers. For online embedded librarians this may mean offering face-to-face technology workshops, suggesting a study group, or, if possible, briefly attending a hybrid class to introduce themselves. Further, students appear to prefer self-paced learning. Creating interactive tutorials with built-in formative evaluation are another way to assess teaching, learning, and level of comfort with new technologies. One teaching object that is often used in online information literacy education is an asynchronous tutorial. If librarians' technology skills are limited, there are many open-source tutorials online for librarians to use; some just requiring a simple request from a colleague at another institution. A freshman composition instructor and librarian at California State University-Stanislaus, for example, developed a research skills session for a fully online course using a series of open source tutorials. They looked for well-designed tutorials that had graphics and interactive elements in which students also had the highest level of control over navigation. To assess learning, the students kept a research log in which they described how each tutorial related to their research. In the end-of-course evaluation, the majority of the students reported that the tutorials had been helpful to them. On the whole the instructor was pleased with the tutorials and thought that the students had improved in their ability to identify a good source (Held, 2010).

With Web 2.0 options, there are many technological choices to support teaching and learning. According to Davis and Smith (2009), over 300 universities established virtual campuses in the Second Life world with courses, library services, and students following. In 2008, at the University of Central Missouri, librarians were embedded in English composition courses that were taught in Second Life. The librarians integrated seven synchronous library "mini-lectures" into the course curriculum and conducted a study to assess the effectiveness of Second Life instruction. A pre- and post-instruction survey evaluated information literacy competencies, student perception of challenges, and research behavior changes. A statistical analysis of the survey results showed no significant change in any of these areas. The authors point out that engaging students in the Second Life environment is difficult, making it problematic to assess the level of attention and to encourage participation.

Librarians have also been offering synchronous library instruction using web conferencing software and assessing the outcomes to improve content and format as well as to solve technical issues. One such institution, Montana State University, used an online evaluation form at the end of each of their synchronous class sessions. The outcomes clarified best practices for teaching with web conferencing software. The optimal length of time for real-time instruction is 45–50 minutes, with sessions taught by two librarians on two computers. One can deliver content, and the other can keep an eye on the chat window and monitor the recording of the session, allowing students to watch or review it later. Following their initial success, they plan to continue and expand the service (Bonnand & Hansen, 2012).

As new technologies develop, librarians continue to experiment with how these tools can be used in information literacy instruction. It is evident from the literature that assessment of student learning and the tools used to deliver instruction will continue to expand not only at the learning object and course-level but at the program level as well.

Program Assessment

Online embedded librarian programs often grow organically from the seeds of one or two interested librarians who offer their services to a single class. One example of this model is a service offered at Valdosta State University (Wright & Williams, 2011). After a successful collaborative experience with a College of Education faculty member, librarians developed several best practices and refined their program to meet the needs of the students. Initially, librarians worked independently, but the structure evolved into a more sustainable model that included greater collaboration and support within the library. This cooperation, at a broader system level, enhanced the variety and quality of instruction and formed the foundation of their online embedded librarian program. Program assessment included a mixed-methods survey instrument that was used to "improve the quality of service by creating richer content for students and reaching to faculty to foster a more collaborative experience" (Wright & Williams, 2011, p. 10).

Other programs are intentionally designed, as was the case at Miami University Middletown (Tumbleson & Burke, 2010). In this model, librarians collaborated with several faculty members across different courses and sections to reach more than 200 students. Librarians employed both formal and informal assessments of the program at the end of each term. Student and faculty evaluations proved to be positive and helpful in making program improvements. The authors stress the importance of regular and sustainable assessment of online embedded programs, calling it "crucial to its growth and development" (p. 980).

Program assessment evaluates the impact of online embedded librarians on student learning, and it is also useful for evaluating workload. Because many of these services are labor intensive such as creating tutorials or LibGuides, administrators may use program assessment data to determine what type of online embedded services the library can realistically provide and sustainably offer. Increasing the role of the online embedded librarian frequently means an adjustment to other library services, unless the budget allows for additional staffing. Many librarians warn that embedding programs can be time consuming, leading to workload issues (Drumm & Havens, 2005; Guillot et al., 2010).

An accepted best practice for sustainability of online embedded librarianship programs is a strategic selection of courses, targeting those where the most impact will be felt. Librarians have been effective in courses that are writing-intensive (Lorenzetti, 2012), for example, and courses that require students to complete a research assignment (York & Vance, 2009). At the same time, a robust program may run the risk of saturation, as was discovered at the College of DuPage (Kelley, 2012). In this case, an outcome of this type of program assessment was to alter the marketing and placement of embedded tutorials.

What's Ahead

If the past is any indication, the future of online embedded librarianship will be defined by technical developments as well as advancing pedagogy. Within the literature of the last 10 years, online embedded librarianship has been touted as the next big thing as well as the future of the reference desk and subject liaison work, and academic libraries as a whole (Edwards, 2011; Rudasill, 2010; Shumaker, 2013; Siess, 2010). Early pioneers in this area may be surprised to discover technologies that were once cutting edge are now commonplace working tools for many librarians. Likewise, library professionals, technology experts, and teaching faculty are currently planning and developing resources and services that will likely become common practice in the years to come.

As librarians adapt to emerging technologies and the evolution of online education, a significant driver of change continues to be campus learning management systems. Pickens-French and McDonald (2013) describe a migration from a proprietary LMS to Sakai, an open-source product. Because of the new learning environment, librarians developed new teaching objects and redesigned the library's Facebook page to include course pages from the LMS. Other examples of new technologies being used in online embedded librarian services include Skype (Cordell, 2012), Twitter (Filgo, 2011), LibGuides (Bowen, 2012), screencasting (Hedreen, 2012), and electronic textbooks (Ratto & Lynch, 2012).

The availability of webcasting software has made a tremendous difference in the delivery of instruction to distance students and as a class supplement for students who meet face to face. Librarians have adapted to the use of webinars through professional training and are now beginning to use them to meet and teach students online (Montgomery, 2010). Social networking sites such as Facebook and MySpace as well as Second Life virtual environments present similar opportunities for communication with students and collaboration with researchers. In addition to social networks, there are also "micro-social networks that focus on niche groups of researchers" (Kesselman & Watstein, 2009, p. 393). These groups facilitate contact with other researchers and the possibility of collaboration.

Librarians may find a niche in these micro-social networks. Kesselman and Watstein (2009) also point out that the advent of social networks has given rise to the emerging technology of social operating systems. This technology organizes, interprets, and evaluates connections between people to foster collaboration and is considered transformative to the academy:

> It will change the way we relate to knowledge and information; the way we do research and evaluate credibility; the way educators and students interact with each other; and the way students learn to be professionals in their chosen fields. (New Media Consortium and EDUCAUSE Learning Initiative, 2008, p. 27)

Academic librarians will want to be involved in the development and support of these systems.

Massive open online courses (MOOCs) are another area where librarians may find a space and place for embedded activities and services. Researchers believe that MOOCs are a learning environment that is ideal for enacting teaching methods that focus on building networks between learners rather than simply transmitting and acquiring information (Mahraj, 2012). Within this landscape, librarians may approach faculty teaching in MOOCs and offer asynchronous tutorials and links to open access research guides. It is suggested that librarians will have to "make the transition from open content to open instruction to participate more fully in shaping the future of higher education and helping online educators provide a valuable learning experience to students" (Mahraj, 2012, p. 364).

The Online Computer Library Center (OCLC) organized a conference in 2013 at the University of Pennsylvania entitled "MOOCs and Libraries: Massive Opportunity or Overwhelming Challenge?" There, librarians from all over the world discussed students, faculty, and what role academic librarians could play in the MOOC phenomenon (Howard, 2013). In a summary document, the next steps for developing librarian roles in MOOCs were identified: Start talking, sharing, and collaborating between libraries; take MOOCs; become experts on licensing and access issues in MOOCs; create a MOOC; support faculty and students in MOOCs; create in-person support opportunities to work with MOOCs; and re-assess library assumptions and practices surrounding MOOCs (Proffitt, 2013).

In an issue brief, the Association of Research Libraries (2012) pointed out that MOOCs raise legal and policy questions for research libraries that included "the proper application of fair use, the transition to open access as the default mode of scholarly publishing, and the provision of equal access to learning materials for students with and without disabilities" (p. 1). But in spite of challenges, the association admonished libraries that it is better to be involved in the adaptation to new demands than left out of the conversation.

While formal, peer-reviewed literature on the topic of MOOCs is still emerging, library-based blogs and discussion lists are rich in conversation about them and what they will mean to librarianship. McKiernan's (2013) *MOOCs and Libraries* blog (http://moocsandlibraries.blogspot.com), for example, is devoted to the intersection of librarians and MOOCs as well as identifying workshops at library conferences that both explore the impact of MOOCs on library services and on the design of those services. A recent post to a "MOOCs and Librarianship Google group" reported successful creation and delivery of a mini-MOOC designed to teach web literacy by librarians at Wake Forest University. The MOOC was marketed to both parents and alumni of the Wake Forest community as a supplement to bib-

liographic instruction. Librarians also reported that some parts of their mini-MOOC were used by librarians in a "flipped classroom" exercise for face-to-face instruction (Wake Forest University, 2013). (For a deeper exploration of this topic, please see this book's Chapter 12, "MOOCs: Getting Involved.")

Conclusion

Over the past decade, the growing number of articles, books, conference papers, and blog postings related to online embedded librarianship reflects the increasing presence of information professionals in this arena. Unique environments mean different characterizations, levels of service, and approaches that embrace a wide range of activities. At the same time, the diverse words and phrases surrounding these activities have begun to enter the common lexicon. Most of the projects, programs, and initiatives identified in this literature review involved online teaching and learning using specialized educational technologies. And while most of the studies reviewed were oriented towards a library presence in a course management system, there are a growing number of examples in which librarians engaged with students in other types of spaces. Similarly, while the best practices and assessment methods reported here may appear to be most applicable to librarians and students in LMS settings, they are not the only environment where these activities occurred or will occur in the future.

The current understanding of the field encompasses a range of services and activities. As online embedded librarianship continues to develop and mature—with its own frameworks, learning tools, best practices, and assessment methods— the need to compare it to more established forms of librarianship will diminish. The promise rests in the potential for using technology in ways that promote meaningful learning. Meeting with students wherever they are—whether in-person or virtually—and on whatever device or platform they use will simply be part of what librarians do.

REFERENCES

Allen, I.E., & Seaman, J. (2013). *Changing course: Ten years of tracking online education in the United States*. Retrieved from Sloan Consortium website: http://sloanconsortium.org/publications/survey/changing_course_2012

Appleton, L. (2005). Using electronic textbooks: Promoting, placing and embedding. *Electronic Library, 23*(2), 54–63.

Association of Research Libraries. (2012, October). *Massive open online courses: Legal and political issues for research libraries* (Issue Brief). Washington, DC: B. Butler. Retrieved from http://www.arl.org/storage/documents/publications/issuebrief-mooc-22oct12.pdf

Bonnand, S., & Hansen, M.A. (2012). Embedded librarians: Delivering synchronous library instruction and research assistance to meet needs of distance students and faculty. In H. Wang (Ed.), *Interactivity in e-learning: Case studies and frameworks* (pp. 326–339). Hershey, PA: Information Science Reference.

Bowen, A. (2012). A LibGuides presence in a Blackboard environment. *Reference Services Review, 40*(3), 449–468.

Bozeman, D., & Owens, R. (2008). Providing services to online students: Embedded librarians and access to resources. *Mississippi Libraries, 72*(3), 57–59.

Chisholm, E., & Lamond, H.M. (2012). Information literacy development at a distance: Embedded or reality? *Journal of Library & Information Services in Distance Learning, 6*(3-4), 224–234.

Clark, S., & Chinburg, S. (2010). Research performance in undergraduates receiving face to face versus online library instruction: A citation analysis. *Journal of Library Administration, 50*(5-6), 530–542.

Cordell, D. (2012). Skype and the embedded librarian. In B.J. Hamilton (Ed.), *Embedded librarianship: Tools and practices* (pp. 8–11). Chicago, IL: ALA TechSource.

Corinth, J. (2003). The lurking librarian project. *Academic Exchange Quarterly, 7*(1), 278–281.

Daly, E. (2010). Embedding library resources into learning management systems: A way to reach Duke undergrads at their points of need. *College & Research Libraries News, 71*(4), 208–212.

Davis, M.G., & Smith, C.E. (2009). Virtually embedded: Library instruction within Second Life. *Journal of Library & Information Services in Distance Learning, 3*(3-4), 120–37.

DeBonis, R., Miller, R., & Pomea, N. (2013). Keep it streamlined for students: Designing library instruction for the online learner. *Proceedings of the ACRL 2013 Conference*. Retrieved from http://www.ala.org/acrl/sites/ala.org.acrl/files/content/conferences/confsandpreconfs/2013/papers/DebonisMillerPomea_KeepIt.pdf

Dennie, D. (2011). Chat widgets as student/librarian communication tools. *Library Hi Tech News, 3*, 13–19.

Dewey, B.I. (2004). The embedded librarian: Strategic campus collaborations. *Resource Sharing & Information Networks, 17*(1), 5–17.

Drewes, K., & Hoffman, N. (2010). Academic embedded librarianship: An introduction. *Public Services Quarterly, 6*(2), 75–82.

Drumm, M., & Havens, B.C. (2005). A foot in the door: Experiments with integrating library services into the online classroom. *Journal of Library & Information Services in Distance Learning, 2*(3), 25–32.

Edwards, M.E. (2011). *Online embedded librarian case study: A descriptive evaluation* (Unpublished doctoral dissertation). University of Florida, Gainesville, FL.

Edwards, M.E., & Black, E.W. (2012). Contemporary instructor-librarian collaboration: A case study of an online embedded librarian implementation. *Journal of Library & Information Services in Distance Learning, 6*(3-4), 284–311.

Edwards, M.E., Kumar, S., & Ochoa, M. (2010). Assessing the value of embedded librarians in an online graduate educational technology course. *Public Services Quarterly, 6*(2), 271–291.

Filgo, E.H. (2011). #Hashtag librarian: Embedding myself into a class via Twitter and blogs. *Computers in Libraries, 31*(6), 78–80.

Francis, M. (2012). Making embedded librarians a part of an online community of learners. *Journal of Library & Information Services in Distance Learning, 6*(1), 19–27.

Guillot, L., Stahr, B., & Meeker, B.J. (2010). Nursing faculty collaborate with embedded librarians to service online graduate students in a consortium setting. *Journal of Library & Information Services in Distance Learning, 4*(1-2), 53–62.

Hawes, S.L. (2011). Playing to win: Embedded librarians in online classrooms. *Journal of Library & Information Services in Distance Learning, 5*(1-2), 56–66.

Haycock, L., & Howe, A. (2011). Collaborating with library course pages and Facebook: Exploring new opportunities. *Collaborative Librarianship, 3*(3), 157–162.

Hearn, M. (2005). Embedding a librarian in the classroom: An intensive information literacy model. *Reference Services Review, 33*(2), 219–227.

Hedreen, R. (2012). Timezones, screencasts, and becoming real: One distance librarian's experiences and lessons learned. *Urban Library Journal, 18*(1). Retrieved from http://ojs.gc.cuny.edu/index.php/urbanlibrary/article/view/1350

Held, T. (2010). Blending in: Collaborating with an instructor in an online course. *Journal of Library & Information Services in Distance Learning, 4*(4), 153–65.

Hemming, W., & Montet, M. (2010). The "just for me" virtual library: Enhancing an embedded eBrarian program. *Journal of Library Administration, 50*(5-6), 657–669.

Herring, S., Burkhardt, R., & Wolfe, J. (2009). Reaching remote students: Athens State University's electronically embedded librarian program. *College & Research Libraries News, 70*(11), 630–633.

Hoffman, S. (2011). Embedded academic librarian experiences in online courses: Roles, faculty collaboration, and opinion. *Library Management, 32*(6-7), 444–456.

Hoffman, S., & Ramin, L. (2010). Best practices for librarians embedded in online courses. *Public Services Quarterly 6*(2), 292-305.

Howard, J. (2013). For libraries, MOOCs bring uncertainty and opportunity. *The Chronicle of Higher Education.* Retrieved from: http://chronicle.com/blogs/wiredcampus/for-libraries-moocs-bring-uncertainty-and-opportunity/43111

Ismail, L. (2011). Getting personal: Reaching out to adult learners through a course management system. *Reference Librarian, 52*(3), 244–262.

Kadavy, C., & Chuppa-Cornell, K. (2011). A personal touch: Embedding library faculty into online English 102. *Teaching English in the Two-Year College, 39*(1), 63–77.

Kealey, S. (2011). Continual evolution: The experience over three semesters of a librarian embedded in an online evidence-based medicine course for physician assistant students. *Medical Reference Services Quarterly, 30*(4), 411–425.

Kelley, J. (2012). Off the shelf and out of the box: Saving time, meeting outcomes and reaching students with information literacy modules. *Journal of Library & Information Services in Distance Learning, 6*, 335–349.

Kenefick, C. (2011). The case for embedded hospital librarianship. *Journal of Hospital Librarianship, 11*(2), 195–199.

Kesselman, M.A., & Watstein, S.B. (2009). Creating opportunities: Embedded librarians. *Journal of Library Administration, 49*(3), 383–400.

Knight, V., & Loftis, C. (2012). Moving from introverted to extraverted embedded librarian services: An example of a proactive model. *Journal of Library & Information Services in Distance Learning, 6*(3-4), 362–375.

Konieczny, A. (2010). Experiences as an embedded librarian in online courses. *Medical Reference Services Quarterly, 29*(1), 47–57.

Kvenild, C. (2012). The future of embedded librarianship: Best practices and opportunities. Retrieved from http://www.cclibinstruction.org/wp-content/uploads/2012/02/CCLI2012proceedings_Kvenild.pdf

Kvenild, C., & Calkins, K. (2011). *Embedded librarians: Moving beyond one-shot instruction.* Chicago, IL: American Library Association.

Lee, S.J., Srinivasan, S., Trail, T., Lewis, D., & Lopez, S. (2011). Examing the relationship among student perception of support, course satisfaction, and learning outcomes in online learning. *Internet and Higher Education, 14*, 158–163.

Lillard, L., Norwood, S., Wise, K., Brooks, J. & Kitts, R. (2009). Embedded librarians: MLS students as apprentice librarians in online courses. *Journal of Library Administration, 49*(1-2), 11–22.

Lorenzetti, J. P. (2012). Do your online courses need an embedded librarian? *Distance Education, 16*(11), 1–2.

Machovec, G. (2001). Course management software: Where is the library? *Online Libraries & Microcomputers, 19*(10), 1–2.

Mahraj, K. (2012). Using information expertise to enhance massive open online courses. *Public Services Quarterly, 8*(4), 359–368.

Matos, M.A., Matsuoka-Motley, N., & Mayer, W. (2010). The embedded librarian online or face-to-face: American University's experiences. *Public Services Quarterly, 6*(2), 130–139.

Matthew, V., & Schroeder, A. (2006). The embedded librarian program. *EDUCAUSE Quarterly, 29*(4), 61–65.

McKiernan, G. (2013). *MOOCs and libraries* [Blog]. Retrieved from http://moocsandlibraries.blogspot.com/

Midler, Z. (2012). Case profile: Zoe Midler and Google Docs. In B.J. Hamilton (Ed.), *Embedded librarianship: Tools and practices* (pp. 12–15). Chicago, IL: ALA TechSource.

Montgomery, S.E. (2010). Online webinars! interactive learning where our users are: The future of embedded librarianship. *Public Services Quarterly,*

6(2), 306–11.

New Media Consortium and EDUCAUSE Learning Initiative. (2008). *Horizon report*. Retrieved from http://www.nmc.org/pdf/2008-Horizon-Report.pdf

Pickens-French, K., & McDonald, K. (2013). Changing trenches, changing tactics: A library's frontline redesign in a new CMS. *Journal of Library & Information Services in Distance Learning, 7*(1-2), 53–72.

Proffitt, M. (2013). MOOCs and libraries event summarized in series of six hangingtogether.org blog posts. Retrieved from http://www.oclc.org/research/news/2013/04-19.html

Ratto, B.G., & Lynch, A. (2012). The embedded textbook: Collaborating with faculty to employ library subscription e-books as core course text. *Journal of Electronic Resources Librarianship, 24*(1), 1–16.

Robertson, A., McMurray, I., Ingram, J., & Roberts, P. (2012). Embedding a curriculum-based information literacy programme at the University of Bedfordshire. *Journal of Pedagogic Development 2*(1). Retrieved from http://issuu.com/uniofbeds/docs/jpd-vol2-issue2

Rudasill, L.M. (2010). Beyond subject specialization: The creation of embedded librarians. *Public Services Quarterly, 6*(2-3), 83–91.

Schulte, S.J. (2012). Embedded academic librarianship: A review of the literature. *Evidence Based Library and Information Practice, 7*(4), 122–138. Retrieved from http://ejournals.library.ualberta.ca/index.php/EBLIP/article/view/17466

Shank, J.D., & Dewald, N.H. (2003). Establishing our presence in courseware: Adding library services to the virtual classroom. *Information Technology and Libraries, 22*(1), 38–43.

Shell, L., Crawford, S., & Harris, P. (2013). Aided and embedded: The team approach to instructional design. *Journal of Library & Information Services in Distance Learning, 7*(1-2), 143–155.

Shumaker, D. (2012). *The embedded librarian: Innovative strategies for taking knowledge where it's needed.* Medford, NJ: Information Today.

Shumaker, D. (2013, February 19). Para-librarians and embedded librarians, part 3 [Blog post]. Retrieved from http://embeddedlibrarian.com/2013/02/

Shumaker, D., & Talley, M. (2009). *Models of embedded librarianship: Final report.* Retrieved from Special Libraries Association website: http://hq.sla.org/pdfs/EmbeddedLibrarianshipFinalRptRev.pdf

Si, L., Xing, W., Zhou, L., & Liu, S. (2012). Embedded services in Chinese academic libraries. *Journal of Academic Librarianship, 38*(3), 175–182.

Siess, J. (2010). Embedded librarianship: The next big thing? *Searcher, 18*(1), 38–45.

Sullo, E., Harrod, T., Butera, G., & Gomes, A. (2012). Rethinking library service to distance education students: Analyzing the embedded librarian model. *Medical Reference Service Quarterly, 31*(1), 25–33.

Tumbleson, B.E., & Burke, J.J. (2010). When life hands you lemons: Overcoming obstacles to expand services in an embedded librarian program. *Journal of Library Administration, 50* (7-8), 972–988.

Wake Forest University. (2013). ZSRx: The cure for the common web. Retrieved from https://sites.google.com/a/wfu.edu/zsrx13/

Wright, L. B., & Williams, G.H. (2011). A history of the embedded librarian program at Odum Library. *Georgia Library Quarterly, 48*(4), 7–11.

York, A.C., & Vance, J. (2009). Taking library instruction into the online classroom: Best practices for embedded librarians. *Journal of Library Administration, 49*(1-2), 197–209.

Embedded Librarians: Evolving and Expanding in Higher Education

Audrey Donaldson and Alyssa M. Valenti

Libraries have changed dramatically in response to the needs of the populations they serve. In recent decades, technology has greatly influenced the ways in which librarians support and instruct students. Electronic tools, online communication, and various elements of learning management systems (LMS) continue to challenge librarians to identify and develop new strategies to address the needs of increasingly diverse user populations. Embedded librarians must consider emerging technologies and the adoption of ever-evolving instructional strategies and tools for supportive measures. In order to capture and retain the attention of students, embedded librarians remain abreast of new tools and strategies applying creativity and innovation to support students' understanding of many complex and diverse information resources.

Both the level of service and the format of embedded services vary. Librarians can be found in physical spaces within departments or divisions working closely in conjunction with course instructors and students. Continually evolving in response to the need for online support, embedded librarians are also interacting with users in virtual spaces like the LMS, serving as consultants, problem solvers, collaborators, guides, and instructors. Virtually embedded librarians establish themselves on college campuses primarily to provide educational support to the online environment.

As academic libraries and library resources change in response to user needs, educational trends, and technological innovations, the embedded librarian's dynamic role relies heavily on creativity, specialization, and instruction to address the needs of online students. This chapter focuses on the role of the online embedded librarian in support of college-level coursework within the online learning environment. The responsibilities, challenges, and considerations for the academic, online embedded librarian highlight a student-centered approach. The overview, examples, and best practices presented here emphasize library services, information resources, instructional support, and innovative strategies.

Current Practices

In the academic environment, embedded librarians support teaching and learning by planning, managing, and coordinating a variety of elements related to reference and instruction, technology, and collaborative agreements with course instructors and facilitators. While current practices differ on an institutional basis and vary from course to course, overall the integration of a librarian within an online course benefits the student, the course facilitator, and the institution (Ralph, 2012; York & Vance, 2009). Depending on the functionality of an institution's LMS, library support can be integrated in face-to-face or virtual classrooms. In the true spirit of embeddedness, specialized library services, along with a librarian who maintains a consistent presence throughout the duration of a course, can positively enhance a student's understanding of how to access and evaluate information resources.

The effective use of LMS features allows the online embedded librarian to provide support and establish visible library presence. The announcements area can introduce and clarify the role of the embedded librarian as well as provide a space to help to share pertinent, timely information throughout the duration of the course. As students develop information literacy skills, other content areas such as the discussion board or forum can be designated to serve a specific role to support student inquiry, research, and understanding. Embedded librarians, as proponents of information literacy, enhance the teaching and learning environment by offering guidance and services that directly relate to the required coursework and assignments. For example, a slideshow on plagiarism, a link to citation guides, and a research tutorial containing screencasts on how to access subject specific databases might be basic components to include in a discussion forum designated for library services and research support. Streaming videos, a bibliography, or an invitation to a book talk are other features that can be added to address the specific needs of an assignment. In general, the LMS provides for the delivery of library instruction and services and offers opportunities for students to "expand their knowledge, ask informed questions, and sharpen their critical thinking for still further self-directed learning" (ACRL, 2000).

The embedded librarian's role may call for direct instruction, library services, and guided support throughout the duration of the course. Four subject area librarians at Purdue University provided semester-long research support for students working on an agribusiness project (Dugan, 2008). Embedded librarians at the University of Michigan served as information consultants over the course of a semester for various teams of students (Berdish & Seeman, 2008). The main ben-

efit to the students seeking to locate research for very specific and somewhat narrow subject areas was the research instruction and ongoing support the librarians provided.

Each individual course requires the course instructor and the embedded librarian to enter into an agreement regarding technological issues and aspects of library support. The agreement should include specifics related to the methods and techniques the embedded librarian will use to engage students. Ultimately, the goal of a successful embedded librarian is to establish a supportive role within the learning community in which he or she has become a member.

Collaboration and communication with the course instructor help to determine how the embedded librarian will serve the students. To offer clarification, the embedded librarian can propose a plan with examples of tools, services, resources, and strategies. This approach presents the course instructor with a clear idea of how the embedded librarian's services can benefit students. As a result, informed instructors are in a better position to select the appropriate level of service, resources, and approaches to support their students. Librarian and instructor collaborations help to define the level of support and to discuss strategies for the delivery of library services to support learning outcomes (Edwards & Black, 2012).

Delivery of Services

Decisions related to the delivery of library support vary from one institution to the next. The implementation of embedded librarian services may be the result of a marketing effort in response to an expressed need or from word-of-mouth recommendations. It is possible for a coordinator or liaison to be the contact responsible for arrangements that establish embedded librarian services. In the LMS, provision and set up of the space and delivery of library services can directly occur based on the embedded librarian or course facilitator's expertise and authorization. However, this set up sometimes requires intervention from instructional designers, technologists, or the IT department. When the embedded librarian is responsible for maintaining the library space in an online course environment, the instructor or campus technology team may need to grant course access to the librarian as well as ensure accurate permissions in order to create, modify, or add course content. At the basic level, the embedded librarian should be able to develop and moderate a forum in which content may include resources from internal or external origination.

It is up to the course instructor to use a welcoming, inviting approach upon introduction of an embedded librarian. When the instructor emphasizes the significance of embedded librarian services, the likelihood of student interactions increases (Bennett & Simning, 2010). Students are more apt to utilize embedded librarian services when the instructor announces this service early in the semester (Sullo, Harrod, Butera, & Gomes, 2012). Additionally, an introductory greeting from the embedded librarian can potentially reinforce the initial announcement from the course instructor, highlight specific services, and invite students to ask questions.

In some cases, course instructors take the initiative to provide their students access to library resources from within the LMS, for example, through the creation of a library resources forum. Within this forum students can access library-specific information and links to other services such as chat reference, a research tutorial, or the library homepage. The instructor can provide selected course-specific information such as websites, films, databases, and other e-resources directly related to the topic or assignments. In cases where an embedded librarian program is not in place, this practice helps to facilitate access for students who can benefit from the provision of vital information resources. However, for institutions offering embedded librarian services, both course facilitators and online students benefit from the specialized services, resources, and individualized support provided by an embedded

librarian. Through collaborations with the course instructor, the embedded librarian can identify ways to meet the specific needs of each student by establishing communication options that encourage students to ask questions. This fosters a direct and immediate connection between the student and librarian.

Instruction

The Association of College and Research Libraries (ACRL) describes the educational role for libraries as a partnership "in the educational mission of the institution, to develop and support information-literate learners who can discover, access, and use information effectively for academic success, research, and lifelong learning" (2000). Once the embedded librarian is established within the online course environment, he or she can align her services to match this ACRL principle through instruction provided in a variety of formats. This can include self-paced tutorials, recorded lectures, helpful links, and direct, supportive student interactions with the librarian either through the discussion forum or another means of virtual communication. Virtual communication could include synchronous online or in-person class meetings, group work, one-on-one video chat, or instant messenger.

Opportunities for instruction often arise in response to student inquiries, which the librarian can subsequently respond to through appropriate means. The response to a question about a citation may lead to instruction regarding the criteria for credible resources or a brief lesson on MLA format presented as a podcast. A broader question related to the research process may require several stages of instruction and guidance. Since the depth of instruction varies, the embedded librarian might also choose to offer telephone, instant messenger, or video chat support as an option.

Embedded librarians are challenged to continually identify relevant methods of instruction along with strategies for their assessment.

Information literacy learning objectives should be established in addition to the course learning objectives. Coordination amongst the stakeholders such as other librarians, teaching faculty, or instructional designers remains a key element in determining how the embedded librarian's role aligns with the course, institutional goals, and ACRL information literacy standards. Through meaningful collaborations with the course instructor and a clear understanding of the course outcomes, embedded librarians can apply effective strategies to support students' acquisition of information literacy skills. Intentionally using a student-centered approach aids in the successful integration of relevant library resources and examples of their implementation in academic achievement.

Reference Questions

Reference support should be offered to students in a manner that conveys availability and willingness to help students to reach their learning goals. Embedded librarians serve students with teaching strategies and tools to promote higher-order thinking skills (Alshraideh, 2009), support the development of research questions (Lipowski, 2008), and encourage intellectual development as a vital component of research activity (Wu & Hsieh, 2006). When librarians model effective inquiry practices, demonstrate critical thinking, and explain new concepts, students benefit from the positive interactions and find value in the level of service provided (Bennett & Simning, 2010).

Preparation for embedded librarianship includes an understanding about the need to support international students with no previous library or research experience, students educated in regions of the U.S. impacted by the closure of school libraries, as well as others who simply do not have a foundation in information literacy skills (Salisbury & Karasmanis, 2011). As a result, students who lack basic skills such as an understanding of the meaning of question words (Morgan, Moni, & Jobling, 2009) and those with limited opportunities to practice inquiry skills require direct instruction to address learning barriers (Ketelhut, Nelson, Clarke, & Dede, 2010). Explicit encouragement and support for questions with a variety of tutorials, tools, and resources provided is sometimes required to level the playing field for underserved and underprepared populations (Donaldson, 2012).

The University of Central Florida (UCF, 2013) identified reiteration as a salient feature for course delivery. Farnsworth and Bevis (2006) also promote repetition as an essential strategy to support online students. The use of custom-built learning objects in the online classroom is another strategy that embedded librarians can use to save time and reduce the need for repetitive instruction. Learning objects are stand-alone tools that cover one specific topic in an isolated fashion. An example of a learning object for an online course would be one that focuses on developing keywords. The learning object is interface agnostic and stresses the skills students need to learn instead of a roadmap of where to click. Resources that are clearly identified can be repurposed for availability in multiple areas of the learning environment. Instructional support, as well as messages regarding reference and library resources, may appear in strategic locations in the research forum or discussion board.

An important feature of delivering asynchronous library instruction or reference is that of timeliness. At times, the increased monitoring and response time for an embedded librarian are aligned with deadlines for the project or assignment. Other factors for establishing response times can be related to the scheduling and availability of the embedded librarian. There are many ways in which an embedded librarian can manage the time requirements of connecting and building relationship with students online. Efforts to facilitate communication include information regarding modes of inquiry and expectations for response. This applies to both student response time as well as turnaround time from the librarian. A strategic method to communicate timeliness

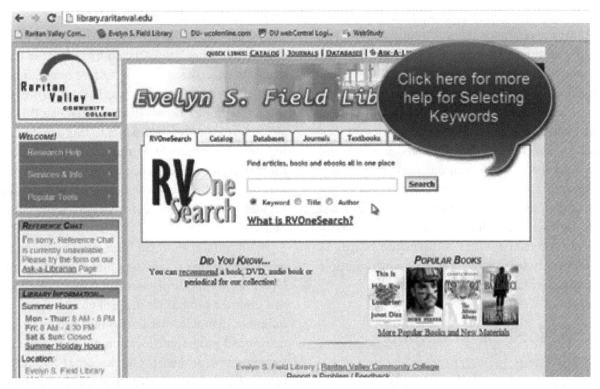

Figure 2.1. Developing keyword instruction. Screenshot of a screencast linked to an external learning object that is solely dedicated to keyword generation.

consists of providing details of availability in the initial "welcome" message, the discussion board post, and in designated content areas in which students are likely to ask questions. Sometimes the course instructor will include the embedded librarian's availability and response time expectations in the announcements, syllabi, learning units, or in other course communication tools. For example, by providing the following message or something similar to the "Library Resources" content area—"Feel free to ask questions at any time. I will respond to your questions within 24 hours"—the embedded librarian clearly indicates the turnaround time. The message could continue with contact information including the hours for phone inquiries with the time zone.

Assessment of Instruction

Assessment of an embedded librarian program is vital for its growth and continued development. Feedback collected from both course instructors and students can be useful for further improve-

ments and enhancements. Feedback can range anywhere from constructive criticism highlighting areas that need extra attention such as student learning barriers to challenges for the online embedded librarian.

Services and support for online students should be assessed continually. An evaluation of reference services includes an assessment of factors such as empathy, various aspects of the learning environment, service reliability, and responsiveness (Gilbert, Liu, Matoush, & Whitlatch, 2006). Instruction must also be assessed to evaluate the delivery and effectiveness for various types of tools, modes, and strategies (Hines, 2008). Assessment tools should be designed to capture both the student learning experience and the collaborative teaching experience for the course instructor.

Surveys are a great tool and can be conveniently provided at key points, such as pre-test, midterm, or post-test. In addition to Likert scale and multiple-choice options, open-ended questions enable users to share their experiences, reactions, and perceptions whether positive or negative of reference services or instruction. One of the authors (AD) demonstrated effective use of survey as assessment when she was embedded in an online English course. She set up a content area called "Library Resources," which included tutorials, a link for chat reference services, a citation tip sheet, other course-related support, and finally, a discussion forum was provided to *Ask a Librarian*. However, after receiving feedback from the instructor through the survey, the author and the instructor decided to also include a library question forum within the discussion board. As a result, students were presented with multiple locations from which to make inquiries.

Embedded Librarian and Reference Librarian: A Comparison

Embedded librarians and reference librarians both share some common responsibilities among which are primary concerns related to information delivery for the provision of service at the student's point of need. In each of these roles, a welcoming environment and efficient response time from the librarian is vital. Each of these librarians relies on effective methods, strategies, and resources to foster information literacy skills (ACRL, 2000). However, there are aspects of the embedded librarian position that require more focused attention to the subject-specific nature of the course material, learning activities, and outcomes.

While the reference librarian often provides reactive services to students, the embedded librarian is challenged to employ proactive approaches to identify and address anticipated student needs and questions. This includes responding to the need for skills development and the reinforcement of research skills and strategies that are directly related to a specific subject or course. An example of the information sources provided for online students are research tutorials, a slideshow

on plagiarism, and citation support links for each individual course. These resources are often available in the forum before the course begins so that students have the opportunity to explore them prior to starting course assignments. However, this same librarian taking on a reference role is also prepared to refer students to these materials but does not explicitly set out to identify each of these resources in reference interactions. Embedded librarians present a selection of materials in advance for online students to access at the point of need.

Continual assessment is essential for both the reference librarian and the embedded librarian. However, the mode of assessment for the embedded librarian program is more likely to require an online or digital format due to the asynchronous nature and geographic location of many distance learning environments. On the other hand, for face-to-face reference interactions, a survey could be available in print as well as online for users visiting the library. The frequency of assessing the embedded librarian program may also be greater due to the need to iteratively tweak and update strategies, resources, and technology tools in a timely manner. Whereas the reference librarian may introduce new tools, resources, and strategies at any point, an embedded librarian needs to provide a consistent set of resources available to online students to establish reliability and trust. Modifications to the online materials used in the LMS should occur between semesters and not in the middle of the course progression. Updates and enhancements that are easily navigated in face-to-face interactions may cause confusion for online students who have already begun to familiarize themselves and rely on items that were previously introduced in the course. For example, the decision to replace a video on plagiarism with a self-paced tutorial should be reflected in subsequent courses throughout the curriculum. A seamless transition is more appropriate to support online learning.

Perhaps one of the most obvious differences between the reference librarian and the embed-

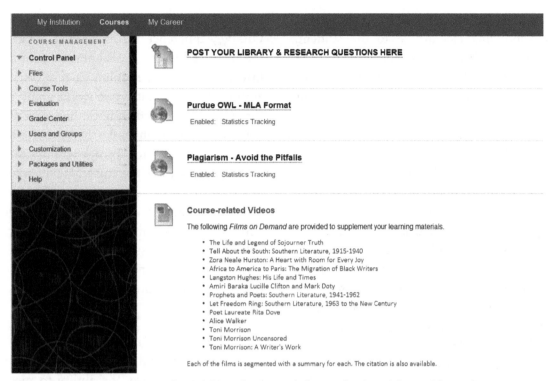

Figure 2.2. Research support. Screenshot of a research forum developed for an African American Literature course.

ded librarian is related to how each responds to questions. Reference librarians may consider the mode of communication as well as the question. For example, a response to the question— "Where can I find a book about… ?"—might include specifics regarding how the patron may locate a book or an e-book. For print, the reference librarian can write down the call number and accompany the student to the stacks. If the student is interested in an e-book, the reference librarian can provide a demonstration on how to navigate the library resources to locate an e-book. Both of these responses are appropriate for face-to-face interactions. However, in an e-learning environment, the response to virtual requests should focus on the steps required to locate e-books, unless otherwise indicated. Time factors regarding receipt, response, clarity, and accuracy for virtual communication are of critical importance. Instead of engaging in a reference interview or a question-and-answer exchange, an embedded librarian's responses are often most efficient when considerations are taken for various aspects of the student's needs and experience. For exam-

ple, in responding to the question—"Where can I find news information?"—an embedded librarian might begin the reply by including step-by-step directions along with a link to the library research resources within the LMS course shell prior to identifying the specific databases for news articles. This strategy will support a student with little experience accessing these resources, including first-year and transfer students.

Directional questions, in general, are interpreted differently by reference librarians and embedded librarians. For example, when a student asks how to get to the bookstore, the reference librarian may be able to refer to a map or simply point in the direction of the bookstore's physical location. For the embedded librarian's response, directing a student to the bookstore could consist of providing a link to the campus bookstore's website.

For questions that require interpretation of assignments, both the reference librarian and the embedded librarian are challenged to convey the importance of directing this question back to the course instructor. While the reference librarian may have the advantage of "saying it nicely" when responding face-to-face to the student, the embedded librarian is challenged with the potential pitfalls of misinterpretation of textual messages. For example, a response such as "Your course instructor will be able to explain exactly what the assignment means. I do not want to mislead you with my interpretation" may come across harshly to an online student in desperate need of timely advice and support. This type of response could also be misinterpreted as an unwillingness to help, which does not foster the welcoming environment the embedded librarian tries so hard to create and maintain. Awareness of the nuances that influence user perception of responses can help the embedded librarian to deliver messages that are perceived as caring, respectful, and engaged (Waugh, 2013).

Embedded librarians respond to user needs from within the online learning spaces devoted to the specific course (Shumaker, 2009). In doing so, some of the resources and strategies employed are the same as those used by, and perhaps devel-oped or identified by, the reference librarian. One key difference for embedded librarians is the increased level of collaboration with course instructors. In another online English course, the author (AV) moderated two weeks of discussion forums and provided a rubric for appropriately crafted responses, which she then shared with the instructor. She created an opportunity to highlight the expertise of the embedded librarian, but this type of interaction is only possible through prior communication and by working out details with the course instructor. Communication between these professionals can help to address a variety of specific concerns and identify issues for future consideration.

Critical Concerns and Issues

While the demand for embedded librarian services may increase, the ability to meet the demand presents a significant challenge (Shumaker, 2009). In marketing plans, library leaders and librarians need to take into account

Criteria	Excellent	Average	Needs Improvement	Rating
1. Frequency & Timeliness	✓ Posts on time or early ✓ Answers all questions completely	✓ Posts on time ✓ Most questions answered	✓ Does not enter forum or post anything	
2. Participation	✓ Replies to librarian ✓ Replies to other students	✓ Replies only to librarian	✓ Does not enter forum or post anything ✓ Does not reply to any posts	
3. Content	✓ Answers all questions ✓ Lists 3-5 appropriate keywords ✓ Shows evidence of learned research skills from watching screencasts	✓ Answers questions ✓ Does not seek further information ✓ Unverified if student watched screencasts	✓ Does not enter forum or post anything ✓ Posts irrelevant or off-topic content ✓ Shows no learned research skills and lacks proof of viewing screencasts	
4. Clarity & Mechanics	✓ Uses complete sentences ✓ Shows well-thought out responses ✓ Poses questions to provoke critical thinking in self and other students	✓ Posts complete sentences and answers all questions ✓ No further questions or comments for more research	✓ Does not enter forum or post anything ✓ Posts too little, or too long and unorganized information	
5. Development of ideas	✓ Shows well-developed topic with support for further exploration ✓ Shows evidence of learned research skills	✓ Replies with one word answers ✓ Does not show evidence of learned research skills	✓ Does not enter forum or post anything ✓ Posts only one poorly-formed topic	
Totals	_ out of 12	_ out of 10	_ out of 10	

Figure 2.3. Rubric for librarian-led discussion forum. Rubric for an online English class used to assess student participation in the library forum.

the feasibility of responding to the demand for embedded librarian services (Matthew & Schroeder, 2006). A critical concern for an embedded librarian program is related to balance (Berdish & Seeman, 2008). Workload balance and the consistent availability of librarians to share responsibilities such as reference, information literacy instruction, and embedded librarian services are key factors for consideration.

It is not uncommon for students to create bonds with familiar resources. Students who have grown accustomed to Wikipedia, YouTube, and Google may be reluctant to explore new resources, which an embedded librarian has the distinct advantage to address when appropriately prepared for this challenge. For example, a course assignment can direct students to explore multimedia, such as streaming video. A keen awareness of the needs of both the course instructor and students prompts the embedded librarian to share educational streaming videos as well as information on how to locate credible information sources. This type of assignment is a great opportunity for librarian and faculty collaboration. Planning, proactive efforts, and a clear understanding of course assignments are essential to identify key teaching and learning opportunities. Sometimes explicit direction in the assignment such as "you are required to use resources provided by the library" can reduce the student's reliance on YouTube as the only video source they know. Embedded librarians can help to change user attitudes and behavior by educating both course facilitators and students about the value of accessible, credible resources.

Librarians and course facilitators share goals of providing access to tools and technology, skills to navigate information resources, and strategies for research success to students. One major concern in meeting these goals is the preparation of librarians to fulfill the role of embedded librarian. Efforts to balance the workload are critical to provide the appropriate level of support, not only for the population served but for the embedded librarians engaging in the wide range of activities

to establish and maintain a high level of support as required (Shumaker, 2009).

Planning and implementation of online embedded librarian services require special considerations. This includes the identification of appropriate resources, strategies, and innovative approaches (Shumaker, 2009). Meanwhile, the adoption of best practices offers guidance from planning through delivery phases (EDUCAUSE, 2013; York & Vance, 2009).

Effective Strategies/Best Practices

Building an effective embedded librarian program requires significant research and planning. From the development phase through the assessment phase, embedded librarians need to prepare for an effective program with the support of key personnel including other librarians, course instructors, technology personnel, and administrators who all serve in vital supportive roles throughout the stages of the process.

The planning phase involves internal and external investigations, including communication with curriculum planning teams, course instructors, and with others fulfilling an embedded librarian role in the academic setting. Part of this phase includes the development of an efficient system for course facilitators to request the services of the embedded librarian, which includes the adoption and establishment of policies and procedures.

Embedded library services can be launched in numerous ways, but identifying the needs of a specific population will determine how to pilot the program. The embedded librarian program can be carefully launched, starting small and expanding gradually. Depending on the purpose and demand, development of the program can be introduced on a multi-phasic basis. For example, the initial program can consist of a single course served by a librarian who collaborates with a course instructor with an increase in the number of courses identified for the following semester or terms.

As the program matures, decision-making challenges include considerations for marketing to increase awareness or opportunities campuswide. At the Community College of Vermont, embedded librarian services grew from three courses to 43 courses in two years due to marketing efforts (Matthew & Schroeder, 2006). With each iterative program evaluation cycle, services and supportive strategies may be identified to increase effectiveness. Ideally, embedded librarian services will develop as a customized service in which the level of engagement, support, and resources vary from course to course or instructor to instructor. It is essential to adopt and develop standards for embedded librarian services that meet the needs specific to the course, program, and institution served.

Public Relations and Marketing

A public relations plan serves the library as well as the institution. A study conducted by Tyler and Hastings (2011) revealed student observations and suggestions for more advertising about the library. Announcements to distribute, post, and e-mail include brochures, fliers, podcasts, and posters. The embedded librarian program can also be promoted in presentations through liaison programs, new-employee orientation sessions, or campus events (Shumaker, 2009).

A full-fledged marketing effort will help to promote the benefits of using embedded librarian services. The author (AV) tried to grow her embedded librarian program through e-mail blasts, a faculty development workshop, and, finally, individualized and specialized presentations for specific academic departments. Marketing her services in this manner helped spread knowledge about the program through word of mouth and proven success from the pilot courses.

The promotion of one prominent feature of the embedded librarian program is the expertise of the embedded librarian. This includes the ability to identify and select resources that specifi-

cally relate to student needs. In addition, embedded librarians provide the information in context with efficiency (Zabel, Thomas, Bird, & Moniz, 2012). When course instructors and students value the embedded librarian as a component of learning, the program has greater opportunity to thrive. Assessment of the program helps to generate data to highlight the value of specific features of the program as well as opportunities for modifications.

Assessment of the Program

Assessment of the embedded librarian program is essential and needs to include feedback from both course instructors and students, which can be used to further develop and enhance the program. Analysis of the responses may also help to determine the future of the embedded librarian program in terms of whether any revisions are needed to the services provided, issues related to instructional and communication strategies, and the selection of resources for the embedded librarian forum.

An example of implementing new features based on assessment surveys occurred when the author (AD) was embedded in an online English class that had a stand-alone forum for research questions. At the suggestion of the instructor, she changed the location of the stand-alone forum to be included as a thread within the main course discussion board. The intent was to increase the opportunities and access to library support by establishing communication within an area that students entered into and engaged with on a regular basis. Informal and formal feedback both supported development of the program. A formal evaluation of the embedded librarian program should also take into account various aspects of current library trends, institutional factors, and new technologies. Examining this information can save the librarian time from "reinventing the wheel" and learning what has and has not worked at institutions with similar missions. Feedback can help to identify new tools, approaches, and strategies to address user needs and areas for improvement.

Through collaborations between the embedded librarian and course instructor, an appropriate method of evaluation may be established. For example, the use of surveys can be implemented in many different ways including the library resources forum and e-mail tool to capture data from students and instructors alike. The author's (AD) experience includes one case in which she communicated with the instructor who, in turn, provided students with directions for the completion of the survey. As a result of this collaboration, data was collected in a manner that was acceptable to both parties. Many LMS providers have built-in evaluation components. When students are requested to complete a full-course survey, the instructional designers can include a few questions regarding assessment of embedded librarian services.

Collaboration

Communication and coordination with course instructors is essential to promote effective learning strategies for students, which helps to create a culture of inquiry (Pedrosa de Jesus, Almeida, & Watts, 2004). As a result of successful communication, the embedded librarian is better positioned to offer support. For example, when course instructors introduce the embedded librarian at the beginning of a course, the librarian is in place to establish himself or herself as a member of the learning environment. In addition, students might be more apt to contact the librarian once the course instructor acknowledges the value of the available services. Course announcements are another way through which students may be prompted to use the embedded librarian services (Matthew & Schroeder, 2006). At key points, when assignments are due, announcements can be used to remind students to consult with librarians for instruction, support, and service.

Effective collaborations between the embedded librarian and the course instructor require clarity and purpose, whether online, via phone, or face to face. Graphic displays may help to demonstrate how the embedded librarian supports the course and how library resources are integrated. A concerted effort between the course facilitator and the embedded librarian allows for opportunities to create a space that conveys and fosters a symbiotic environment (Berdish & Seeman, 2008). Librarian awareness of both the course instructor's needs and student needs helps to prepare for the delivery of impactful services and support.

Collaborations with instructors should take into account student attitudes and behavior. For example, when instructors assign their students to ask the embedded librarian questions, the interaction that occurs initiates a critical process in the acquisition and development of information literacy skills. Students gain from the practice while others benefit from observing how their classmates articulate questions. This learning experience is meaningful when the students are tasked to make inquiries associated with an assignment (Matthew & Schroeder, 2006).

Building relationships is vital to the growth and development of embedded services (Kvenild & Calkins, 2011). Efforts to solidify the partnership between the embedded librarian and the course instructor are evident when the embedded librarian program is launched in a manner that benefits the students throughout the duration of the course. The embedded librarian can offer recommendations to the course instructor for effectively implementing the embedded services. The following is a sample communication used by the author (AD) to gain support from the course instructor:

Your students will be encouraged to use the library resources for this course when you

- *introduce the embedded librarian in the introduction and announcements;*
- *encourage use of the services in the course syllabus;*

- *require that students formulate inquiries related to a course assignment and submit at least one question to the librarian, or provide examples of keywords and resources used in case they have no questions;*
- *remind students that the library resources will help them to complete their research papers.*

This strategy will support library and research practices. Item c (above) will enable students to specifically engage in activities to develop information literacy skills. Requiring students to generate inquiries is directly aligned with and related to ACRL Information Literacy Standard One (ACRL, 2000), which states, "the information literate student defines and articulates the need for information." Subsequent activities can build upon previous learning activities to demonstrate that students meet the fourth outcome of Standard One: "The information literate student reevaluates the nature and extent of the information need." Incorporating requirements to meet ACRL's Information Literacy Standard Two promotes demonstration that "the information literate student accesses needed information effectively and efficiently"

This level of collaboration highlights the supportive roles of both the librarian and the course instructor. The integration of the embedded librarian services may include course requirements that are directly linked to the embedded librarian forum. This strategy seeks to promote student awareness of the library resources, encourage use of the services, and increase the development of information literacy skills through practice.

Student-Centered

A student-centered approach begins with learning objectives that are aligned with ACRL's *Information Literacy Competency Standards for Higher Education* (2000). This can include tools, resources, and support based on effective teaching strategies and best practices for e-learning. Guidelines, standards, and best practices prepare online embedded librarians for engaging in a manner that supports learning. In addition to information literacy skills, Tyler and Hastings (2011) recommended "online learning students… participate in training to increase skills in the use of computer applications and online library resources" (p. 28). In response, the embedded librarian is challenged to identify pertinent skills and appropriate resources to address course-specific learning outcomes.

Mini-lessons, lectures, self-paced tutorials, and learning objects are other ways to instruct students on library concepts, information navigation, and research strategies. Thoughtful preparation, awareness, and understanding about aspects of the population served and the course requirements help to identify, create, and include accessible materials to teach relevant information in a timely manner. A set of prepared responses may be generated to facilitate support efforts, which can then be edited and repurposed to address the specific needs for each interaction.

In addition to communicating the goal to provide reference support, it may benefit the student to access examples of how the reference exchange works. A podcast or sample scripts that demonstrate the level and types of questions asked by students provides a model for students. To effectively address the diverse learning styles and preferences of students, the embedded librarian is challenged to utilize and consider appropriate technologies to support all students no matter their skill level or ability. An embedded librarian ensures that the materials provided are ADA compliant, browser agnostic, and sometimes available offline, i.e. screencasts, downloadable videos, and others.

Universal design and ADA compliance should be evident as students navigate and access resources within the realm of the supportive environment. Along with learning preferences, the design of the online support module should take into consideration word choice, clarity, and other communication features to address issues of access and equity. Communication with students should convey a tone that is open, welcome, and non-threatening. Information should be presented in several ways, and students should have multiple options for communicating and engaging in the learning process (Rose & Gravel, 2010). Since the embedded librarian serves all students he or she should demonstrate flexible approaches to support students with specific learning preferences or additional requirements.

Another way to address student-learning needs is through open communication. Students often share information with instructors that can be useful to elucidate students' concerns as well as in the assessment of learning preferences. Once identified, learning preferences and challenges related to language barriers may be supported with tools and strategies directed to address those needs.

When students are tasked to interact with the librarian, they are provided with an opportunity to gain familiarity with a process that might lead to additional inquiries. Bennett and Simning (2010) describe a case where an online embedded librarian provided an activity designed to increase interaction between him and the students. This activity was intended to support the students' development of library and research skills. In addition to the learning activity, students were also assigned to view introductory tutorials and guides. The culmination of this learning activity required the students to share their experiences by posting to the designated threads in the course discussion forum. This presented the embedded librarian an opportunity to respond to each student and helped the librarian to learn more about student needs.

Embedded librarians can serve a powerful role in supporting first-year students and new researchers. Recognizing that prior research experiences differ, librarians are in a position to provide opportunities to fill the gaps and support skills building (Salisbury & Karasmanis, 2011).

Because the nature of the embedded librarian is to meet the users where they are, embedded librarians can tailor every bit of service they provide. If a librarian notices that a specific class

struggles with appropriate keyword generation, lessons can be added or revised to address this skill. Similarly, if another class demonstrates a need for narrowing research topics, the librarian can again adjust as necessary for this added characteristic. For example, the author (AD) found an opportunity for this type of service when she created a PowerPoint presentation to help students understand that college-level research requires a variety of resources, some of which are scholarly and more appropriate for the purposes of academic research than Google or Wikipedia. Another example is when the author (AV) found herself embedded in a similar situation where students were asked to identify and post a citation for one scholarly, peer-reviewed article for an assignment. She and the course instructor found that many students were using popular sources. A quick, revised and updated screencast explaining what was *not* appropriate as a scholarly, peer-reviewed source helped the students before they got too far off course.

A broad range of resources can help students to understand specific concepts, processes, and strategies related to library services and research activities. A helpful approach strikes a balance between monitoring and hovering, and support should be easily accessible. Considerations for the adoption of best practices may include the following:

- Establish presence.
- Welcome questions.
- Check in consistently.
- Respond with relevance.
- Determine how to address student difficulties.

For example, if an embedded librarian observes conversations in the discussion board that reveal student difficulties with a specific concept, skill, or resource, a carefully crafted response can help students to stay on track. To support student needs, the embedded librarian may provide a podcast or tutorial in a research forum to raise the level of awareness and understanding of all students. In general, embedded librarians should

Figure 2.4. Identifying scholarly articles. Screenshot of a screencast used to help students more accurately identify scholarly articles.

regard student difficulties and inquiries related to information literacy, research, or library services as a prompt for support. Multiple modes of communication may need to be implemented to interact with students. A welcoming learning climate is introduced and maintained with clearly stated expectations for response time and the scope of questions that are appropriate within the forum.

Students are also directed to submit inquiries about the course content, assignment parameters, and grades directly to the course facilitator. If a student directs these types of questions to the librarian, it is sometimes appropriate to forward the message to the instructor with a reply to the student that they should direct these types of inquiries to the appropriate person. Further, through collaborations with the course facilitator, these guidelines can be clearly articulated in the syllabus and other course documents.

Embedded librarians increase opportunities to establish rapport and build trust when their responses are direct, respectful, and timely. Awareness about student needs is reflected through the resources and tools provided with the "research forum." When the embedded librarian knows of such factors as students' prior learning experiences and inquiry skills (experience, behavior, and attitudes), he or she can promote increased awareness in conversations regarding student-centered approaches to teaching. Definitions and explanations can support student understanding of library concepts and words like stacks, interlibrary loan, and reference. Clarity is particularly significant for online students in regards to misinterpretation of textual meaning, and especially considering the lag time between the time the question is submitted and when the answer is provided in an asynchronous discussion forum.

Embedded librarians serve as an integral support mechanism. Berdish and Seeman (2008) describe embedded librarians critical role as one responsible for bridging the "divide between libraries and distance learners." The integration of this set of specialized services offers a benefit for students, support for instructors, and instruction to develop information literacy.

Questions

As librarians establish relationships with library users, they increase their awareness of user needs, behaviors and attitudes. When students conceive questions but are reluctant to ask, embedded librarians can identify some common questions and promote clarity by providing the answers that will help students to succeed in their efforts to navigate library resources (Shumaker, 2009). Solutions may be addressed in a proactive approach as librarians anticipate issues, concerns, and questions that students are likely to present. Question threads may be established to engage students in dialog to promote understanding. Another benefit of displaying this dialog within the discussion board is that it provides examples of the question and answer exchange between students and the embedded librarian. Efforts to accommodate those who lack articulation skills and experience help students to overcome barriers to learning (Donaldson, 2012).

A list of frequently asked questions (FAQs) may also be a useful tool to add to the library resources forum (University of Maryland University College, 2010). The availability of FAQs demonstrates to students how they may approach asking the appropriate questions that will support them as they engage in research. This includes guidance with formulating effective queries through databases when searching for information (Lipowski, 2008). For example, a student may understand that they need resources for a research paper but may not understand the research process, and many have limited experience with asking questions related to research. Questions listed in the FAQ can be as simple as "Where do I find my password for my library account?" to more complex questions like "How long does it take for a journal article or book requested through interlibrary loan to arrive from another library?"

In addition to providing a direct answer to the question, the FAQ response can also introduce the concept of interlibrary loan to students

unfamiliar with the service. From simplistic to complex, the level of questions listed in the FAQ may serve as useful examples for students to follow and adapt for their own purposes. The FAQ may further serve to reinforce the idea that questions are welcome (Nadelson, 2009).

Demonstrations of search strategies, navigation tips, and resourceful tools can help to answer questions or generate new questions. An automatic question submission tool may help to encourage those who wish to remain anonymous. A "click here to submit a question" feature can be provided so that the question is automatically submitted to the embedded librarian whose response will be automatically returned to the sender. Additional strategies to increase effort to address questions should be implemented as a proactive approach to reach students who are too shy or reluctant to make inquiries. Reference features such as instant messaging and Facebook also facilitate inquiries by providing easy, anonymous access.

Embedded librarians can also expect to encounter challenging questions or technical difficulties that inhibit a timely response. "I don't know" is a valid response. Additional ways to indicate that an answer to the question is not immediately available include

- tell the patron that you will need more time to research,
- refer the question,
- request contact information and respond at a later date.

Ralph (2012) describes a best-case scenario approach where library and research orientation is offered early, prior to the point of need, then followed with virtual support. The idea to offer greater, tiered support for novice researchers or first-year students will help familiarize students with the library resources and services while also preparing them for research.

Considering the potential for an increase in students lacking experience with questions and inquiry skills, the embedded librarian forum can be made scalable to allow for opportunities to develop this vital skill-set. For most institutions of higher education, the expectation that first-year college students have achieved some level of proficiency with question development is not unreasonable (Lord & Baviskar, 2007). However, a study of student behaviors, attitudes, and experiences suggests that some students do not perceive the library as a place to ask questions. Instead, some students believe it is their responsibility to use computers or books to find answers (Donaldson, 2012). Through the use of tutorials and FAQs students may gain clarity on approaches to determine what to ask and how to ask (Petress, 2006). Meanwhile, professional development opportunities can prepare embedded librarians and those looking to become embedded with updated information about the student populations they serve.

The variety of communication options available is handy from a student perspective, but can make it difficult to track student use of library resources. Enhancements to the embedded librarian program should take into consideration that the intent is to support student learning and access. In order to enhance her visibility and availability in offering services, resources, and support in alignment with learning activities and assignments, the author (AD) found she needed to increase her activity within the discussion board. She addressed this concern by looking for opportunities to support student needs as identified in conversations with the course instructor by posting materials and links to support current and upcoming assignments and in response to discussion board conversations. The goal in this case was to determine if her presence increased awareness about the wealth of relevant library resources. As in any project where time is a critical concern, piloting a move to increase time spent needs to be carefully tracked and documented for future outcomes. Continuous assessment of the virtual environments served will help the embedded librarian to provide the appropriate level of support, resources, and

services. Decision-making to enhance services may include global research efforts and local observations. The following list of questions may help to stimulate discussions and ideas in support of enhancements to embedded librarian programs.

Questions to Ask about Your Embedded Librarian Program

When considering planning and implementation for an embedded librarian program, ask yourself the following questions:

- How does the level of information literacy, research support, and service align with the college mission?
- Concerned about equitable resources for online students? What resources, strategies, and other learning opportunities are online students missing?
- Can you share concepts and experiences via podcast, screencasts, or links? For example, an exploration of print format, encyclopedia use, journals, books, etc.
- What is the appropriate level of information literacy education for the class?
- What is the best way to assess the program?

Best practices are based on experience, assessment, and research. Continued research, communication, and coordination are key elements to maintain an effective embedded librarian program. Adherence to best practices requires a proactive approach to the identification of relevant, accessible resources and services. A clear understanding of student needs and solid communication with the course instructor promotes consistent and timely response. Acknowledgement that each situation has specific and varying requirements prepares the embedded librarian to effectively serve. Professional development will help to prepare a team of embedded librarians to engage effectively in this new and expanding role. The following checklist may serve as a guide.

Embedded Librarian Checklist

Pre-Course Delivery Preparations

- Collaborations
- Alignment with curriculum
- Access to the course
- Development and identification of resources, services, instructional strategies, support, communication modes

Early Phase of Course Delivery

- Give personal introduction.
- Share tips and tools to facilitate the navigation of resources.
- Provide contact information and notification of response time.

Mid-Course

- Model and demonstrate effective research strategies.
- Provide direct instruction as required.
- Communicate with course instructor to determine additional needs.

End of Course

- Surveys
- Evaluations
- Assessment
- Reflections

Embedded librarians are encouraged to adopt best practices to support themselves as they set out to develop effective programs. In addition to collaborations and partnerships on campus, librarians can benefit from the expertise of library specialists external to their college environment. Through interactions, projects, and information sharing, embedded librarians can gain valuable feedback, strategies, and tools. Models aligned with best practices can enhance the journey.

Conceptual models not only guide the process but may be used to demonstrate and communicate the process to course instructors. A basic conceptual model created by the authors—the Embedded Librarian CSE Model (Collaborate, Support, Evaluate)—illustrates the librarian's dynamic role using a student-centered approach. Once services are requested, the librarian actively collaborates with course instructors to gain an understanding of the learning objectives and outcomes. Through agreements and with the establishment of parameters, the librarian's supportive role includes the creation of a space in which to deliver resources identified to support the learning outcomes. Instructor feedback, student surveys, and the librarian's observations and reflections can be used to evaluate the program. With each cycle, the experiences and feedback are vital elements to further enhance and expand the embedded library program and associated resources.

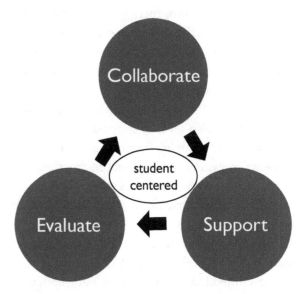

Figure 2.5. Embedded Librarian CSE Model. Key processes required to maintain a student-centered embedded librarian program within an online learning environment.

Future Considerations

As the demand for online research support increases so too will opportunities for embedded librarians. In the online learning environment, provision of library support and services will require technical skills as well as teaching and reference experience. Librarians seeking to address the time commitment for this specialized role can create a set of common responses that are readily available for posting (Bennett & Simning, 2010). Embedded library services within physical spaces often require subject specialization and interpersonal skills to serve in a role that requires close interaction and alignment within academic divisions or departments.

Future demands for research support for students in face-to-face courses can offer increased opportunities for librarians. As the flipped classroom is becoming more prominent in higher education, the virtual embedded librarian can serve in a unique position when this technique is implemented. By delivering online library support outside of the classroom, there is more time in the classroom to put the skills to use and practice. As Ralph (2012) observed, even doctoral students require support beyond the one-shot information literacy session. Embedded librarian services to supplement the one-shot information literacy session might also serve to support accreditation for institutions of higher learning. This will enable students to gain access to direct instruction and support from within the LMS that houses many of their assignments, discussions, and learning resources.

Student survey feedback and other assessment data are vital to shape the expanding role of the embedded librarian. This information is significant both for internal assessments and accreditation reviews (York & Vance, 2009). Future efforts to gain statistics on the correlation between student success or student retention and library and embedded librarian services may be more effectively addressed in surveys that assess specific courses and learning outcomes or campus-wide assessments.

Staying up to date with emerging technologies and library trends supports the planning and development efforts for new services, tools, and strategies. With new technologies and educational configurations, attention to access and equity remains a significant consideration. Staying informed of reading comprehension issues and attention deficits can bring forth awareness for the need to identify audio and visual media

to support student-learning needs. Future learners may present a new set of learning preferences for consideration. Embedded librarians can play a role in the identification and development of tools and techniques to support the needs of online students.

Where provided, course facilitators may also choose to secure the services of an embedded librarian to provide direct support in their course. However, as the demand for embedded services increases so might the necessity for training those seeking to fulfill this specialized role. Meanwhile, the allocation of funds for continued development of embedded librarian programs challenge embedded librarians and library administrators to consider the need for professional development, resources, and other factors required to maintain and expand the program (Shumaker, 2009).

With the development of new technologies to enhance communication, the embedded librarian of the future will have additional tools to facilitate student support. New strategies to promote increased interaction will be available in the online environment for support. For example, the librarian in collaboration with the course instructor may identify critical points in the research process during which students may benefit from librarian support to address specific needs. Evolving needs may necessitate new strategies and configurations.

Just as the emergence of the embedded librarian is attributed to factors related to student needs, aspects of the teaching and learning environment will influence educational technology and learning platforms. As Schulte (2011) recommended based on observations in an academic health science library, "each institution must balance its organizational needs with that of its customers when designing its future services" (p. 279). The future outlook for this dynamic professional is filled with opportunities to instruct and support users through the use of creative and innovative approaches.

REFERENCES

Alshraideh, M. (2009). The effect of Suchmans' inquiry model on developing critical thinking skills among university students. *International Journal of Applied Educational Studies, 4*(1), 58–69. Retrieved from http://www.ijaes.com/

Association of College and Research Libraries. (2000). *Information literacy competency standards for higher education.* Retrieved from http://www.ala.org/acrl/sites/ala.org.acrl/files/content/standards/standards.pdf

Association of College and Research Libraries. (2011). *Standards for libraries in higher education.* Retrieved from http://www.ala.org/acrl/sites/ala.org.acrl/files/content/standards/slhe.pdf

Bennett, E., & Simning, J. (2010). Embedded librarians and reference traffic: A quantitative analysis. *Journal of Library Administration, 50*(5-6), 443–457. doi:10.1080/01930826.2010.491437

Berdish, L., & Seeman, C. (2008). *Spanning the straits of business information: Kresge library's embedded librarian program for MAP (multidisciplinary action program).* Paper presented at the Special Libraries Association Annual Conference, Seattle, WA.

Donaldson, A. (2012). *Inquiry skills: A phenomenological study on the perceptions of first-year community college students* (Doctoral dissertation). Retrieved from ProQuest Dissertations and Theses. (3531379)

Dugan, M. (2008). Embedded librarians in an ag econ class: Transcending the traditional. *Journal of Agricultural and Food Information, 9*(4), 301–309.

EDUCAUSE. (2013, February 5). *Lessons from the field: An analysis of online instructors' "best practices."* Presentation conducted at the EDUCAUSE Learning Initiative Annual Meeting, New Orleans, LA. Retrieved from www.educause.edu/eli/events/eli-annual-meeting/2013/2013/lessons-field-analysis-online-instructors-best-practices

Edwards, M. E., & Black, E. W. (2012). Contemporary instructor-librarian collaboration: A case study of an online embedded librarian implementation. *Journal of Library & Information Services in Distance Learning, 6*(3-4), 284–311.

Farnsworth, K. & Bevis, T. (2006). *A Fieldbook for Community College Online Instructors.* American Association of Community Colleges.

Gilbert, L., Liu, M., Matoush, T., & Whitlatch, J. (2006). Assessing digital reference and online instructional services in an integrated public/university library. *Reference Librarian, 46*(95-96), 149–172.

Hines, S. S. (2008). How it's done: Examining distance education library instruction and assessment. *Journal of Library Administration, 48*(3-4), 467–478.

Ketelhut, D., Nelson, B., Clarke, J., & Dede, C. (2010). A multi-user virtual environment for building and assessing higher order inquiry skills in science. *British Journal of Educational Technology, 41*(1), 56–68. doi:10.1111/j.1467-8535.2009.01036.x

Kvenild, C., & Calkins, K. (2011). *Embedded librarians: Moving beyond one-shot instruction.* Chicago, IL: Association of College and Research Libraries.

Lipowski, E. (2008). Developing great research questions. *American Journal of Health-System Pharmacy, 65*(17), 1667–1670. doi:10.2146/ajhp070276

Lord, T., & Baviskar, S. (2007). Moving students from information recitation to information understanding: exploiting Bloom's taxonomy in creating science questions. *Journal of College Science Teaching, 36*(5), 40-44. Retrieved from http://www.nsta.org/college/

Matthew, V., & Schroeder, A. (2006). The embedded librarian program. *EDUCAUSE Quarterly, 29*(4), 61–65. Retrieved from http://net.educause.edu/ir/library/pdf/EQM06410.pdf

Morgan, M., Moni, K., & Jobling, A. (2009). Who? Where? What? When? Why? How? Question words—What do they mean? *British Journal of Learning Disabilities, 37*(3), 178–185. doi:10.1111/j.1468-3156.2008.00539.x

Nadelson, L. S. (2009). How can true inquiry happen in K-16 science education? *Science Educator, 18*(1), 48–57. Retrieved from http://www.nsela.org

Pedrosa de Jesus, H., Almeida, P., & Watts, M. (2004). Questioning styles and students' learning: Four phenomenological studies. *Educational Psychology, 24*(4), 531–548. Retrieved from http://www.tandf.co.uk/journals/carfax/01443410.html

Petress, K. (2006). Questions and answers: The substance of knowledge and relationships. *College Student Journal, 40*(2), 374–376. Retrieved from http://www.projectinnovation.biz/csj.html

Ralph, L. (2012). Using education informatics to improve library services to doctoral students: An embedded approach. *International Journal of Doctoral Studies, 7*, 235–244. Retrieved from http://ijds.org/Volume7/IJDSv7p235-244Ralph0354.pdf

Rose, D.H., & Gravel, J.W. (2010). Universal design for learning. In P. Peterson, E. Baker, & B. McGaw (Eds.), *International encyclopedia of education (pp. 119–124).* Oxford, England: Elsevier.

Salisbury, F., & Karasmanis, S. (2011). Are they ready? Exploring student information literacy skills in the transition from secondary to tertiary education. *Australian Academic & Research Libraries, 42*(1), 43-58.

Schulte, S. J. (2011). Eliminating traditional reference services in an academic health sciences library: A case study. *Journal of the Medical Library Association, 99*(4), 273–279. doi:10.3163/1536-5050.99.4.004

Shumaker, D. (2009). Who let the librarians out? Embedded librarianship and the library manager. *Reference & User Services Quarterly, 48*(3), 239–242.

Sullo, E., Harrod, T., Butera, G., & Gomes, A. (2012). Rethinking library service to distance education students: Analyzing the embedded librarian model. *Medical Reference Services Quarterly, 31*(1), 25–33.

Tyler, K., & Hastings, N. B. (2011). Factors influencing virtual patron satisfaction with online library resources and services. *Journal of Educators Online, 8*(2), 1–34. Retrieved from http://www.thejeo.com/Archives/Volume8Number2/TylerandHastingsPaper.pdf

University of Central Florida. (2013). Design of an online course. *Teaching Online.* Retrieved from http://teach.ucf.edu/pedagogy/design-of-an-online-course/implementation-delivering-your-course/

University of Maryland University College. (2012). Best practices for online teaching. Retrieved from http://www.umuc.edu/ctl/upload/bestpractices.pdf.

Waugh, J. (2013). Formality in chat reference: Perceptions of 17- to 25-year-old university students. *Evidence Based Library and Information Practice, 8*(1), 19–34. Retrieved from http://ejournals.library.ualberta.ca/index.php/EBLIP/article/view/17911

Wu, H., & Hsieh, C. (2006). Developing sixth graders' inquiry skills to construct explanations in inquiry-based learning environments. *International Journal of Science Education, 28*(11), 1289–1313. doi:10.1080/09500690600621035

York, A. C., & Vance, J. M. (2009). Taking library instruction into the online classroom: Best practices for embedded librarians. *Journal of Library Administration, 49*(1-2), 197–209. doi:10.1080/01930820802312995

Zabel, D., Thomas, E. A., Bird, N., & Moniz, R. J., Jr. (2012). Informationists in a small university library. *Reference & User Services Quarterly, 51*(3), 223–225.

part two:
developing programs in the online embedded environment

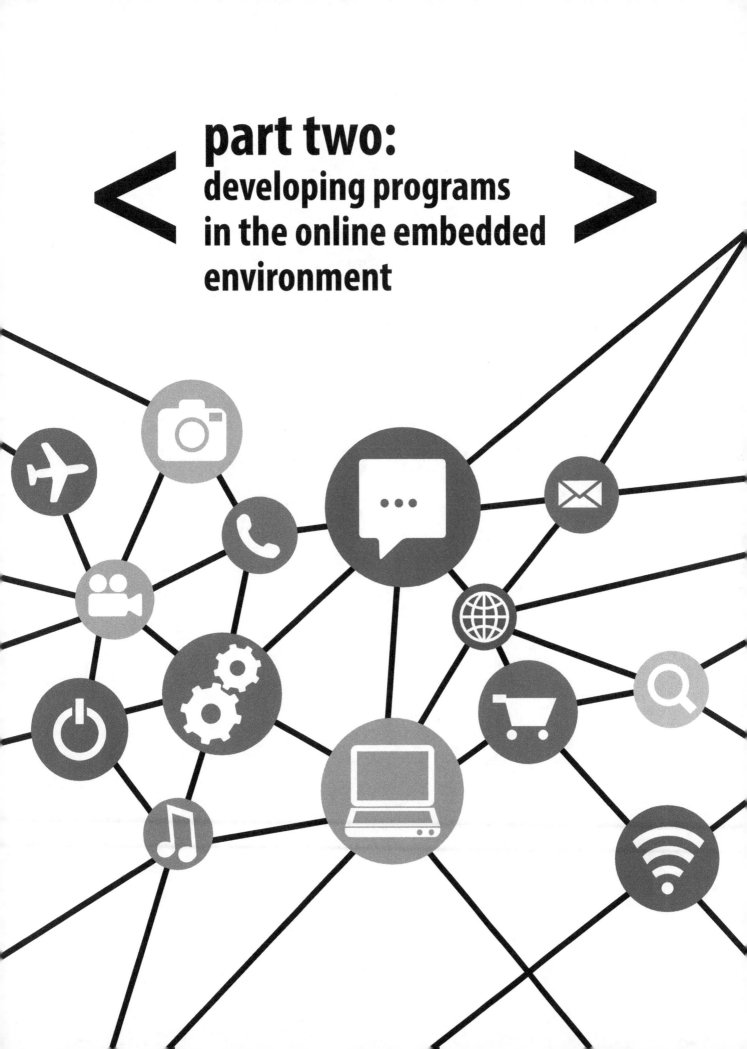

Sustainable Embedded Librarianship to Foster Research Skills in an Online Graduate Program

Swapna Kumar, Kristin Heathcock, and Marilyn N. Ochoa

Online education in the United States has seen unprecedented growth in the last decade with over seven million students taking an online course in the fall 2011 semester, at least four times more than those 10 years ago (Allen & Seaman, 2013). Online students often study at a distance for convenience and access and work full-time or have other commitments: Therefore, they are not always familiar with access to resources at their academic institution. However, online students' perception of connectedness to an institution plays an important role in student completion of online courses and student satisfaction in an online program (Cain & Lockee, 2002; Tait & Mills, 2003). Institutions of higher education thus strive to provide various forms of support at the institutional, program, and course level in order to provide online students with a quality online learning experience. This chapter presents one such effort: the collaboration between librarians and the coordinator of an online doctoral program to provide library services and skills to online doctoral students.

Information Literacy and Doctoral Students

Information literacy is defined as "the ability to locate, evaluate, and use effectively the needed information" (American Library Association, 1989, para. 3). According to Kuruppu and Gruber (2006), doctoral students' information literacy skills are largely overestimated by doctoral students and their faculty. Green (2010) used the term "information illiteracy" to describe doctoral students' lack of information literacy skills, asserting that new doctoral students' information literacy skills could sometimes be similar to undergraduates. She quotes a faculty member in her study, as stating,

> I think that what is a bit scary is how little they know... how few databases they're using and that sort of thing.... It seems to turn out that quite often they don't know much, and they're using Google and Google Scholar.... I think there is a lot of illiteracy out there. (Green, 2010, p. 315)

Doctoral studies can be challenging and doctoral students experience anxiety in several areas such as research, writing, persistence, and, more recently, technology (Gottlieb, 1994; Nelson & San Miguel, 2003; Onwuegbuzie, 1997; Onwuegbuzie & Jiao, 1998). Furthermore, doctoral students as adult learners experience low self-efficacy and "library anxiety" (Collins & Veal, 2004, p. 12) that can prevent them from finding, evaluating, and using appropriate resources in literature reviews and in their research proposals (Onwuegbuzie, 1997). These challenges are magnified in the online environment where doctoral students attempt to design, implement, and write up research in physical isolation from peers and faculty and where they do not have awareness or regular contact with the institutional services available to on-campus students. Such information literacy challenges may be alleviated if online doctoral students have regular interaction with one or more librarians and feel comfortable reaching out to those librarians who provide online instruction and support.

Macauley and Cavanagh (2001) suggest using a liaison librarian (or primary contact) for doctoral students studying at a distance. Such a liaison librarian could specialize in supporting online doctoral students as they navigate the information sources and services required for degree completion (Macauley & Cavanagh, 2001). In the study presented here, an embedded librarian who can fulfill a role similar to the one described by Macauley and Cavanagh and support the research needs of online doctoral students was embedded in the first year of an online doctoral program. The design, implementation, and assessment of the embedded librarian project in an online doctoral program are the focus of this chapter.

Embedded Librarians in Online Education

In the past, librarians have been embedded into different contexts such as colleges, departments, and face-to-face courses to provide information literacy instruction (Dewey, 2004; Drewes & Hoffman, 2010; Dugan, 2008; Freiburger & Kramer, 2009; Kesselman & Watstein, 2009; Love & Norwood, 2007; Matthew & Schroeder, 2006; McMillen & Fabbi, 2010; Shumaker & Talley, 2009). In their literature review on embedded librarianship, half of the articles identified by McMillen and Fabbi (2010) focused on distance and online courses. Prior literature on embedded librarians described how librarians were

embedded in online courses (Hoffman, 2011; Hoffman & Ramin, 2010; Konieczny, 2010). For example, Konieczny (2010) described a health sciences librarian who was embedded in several online nursing and healthcare systems administration courses. The embedded librarian used the discussion board to answer questions throughout the semester; provided library links, subject specific guides, and course-specific websites; and provided a synchronous library instruction session. Additionally, some courses Konieczny (2010) described had weekly research-based assignments that were monitored by the librarian. Hoffman and Ramin (2010) describe the experiences of several librarians embedded more briefly in courses, where the embedments consisted of only providing a synchronous one-shot instruction session or a limited duration text chat session. Several benefits of embedded librarians in online education have also been highlighted in the literature such as supporting online students, fostering connectedness to an institution, and helping students apply information literacy instruction to course activities (Kesselman & Watstein, 2009; Love & Norwood, 2007).

Some studies have also assessed students' satisfaction with embedded librarians and students' information literacy skills. In graduate online instruction, assessment has been conducted with small samples of students. Edwards, Kumar, and Ochoa (2010) used a mixed methods design to assess the impact of an embedded librarian in an online graduate course. They concluded that while the presence of an online embedded librarian was beneficial for both students and faculty, more detailed and rigorous assessment methods are required to assess information literacy skills. Other studies have focused on students' preferred formats for learning in embedded librarianship. On surveying students' satisfaction with various components of an embedded librarian in the first year of an online graduate program, Kumar and Ochoa (2012) reported that students preferred a combination of online tutorials and synchronous instruction where they could ask questions. Similar results were reported by Bonnand and Hansen (2012), who investigated best practices using web conferencing for information literacy instruction.

Studies that assessed the impact of librarians embedding in face-to-face undergraduate courses can also be adapted to assess online embedded librarian instruction. For instance, Bowler and Street (2008) designed several experimental face-to-face embedded librarian instances with differing levels of integration and assessed students using a standardized information literacy rubric. They found that a higher level of librarian integration that included more student interaction with the librarian resulted in a significant improvement in student scores. McMillen and Fabbi (2010) embedded in a face-to-face undergraduate education course and created several library-based assignments in collaboration with the course instructors to assess the learners' application of the library instruction. They reported positive trends in student learning and increased collaboration with faculty (McMillen & Fabbi, 2010).

The First Embedded Librarianship Project in the Online Doctoral Program

The research for this chapter took place in an online doctoral program in education that requires students to complete the following activities related to information literacy: to search, find, critique, and use peer-reviewed publications; to write annotated bibliographies, book reviews, and literature reviews; to frame their research in the context of seminal theories and prior research in the field; and to manage the literature and use appropriate citation styles. To support incoming online students in 2010, the program coordinator and the education librarian collaborated to identify minimum skills and knowledge required by students to succeed in their first year in the online program. Sample topics were access to on-campus resources, understanding how to use available databases, and the use of bibliographic management software available at the university (RefWorks). Simultaneously, as a crucial first step in the instructional design process (Koneru, 2010), incoming students' existing skills were identified using an online survey. Items in the survey assessed online students' perceived ability to use resources, find appropriate literature, and cite and evaluate resources (Kumar, Ochoa, & Edwards, 2012). Moreover, students were asked about their preferred format for online library instruction based on past experiences.

Instruction was designed based on the survey results. First, existing library instructional resources were reviewed for accuracy and appropriateness and linked in the orientation course for incoming doctoral students. The librarian created QuickTime video tutorials and portable documents (PDFs) that contained transcriptions or step-by-step instructions for various topics that did not already exist in the library's instructional tutorials. A library help forum was included in the orientation course that was monitored by the librarian. The librarian conducted two synchronous sessions during the first semester and one synchronous session during the second semester on topics identified by the librarian, faculty, and students as important to student progress. Students thus interacted with the embedded librarian by e-mail, on the library help forum, and during synchronous sessions (Kumar & Ochoa, 2012). A post-instruction survey indicated that the embedded librarian project was successful in improving students' information literacy skills. Students used the search engine Google less and used Google Scholar and other specialized education databases more after the embedded librarian project. Similarly, 89.5% were aware of dissertation databases compared to 28.6% before the embedded librarian project. Students also reported higher confidence accessing and using library resources (Kumar & Edwards, 2013).

The first attempt at embedded librarianship in the online doctoral program was thus successful, but several issues became apparent during the project. First, students did not view online tutorials that were not appropriately placed. That is, online tutorials placed close to assignments that were due or within related modules in their online courses were more likely to be viewed. Second, students were practitioners who had not been engaged in academic pursuits for many years or were not familiar with current online databases or journals in education. Although they were technology-savvy and comfortable searching in public search engines, they did not always know how to search within academic databases (Kumar & Ochoa, 2012). Similar to Green's (2010) conclusion, several were not aware of their low information literacy skills until they participated in the instruction provided by the embedded librarian. In the post-survey, they reported increased confidence but increased anxiety, and some stated they now knew what they didn't know (Kumar & Edwards, 2013). It was thus important that the program coordinator or instructor highlight to students what information literacy meant as well as the importance of information literacy to their success in the doctoral program. Third, students came in with a wide range of skills and interdisciplinary interests as reflected in the needs analysis. It would not be sufficient to provide generic information literacy instruction about access and databases; the embedded librarian would have to address individual challenges faced by students.

The Second Embedded Librarian Project in the Online Doctoral Program

The above experiences prompted the creation of a structured plan for supporting a new cohort of online students in 2012 based on best practices on embedded librarianship in the literature and what had worked in the first implementation in our program.

- The program coordinator first reviewed changes to the curriculum, assignments, and re-identified essential information literacy skills needed to facilitate students' success in the doctoral program (e.g. off-campus access to databases, using APA sixth edition instead of the fifth). Consequently, the embedded librarian reviewed and integrated new resources now available at the library for instruction in those areas; updated any tutorials, videos, or PDFs from the previous implementation that were outdated; and created new resources for new interfaces at the library.

- Similar to the previous implementation, a needs analysis was conducted to survey students' experience and perceived ability to access information online; search and retrieve different types of resources in the field of education; and manage and use library resources in their writing. The needs assessment was hosted online, and all 23 incoming doctoral students completed it.

- The librarian and the program coordinator then met to discuss the results of the survey and finalize the curriculum as well as the formats of embedded librarian interactions for the second group. The needs analysis results indicated that students would benefit from a thorough introduction to the library, online databases in education, online databases in their specific areas of interest, and bibliographic management software. Students reported lack of familiarity and use of the databases available and lack of experience with academic research in the last few years; consequently, multiple formats of instruction were planned. Some decisions were based on areas that had been problematic with the previous group. For instance, Ulrich's International Periodical Directory, a tool that could assist students in determining the quality of articles, would be taught to all students. Also, despite professing a preference for online tutorials when entering the program, previous students had found synchronous sessions more valuable; therefore, it was decided that synchronous sessions would be recommended.

- Based on feedback from previous students, the embedded librarian curriculum began with online tutorials about on-campus access even before the students began the program. A LibGuide was created especially for this group of students with initial topics such as off-campus access, searching strategies, main databases, etc. Two weeks after courses began, students attended a synchronous session with the librarian where they could troubleshoot, ask specific questions, and receive instruction on determining article quality. Videos relevant to assignments in the courses that first semester were strategically available within online modules in the LMS for those weeks. A second synchronous session about RefWorks was taught by the librarian later in the semester. She was also available in a library help forum throughout the semester.

Methodology: Data Collection and Analysis

At the end of six months, students (n = 16) voluntarily participated in an online post-survey of their information literacy skills to measure

- students' satisfaction with the embedded librarian experience,
- students' familiarity and use of library resources after the embedded librarian experience,
- students' confidence and anxiety after the embedded librarian experience.

Survey items included students' satisfaction with various interactions with the embedded librarian and their perceived ability, confidence, and anxiety when applying information literacy

skills. The results of students' perceived information literacy skills in the post-survey were compared to students' responses on the needs analysis at the beginning of the program using descriptive analysis.

Three open-ended questions were also included in the post-survey about students' application of resources provided by the embedded librarian, specifically, how the instruction impacted their approach to using education databases, how students had used the instruction provided during the synchronous sessions, and any suggestions for improving information literacy instruction. The open-ended responses were open coded first and then collapsed to themes that were used to supplement the quantitative results where appropriate (Strauss & Corbin, 1990).

Results
Participation and Satisfaction

Students were asked a variety of questions about their participation and satisfaction with the information literacy instruction provided during their time in the program. Sixteen students completed the survey. Of these students, 93.8% indicated that they had accessed the university's library resources from off campus during the previous six months, while 56.3% indicated that they had accessed the online library tutorials created for their cohort during this same time period.

Students' satisfaction with and perceived value of the different components of the library instruction during their time in the program were examined (Tables 3.1 and 3.2). Seventy-five percent of students indicated that they were satisfied to very satisfied with the initial library instruction, an on-campus, face-to-face introduction to the library. The asynchronous materials provided for the students, which included a LibGuide and video tutorials, were used by 14 of 16 students in the survey. Students' mean satisfaction with these materials was the highest of the three formats—2.21 (Table 3.1)—and no students who used these materi-

Table 3.1. Satisfaction with Library Instruction

Please rate your satisfaction with the library instruction you received for conducting research in Fall 2012.	Attended (n = 16)	Mean (very satisfied = 3; not satisfied = 1; did not attend = 0)
Summer 2012: On-campus introductory one-hour library orientation session	16	1.88
Summer–Fall 2012: Asynchronous materials (LibGuide, video tutorials) provided before and after course began	14	2.21
Fall 2012: Synchronous session	14	2.14

als indicated that they were unsatisfied. Fourteen students reported attending the synchronous session, with a mean satisfaction rating of 2.14, where 85.7% indicated that they were satisfied to very satisfied with this session. Information provided during the session was applied directly to coursework by 76.9% of the students who attended the session. Open-ended responses indicated that students learned information during the synchronous session that was useful for them to find journal articles, access relevant education databases, evaluate peer-reviewed materials using Ulrich's International Periodical Directory, access course reserve materials and research guides, and improve their search strategies.

Students were asked to rate the value of the library instructional components to their ability to complete their assignments during the beginning of the program (Table 3.2). All components of the library instruction were perceived as valuable with the asynchronous materials and synchronous session being perceived as most valuable with mean ratings of 2.36 and 2.29 respectively. Both of these instructional formats were rated as valuable to very valuable by 92.9% of the 14 students who viewed them and attended the session with only one student rating them as not valuable. The on-campus session was also perceived as being valuable with a mean rating of 2.13.

Confidence and Perception of Information Literacy Skills

Students were surveyed about their confidence and perception of research skills both prior to the beginning of the program and after the completion of the first semester (Table 3.3). Students' confidence in their ability to conduct library research using the library catalog increased during their time in the program. When initially they reported their confidence in their research skills using the library catalog (very confident = 4; confident = 3; somewhat confident = 2; and not confident = 1), the mean rating for their skills was a 2.39 (SD = .839). After the first semester in the program, the mean rating for students' confidence increased to 2.75 (SD = .775). While an independent t-test indicates that there is no significant difference in the reported confidence ($t(37) = -1.355, p = .184$), it is worth noting that prior to the program only 43.5% of students reported that they were confident to very confident in their use of the library catalog, but after their first semester in the program with an embedded librarian 68.8% reported that they were confident to very confident.

Likewise, students reported increased confidence in their ability to conduct research using the article databases provided by the university (very

Table 3.2. Value of Library Instruction to Assignment Completion

Please rate the value of the following to your ability to successfully complete assignments in Fall 2012.	Attended (n = 16)	Mean (very valuable = 3; not valuable = 1; did not attend = 0)
Summer 2012: On-campus introductory one-hour library orientation session	16	2.13
Summer–Fall 2012: Asynchronous materials (LibGuide, video tutorials) provided before and after course began	14	2.36
Fall 2012: Synchronous session about peer-reviewed resources	14	2.29

Table 3.3. Perceived Skills and Confidence Using Library Resources

	Pre-survey (n = 23)		Post-survey (n = 16)	
	Mean	SD	Mean	SD
How confident are you in conducting library research using the library catalog? (very confident = 4, not confident = 1)	2.39	.839	2.75	.775
How confident are you in conducting library research using article databases, e.g., Academic Search Premier or Education Full Text? (very confident = 4, not confident = 1)	2.22	.902	2.75	.683
How do you rate your library research skills? (very skilled = 4, not skilled = 1)	2.30	.703	2.56	.814
How do you rate your success with finding research articles that are relevant to your topic? (very successful = 4, not successful = 1)	2.57	.788	2.81	.750

confident = 4; confident = 3; somewhat confident = 2; and not confident = 1). In the pre-survey, 34.8% of students reported that they were confident to very confident in their ability to research using article databases (M = 2.22, SD = .902). In the post-survey, 62.5% of students reported that they were confident to very confident in their ability to use the article databases (M = 2.75, SD = .683). Though an independent t-test indicates that there is no significant difference in the confidence of the students in the pre- and post-surveys (t(37) = -1.994, p = .054), it is apparent from the data that students have increased confidence in their ability to research using the article databases. Compared to 21.7% in the pre-survey who rated themselves as not confident, there were no students in the post-survey that rated themselves as not confident.

Students' ratings of their library research skills improved during their time in the program (very skilled = 4; skilled = 3; somewhat skilled = 2; and not skilled = 1). Prior to their time in the program, students' mean rating for their skills was 2.30 (SD = .703), with 34.7% rating themselves as skilled to very skilled. After their first semester in the program, students' ratings of their skills increased to 2.56 (SD = .814), with 50% reporting themselves as skilled to very skilled. An independent t-test indicated that there was no significant difference in students' rating of their skills (t(37) = -1.057, p = .297).

Students' reported success in locating relevant articles for their research also increased dur-

ing their time in the program (very successful = 4; successful = 3; somewhat successful = 2; and not successful = 1). Initially, students' mean rating for their success was 2.57 (SD = .788), with 47.8% reporting themselves as successful to very successful. After their time in the program, students' mean reported rating was 2.81 (SD = .750), with 62.6% reporting themselves as successful to very successful. Like the other ratings, an independent t-test indicated that there was no significant difference in the students' rating of their success (t(37) = -.983, p = .332).

Awareness and Use of Relevant Databases

Students were presented a list of 14 databases relevant to the subject-matter of the program from which to indicate those that they were aware of and those they used frequently. The pre-survey revealed that students were unaware of the most frequently used databases by doctoral students in educational technology in our program (Table 3.4). The database with which students were most familiar was ERIC (52.2%). Students' awareness of the other key databases was low: Academic Search Premier (17.4%), Dissertations and Theses (13%), Education Full Text (17.4%), Ulrich's International Periodical Database (0%), and Web of Science (0%). In the post-survey, however, students overwhelmingly indicated increased familiarity with the most frequently used education databases: ERIC (87.5%), Dissertations and

Theses (87.5%), Education Full Text (81.3%), Google Scholar (81.3%), Academic Search Premier (56.3%), and the library catalog (50%).

Table 3.4. Awareness of Education Databases

Educational databases of which you are aware (Check all that apply.)	Pre-survey (n = 23)	Post-survey (n = 16)
Academic Search Premier	17.4%	56.3%
Dissertations and Theses	13.0%	87.5%
Education Full Text	17.4%	81.3%
ERIC	52.2%	87.5%
GoogleScholar	30.4%	81.3%
JSTOR	34.8%	56.3%
LexisNexis Academic	30.4%	37.5%
Library Catalog	21.7%	50.0%
PsycInfo	13.0%	25.0%
Social Science Citation Index	4.3%	6.3%
Social Sciences Full Text	13.0%	12.5%
Ulrich's International Periodical Database	0.0%	43.8%
Web of Science	0.0%	6.3%
WorldCat	8.7%	25.0%
Other, please specify (EBSCO)	0.0%	6.3%

Similar to their awareness of databases, students reported little prior use of databases other than ERIC (52%) in the pre-survey. Seven of the 14 databases had never been used by these students (Table 3.5), but after the embedded librarian project, students' responses in the post-survey indicate increased use of databases for research. The most popular database continued to be ERIC, with 81.3% of the students reporting its use. Also reported as frequently used were Google Scholar (75%), Dissertations and Theses (56.3%), Education Full Text (50.0%), Academic Search Premier (37.5%) and JSTOR (25.0%).

Students' responses to the open-ended question—"In what ways did the library instruction provided to you impact your approach to using the above databases?"—revealed that the embedded librarian project introduced them to the databases available at the university and showed them how to access the databases on campus and remotely and how to search the databases. Additionally, students noted that they were now better able to locate peer-reviewed materials. One student stated that the instruction was useful in introducing them to the live library assistance available for them online.

Table 3.5. Use of Education Databases

Educational Databases that you frequently use (Check all that apply.)	Pre-survey (n = 21)	Post-survey (n = 16)
Academic Search Premier	14.3%	37.5%
Dissertations and Theses	0.0%	56.3%
Education Full Text	9.5%	50.0%
ERIC	52.4%	81.3%
Google Scholar	14.3%	75.0%
JSTOR	9.5%	25.0%
LexisNexis Academic	9.5%	6.3%
Library Catalog	4.8%	12.5%
PsycInfo	0.0%	0.0%
Social Science Citation Index	0.0%	0.0%
Social Sciences Full Text	0.0%	6.3%
Ulrich's International Periodical Database	0.0%	12.5%
Web of Science	0.0%	0.0%
WorldCat	0.0%	0.0%
Other, please specify (EBSCO)	0.0%	6.3%

Evaluation, Management, and Citation of Research

Use of peer-reviewed materials is important for students in a doctoral program. As such, students were asked if they were aware what a peer-reviewed journal was along with a question about how to determine quality and authority of a resource. Students in both the pre- and post-survey overwhelmingly indicated their awareness of the definition of a peer-reviewed journal; in the pre-survey 91.3% and in the post-survey 100% of students indicated knowledge of peer-review articles (Table 3.6). Likewise, students in both the pre- and post-surveys indicated that the peer-reviewed status of a journal was important in determining the quality and authority of resources found during their research. In the pre-survey, 60.9% of the students indicated that this was the most important factor, and in the post-survey, 68.8% of the students indicated this was the most important factor.

Table 3.6. Peer-Review Knowledge

Do you know what a "peer-reviewed" journal is?	Pre-survey (n = 23)	Post-survey (n = 16)
Yes	91.3%	100.0%
No	8.7%	0.0%
Which of the following factors do you think is most important for determining quality and authority of a resource discovered?	Pre-survey (n = 23)	Post-survey (n = 16)
Author	13.0%	0.0%
Name of journal	8.7%	6.3%
Peer-reviewed journal	60.9%	68.8%
Publication date	13.0%	12.5%
Publisher	4.3%	0%
Other	0.0%	12.5%

Students' ratings of their ability to evaluate the quality of the research articles found when conducting research were found to have increased in the post-survey (Table 3.7). In the pre-survey, students' mean rating for their ability was 2.65 (excellent = 4; good = 3; fair = 2; poor = 1) (SD = .775), while in the post-survey, it was 2.81 (SD = .981). An independent samples t-test indicated there was no significant difference in the reported abilities of the students ($t(37)$ = -.570, p = .572). Interestingly, there appeared to be a slight increase in students reporting a poor ability to evaluate quality, indicating increased awareness of their evaluation capabilities. Only 4.3% (one student) in the pre-survey indicated they had poor evaluation abilities, while 12.5% (two students) reported poor evaluation abilities in the post-survey.

Students mean rating of their ability to cite academic resources appropriately (Table 3.7) in the pre-survey was 2.87 (SD = .869) and increased to 3.25 (SD = .683) in the post-survey. While an inde-

pendent samples t-test indicated that there was no significant difference in the reported ability of the groups, ($t(37)$ = -1.463, p = .152), fewer students indicated poor ability to cite in the post-survey.

Table 3.7. Evaluation, Management, and Citing of Resources

	Pre-survey (n = 23)	Post-survey (n = 16)
How do you rate your ability to evaluate the quality of research articles found in your academic searches? (excellent = 4, poor = 1)	2.65	2.81
How do you rate your ability to cite your academic resources appropriately (e.g. APA, Chicago, MLA style)? (excellent = 4, poor = 1)	2.87	3.25

When asked to identify which tools were used to organize their research resources (Table 3.8) in the pre- and post-surveys, students reported using a variety of tools for the organization of their research resources. In the pre-survey, the majority of students (84.2%) reported using Microsoft Word for their organizational purposes. After the first semester in the program, fewer students reported using Microsoft Word (37.5%), with the majority now reporting use of RefWorks (50%). A RefWorks video and job aid had been provided in the LibGuide by the embedded librarian.

Table 3.8. Organization of Resources

Which of the following tools, if any, do you use to organize your resources? (Check all that apply.)	Pre-survey (n = 23)	Post-survey (n = 12)
EasyBib	10.5%	12.5%
EndNote	5.3%	0.0%
Microsoft Excel	26.3%	12.5%
Microsoft Word	84.2%	37.5%
RefWorks	10.5%	50.0%
Zotero	0.0%	0.0%
Other, please specify (11 Mendeley, 1 Bibme)	42.1%	12.5%

Students were asked to provide feedback on what worked and what some challenges were or changes needed for the library instruction provided for them during 2012. Students provided a variety of different responses, yet the majority of the responses indicated that the instruction was useful and that additional instruction would be welcomed. No students indicated that the instruction was not beneficial. Instead students requested that there be a longer session provided during their initial campus visit, along with additional instruction on how to better search and navigate the library resources. Some responses by students indicated that instruction on resources other than journal databases would also be useful. For instance, a student wrote, "not all articles were available online," suggesting that the student may be unaware of the interlibrary loan services available, and instruction should be provided on how to more effectively use all of the services available from the library. Students also wrote that they would prefer to participate in synchronous sessions after having watched an introductory tutorial or video. This would allow them to have more of a hands-on instructional experience rather than a synchronous lecture.

Implications for Embedded Librarianship

The embedded librarian project described in this chapter was based on a review of prior embedded librarianship literature and lessons learned from a previous attempt at embedded program-integrated information literacy instruction in the online doctoral program. Students' perceived information literacy skills and confidence when using library resources were assessed at the beginning of the project and after project implementation. Although the statistical analyses indicated no significant difference in the pre- and post-survey, the mean scores on all the items demonstrated an increase in students' skill and confidence after the project. Students reported increased awareness and use of important library databases in educa-

tion and increased confidence in searching, finding, evaluating, and citing resources. They could more successfully differentiate peer-reviewed materials from other types of publication sources after the project. The acquisition of these skills could make a difference to students' success in their doctoral assignments and progress; therefore, from a program perspective, the embedded librarian project was successful.

At the same time, students' reports of their participation, satisfaction, and information literacy skills and confidence in this study suggest that one semester of embedded librarian services is not sufficient to fully meet the information literacy needs of graduate students in an online doctoral program. Students' reports of increased confidence and research skills are evidence that the embedment of the librarian is essential, and comments from students indicate that there is a continuing need for additional information literacy instruction embedded within the program. Based on the results of this research and extending from the literature (Bowler & Street, 2008; McMillen & Fabbi, 2010), future embedded librarian interactions will continue to be designed to include a variety of opportunities for students to learn and use the information literacy skills to succeed in online programs. To support future cohorts of online students and sustain the information literacy support for current online students, student satisfaction, use, and comments about the instruction during this project were analyzed closely.

Students indicated overall satisfaction with the three main components of their library instruction during the program: the on-campus orientation, asynchronous instructional materials, and online synchronous sessions with the embedded librarian. Students' satisfaction was highest with the asynchronous materials, followed by the synchronous session and the on-campus session. For unavoidable reasons, the scheduled on-campus session had to be conducted by a different librarian who did more of a standard orientation to the library. This could be one reason for the lower ratings. From a program perspective, while an embedded librarian is immensely valuable because he or she understands the needs and the curriculum of the online program, it is also problematic if the embedded librarian is unavailable or unable to support those students even for a short time. From a sustainability standpoint, it is not always realistic for one embedded librarian to deal with all the instruction or students in a program. The possibility of two librarians embedding in an online program should be explored, assuming that a library has the resources and an online program enrolls a large number of students.

In the post-survey, only 56.3% of students reported using the tutorials created for this group while 75% reported attending the synchronous session. Unfortunately, there was a problem tracking the use of LibGuides by students. This is an important source of data to include in future embedded librarian offerings in the program because it provides data on actual use of asynchronous materials instead of the reported use of asynchronous materials by students. One reason for the synchronous session being attended by more students than those who viewed the tutorials could be that the program coordinator sent an e-mail to students shortly before the synchronous session highly recommending it and highlighting its value. She also recommended the tutorials at the beginning of the semester but did not send out specific e-mails during the semester. Therefore, in future semesters, it would be important for faculty to constantly reiterate the importance of information literacy to doctoral student's progress in the program in terms of ability to succeed in research assignments. Furthermore, the results suggest that the embedded librarian could reach more students and provide more interactions if she offered additional synchronous sessions. Perhaps the recommendation of one student, to provide a required tutorial prior to the synchronous session, would be beneficial in future offerings. The librarian could encourage students to review online videos and other asynchronous materials prior to a synchronous session. This approach enables more of a hands-on real-time experience that reinforces what students have learned beforehand and allows them to clarify questions.

Ninety-two percent of the students agreed or strongly agreed that the information literacy instruction was valuable for their completion of assignments within the online program. Changes recommended by the students include increasing the time of the orientation session to two hours, making it more of a hands-on session, and covering the peer-reviewed and theses and dissertation information during this time. Overwhelmingly students indicated a need for additional instruction. Particular needs mentioned by students include providing another basic "how-to search" session, advanced search strategies, and subject-term search strategies. From these comments, it is apparent that students in the program continue to be at different information literacy levels, which requires instruction targeted to their different needs. Future interactions will include a variety of methods to discuss and engage students in information literacy topics. The library help forum was available to students so they could ask questions of the embedded librarian. In the future, it could also be used for the librarian to send students reminders or call their attention to resources or materials during a certain week that would be useful to assignments. Future sessions for new cohorts will include longer on-campus sessions to explain some topics in greater detail or to introduce additional topics. That content will also be reinforced via asynchronous resources; this combination allows students to learn and then review the material at their own pace as needed. The more complex library topics such as locating relevant articles and evaluating peer review resources will be reinforced online both synchronously and asynchronously.

We would like to highlight the value of a librarian and program director or coordinator collaboratively designing and implementing an experience that strategically uses different levels of integration to support the research and assignments in a program. The collaborative selection of topics, the collaborative designing of instruction, and the emphasis of the value of information literacy content by the program coordinator to the students in this project greatly assisted the librarian in providing relevant instruction and support. In the online program in this study, the program coordinator not only managed the program but also led the development of curriculum, sequencing of courses, and student development. In other programs such collaborations could occur with any faculty member involved in the curriculum or teaching key research courses.

The assessment of embedded librarian projects is as important as their implementation. Surveys, analysis of student activities, and information literacy tasks can be used to assess students' newly acquired information literacy skills. In this case, the pilot project included collaborative research between the embedded librarian and the program coordinator at every stage of the project, from the design of the needs assessment to the post-survey analysis. For the research on the second offering of the program, a prior online student who is also a librarian contributed to the adaptation of previous research instruments for this study. Her role as a prior student in the online doctoral program coupled with her own work experience was invaluable to the identification of beneficial content. Collaboration for embedded librarianship, therefore, does not have to include only faculty members and the embedded librarian but can also include students or administrators who are familiar with students' specific needs in an online program.

Conclusion

Students' reports of increased confidence and their improved perceptions of research skills provide support for the continued involvement of an embedded librarian with this group and future groups of students in the online program in this study. Administration and faculty members in online graduate programs often place importance on research and social support for master's and doctoral students. However, information literacy

support—providing online students with the skills to use online resources, evaluate them, and use them appropriately in their coursework—is often taken for granted in incoming graduate students and viewed as the students' responsibility. Unfortunately, graduate students do not always possess information literacy skills and are not necessarily able to apply them in academic environments; however, they cannot successfully progress in their academic programs without these skills. This chapter describes one approach to supporting these students by analyzing their incoming existing skills in these areas and providing them with information literacy instruction in the form of an embedded librarian. Despite the small sample, the approach and assessment outlined here by the authors could be applied to other master's and doctoral programs whether online or on-campus and by other administrators or faculty who collaborate with librarians to provide information literacy instruction.

REFERENCES

Allen, I. E. & Seaman, J. (2013). *Changing course: Ten years of tracking online education in the United States*. Retrieved from Sloan Consortium website: http://sloanconsortium.org/publications/survey/changing_course_2012

American Library Association. (1989). *Presidential committee on information literacy: Final report*. Retrieved from http://www.ala.org/ala/mgrps/divs/acrl/publications/whitepapers/presidential.cfm

Bonnand, S., & Hansen, M.A. (2012). Embedded librarians: Delivering synchronous library instruction and research assistance to meet needs of distance students and faculty. In H. Wang (Ed.), *Interactivity in e-learning: Case studies and frameworks* (pp. 326–339). Hershey, PA: Information Science Reference.

Bowler, M., & Street, K. (2008). Investigating the efficacy of embedment: Experiments in information literacy integration. *Reference Services Review, 35*(4), 438–449.

Cain, D. L., & Lockee, B. (2002). Student support services at a distance: Are institutions meeting the needs of distance learners? Retrieved from ERIC database. (ED468729)

Collins, K. M. T., & Veal, R. E. (2004). Off-campus adult learners' levels of library anxiety as a predictor of attitudes toward the Internet. *Library & Information Science Research, 26*(1), 5–14.

Dewey, B. I. (2004). The embedded librarian: Strategic campus collaborations. *Resource Sharing & Information Networks, 17*(1), 5–17.

Drewes, K., & Hoffmann, N. (2010). Academic embedded librarianship: An introduction. *Public Services Quarterly, 6*(2), 75–82.

Dugan, M. (2008). Embedded librarians in an ag econ class: Transcending the traditional. *Journal of Agricultural & Food Information, 9*(4), 301–309.

Edwards, M., Kumar, S., & Ochoa, M. (2010). Assessing the value of embedded librarians in an online graduate educational technology course. *Public Services Quarterly, 6*(2-3), 271–291.

Freiburger, G., & Kramer, S. (2009). Embedded librarians: One library's model for decentralized service. *Journal of the Medical Library Association, 97*(2), 139–142.

Gottlieb, N. (1994). Supervising the writing of a thesis. In O. Zuber-Skerritt & Y. Ryan (Eds.), *Quality in postgraduate education* (pp. 110–119). London, England: Kogan Page.

Green, R. (2010). Information illiteracy: Examining our assumptions. *The Journal of Academic Librarianship, 36*(4), 313–319.

Hoffmann, S. (2011). Embedded academic librarian experiences in online courses: Roles, faculty collaboration, and opinion. *Library Management, 32*(6), 444–456.

Hoffmann, S., & Ramin, L., 2010. Best practices for librarians embedded in online courses. *Public Services Quarterly, 6*(2), 292–305.

Kesselman, M. A., & Watstein, S. B. (2009). Creating opportunities: Embedded librarians. *Journal of Library Administration, 49*(4), 383-400.

Koneru, I. (2010). ADDIE: Designing web-enabled information literacy instructional modules. *DESIDOC Journal of Library & Information Technology, 30*(3), 23–33.

Konieczny, A. (2010). Experiences as an embedded librarian in online courses. *Medical Reference Services Quarterly, 29*(1), 47–57.

Kumar, S., & Edwards, M. E. (2013). Information literacy skills and embedded librarianship in an online graduate program. *Journal of Information Literacy, 7*(1), 3–17.

Kumar, S., & Ochoa, M. N. (2012). Program-integrated information literacy instruction for online graduate students. *Journal of Library & Information Services in Distance Learning, 6*(2), 67–78.

Kumar, S., Ochoa, M. N., & Edwards, M. E. (2012). Considering information literacy skills and needs: Designing library instruction for the online learner. *Communications in Information Literacy, 6*(1), 91–106.

Kuruppu, P. U., & Gruber, A. M. (2006). Understanding the information needs of academic scholars in agricultural and biological sciences. *Journal of Academic Librarianship, 32*(6), 620.

Love, M., & Norwood, S. (2007). Finding our way as "Embedded Librarians." *College & Undergraduate Libraries, 14*(4), 87–93.

Macauley, P., & Cavanagh, A. K. (2001). Doctoral dissertations at a distance: A novel approach from Downunder. *Journal of Library Administration, 32*(1), 331–346.

Matthew, V., & Schroeder, A. (2006). The embedded librarian program. *EDUCAUSE Quarterly, 29*(4), 61–65.

McMillen, P., & Fabbi, J. (2010). How to be an E3 librarian. *Public Services Quarterly, 6*(2), 174–186.

Nelson, C. D., & San Miguel, C. (2003). Designing doctoral writing workshops that problematise textual practices. *Hong Kong Journal of Applied Linguistics, 8*(2), 116–136.

Onwuegbuzie, A. J. (1997). Writing a research proposal: The role of library anxiety, statistics anxiety, and composition anxiety. *Library and Information Science Research, 19*, 5–33.

Onwuegbuzie, A. J., & Jiao, Q. G. (1998). Understanding library-anxious graduate students. *Library Review, 47*, 217–224.

Shumaker, D., & Talley, M. (2009). *Models of embedded librarianship: Final report.* Retrieved from Special Libraries Association website: http://hq.sla.org/pdfs/EmbeddedLibrarianshipFinalRptRev.pdf

Strauss, A. L. & Corbin, J. (1990). *Basics of Qualitative Research.* Sage: Newbury Park.

Tait, A., & Mills, R. (Eds.). (2003). *Rethinking learner support in distance education: Change and continuity in an international context.* London, England: Routledge Falmer.

Embedded Librarian in a Military Distance Education Program

Catrina Whited[†], Bridget A. Powell, and Gail Nicula

In 2002, the Joint Forces Staff College (JFSC), under the National Defense University (NDU), launched its first program for distance learners. This program, Advanced Joint Professional Military Education (AJPME), has evolved over the past 10 years to include an embedded librarian.

Distance learning is a growing part of higher education. According to a report by Allen and Seaman (2013), the "proportion of all students taking at least one online course is at an all-time high of 32.0 percent" (p. 4). The National Center for Education Statistics (2013) issued a report, covering 2010–11 and 2011–12, indicating that 86.08% of undergraduate programs and 82.50% of graduate programs have some distance education courses. Statistics on military distance education programs are more limited, with the added complication that often training and education statistics are not differentiated in the literature.

Brief History of Distance Learning in the Military

The military has a long history of providing educational and training services to service members stationed around the globe. For many years, correspondence training programs were available to military members and civilians across the military services. During the 1940s military services offered print-based correspondence courses. The 1950s brought television courses for the Army Signal School. In the 1970s, the Air Force Institute of Technology, a graduate school and provider of professional and continuing education for the United States armed forces, provided teleteach, classes viewed over a television. Beginning in 1976, the U.S. Army had a correspondence program managed by the U.S. Army Training Support Center at Fort Eustis, Virginia (Duncan, 2005). This early version of "distance" education for the Army consisted of correspondence courses used for learning additional skills or cross-training into a new career field.

These courses were on the cutting edge of educational technology for that time, yet the lack of now standard computing systems limited the distribution of support services to learners. If a writing requirement existed in a course, students were given no support to develop research and writing skills. It was not until the 1990s that technologically based distance learning began to expand in the armed forces.

In the late 1990s, the U.S. government issued specific guidelines regarding the use of technology in education. This guidance came in the form of the Advanced Distributed Learning (ADL) Initiative. Created by Presidential Executive Order 13111 and signed into effect on January 12, 1999, this initiative directed that the Department of Defense (DoD) and other federal agen-

---

†*This author is an employee of the U.S. Government. This work was prepared as part of their official duties. Title 17, USC 105 provides that "Copyright protection under this title is not available for any work of the United States Government."*

cies review and adopt advances in technology with a goal of creating a flexible and responsive workforce. The executive order had two goals: (1) provide employees with opportunities to participate in training programs, and (2) investigate how best to use technology in support of lifelong learning (ADL, 2013, "History," para. 1).

To do this, the ADL Initiative began by exploring ways to "standardize and modernize education and training" (ADL, 2013, "History," para 3). The creation of the ADL Collaborative Lab in Alexandria, Virginia provided an environment where professionals could explore, collaborate, and assess a variety of standards and tools that would best support the DoD. In the spring of 2000, the DoD issued the Implementation Plan for Advanced Distributed Learning. This plan provided a roadmap for providing "high-education and training, that can be tailored to individual needs and delivered cost-effectively, anytime and anywhere" (DoD, 2000, p. ES-1).

Background on Joint Professional Military Education

The Goldwater-Nichols Department of Defense Reorganization Act of 1986 transformed the DoD into an organization more focused on "joint matters" rather than individual military service perspectives. One part of the act mandated joint professional military education (JPME) for active component officers. Muhleman (1994) defined JPME as "focused on the integrated employment of land, sea, air, space, and special operations forces. It refers to PME [professional military education] taught in a joint environment, by a joint faculty, to a joint student body, and from a joint perspective" (p. 108). In 2000, the National Defense Authorization Act directed the Armed Forces Staff College (as the JFSC was then called) to develop academically rigorous in-residence and distance-learning programs for officers from all branches of the service that would encourage cohort development and cross-service acculturation.

The result of this was the development of JPME Phase I and II: JPME "Phase I covers the basic fundamentals needed in joint operations. JPME Phase II covers advanced concepts in joint planning, operations, procedures, and perspectives" (Sheppard, 2004, p. 3).

Background on JFSC

JFSC's charter is to deliver world-class JPME Phase II to members of the U.S. military services. The Phase II programs are designed to provide students with an opportunity to experience all of the planning and operational challenges a staff officer could anticipate over a three-year joint duty assignment whether the assignment is on the Joint Staff, a Joint Task Force, or service component staff.

The JFSC, located in Norfolk, Virginia, is a component of National Defense University (NDU) and is chartered by the Joint Chiefs of Staff. At JFSC there are two certificate courses that provide JPME Phase II. The first course is the Advanced Joint Professional Military Education (AJPME), which is a predominantly online learning course with two face-to-face sessions. The second course is the Joint and Combined Warfighting School (JCWS), an in-resident 10-week course. (Starting in January 2013, a JCWS nonresident satellite program was implemented in Tampa, Florida that is also served by the library.) Additional in-residence programs at JFSC include a yearlong master's degree program, Joint Advanced Warfighting School (JAWS), as well as several other courses such as Joint Command, Control, Communications, Computers and Intelligence Staff and Operations Course; Homeland Security Planner's Course; and the Joint, Interagency, and Multinational Planner's Course.

The primary program at JFSC is the 10-week in-residence JCWS program. This course is one of the key methods for active duty students to receive their JPME Phase II certificate. While it is technically available to members of the Reserve Component (the collective term when referring to the Air, Army, and Navy Reserve and the Air and Army National Guard), the services control the slots in the course and who attends; they do not set aside seats for members of the Reserve Component (RC). Furthermore, since the majority of RC personnel have a full-time job in addition to military duty, it is often difficult to get 10 weeks off to attend the in-residence course.

Course

Recognizing this challenge, the National Defense Authorization Act of 1999 authorized the DoD to develop a course for RC members that was "similar in content but not identical to" the 10-week in-residence JCWS course. The language in the law was deliberately vague as to specifics of the course, allowing the course developers to best decide the details. The result was Advanced Joint Professional Military Education (AJPME): a 40-week blended or hybrid course (using both face-to-face and distance segments) based on the lessons and syllabus from the JCWS course.

The first iteration AJPME began in September 2002. The course has been modified over the years but still retains its basic shape—12 weeks of distance education; one week in-residence at JFSC; 25 weeks of distance education; and a final two-week in-residence session that culminates in a graduation ceremony. Unlike the 10-week JCWS course, which uses three-person teaching teams, AJPME online instructors carry one to two classes solo, with other faculty assisting during the in-residence segments. The college offers four AJPME courses each year. During the past two years the program has grown from two to four seminars per class. Currently there are up to 90 students enrolled in each course, which is divided into "seminars" of approximately 23 students.

One of the authors (BP) has been an AJPME instructor since the inception of the program and provides her insight in the next several sections. During the 2003 course, students were required to complete two writing assignments: a

one- to two-page information paper and a 3000-word joint research paper. However, resources for researching papers were limited at best. While the librarians at the Ike Skelton Library at JFSC were willing to help, there was no single dedicated—embedded—distance librarian. Students who were fortunate enough to have decided on a topic prior to coming to the first face-to-face session were able to use physical library resources. However, obtaining assistance from a librarian was difficult because, due to staffing levels, a librarian was not often available before or after class hours when students were most likely to need library services.

Still, the library staff did not develop a basic instructional program to assist AJPME students. At the beginning of the first face-to-face session, a team of librarians provided each seminar with an overview of the online research tools available to the students as well as a tour of the physical library spaces. Students were also provided the opportunity to check out books for the duration of their course. However, one-on-one research assistance was lacking. Some students were fortunate to live in an area with a fairly robust public or university library system that they could utilize for research assistance, but many students lived overseas or traveled to a degree that made such research impossible. Neither the library nor the instructors had the resources to provide personalized, systematic instruction on how to conduct research, so not surprisingly, the quality of student papers varied.

The librarian's ability to interact with the classes in the beginning was somewhat hit or miss, mostly due to the exploratory nature of the endeavor. The librarian tried a combination of synchronous sessions, e-mails, and telephone calls. Even these basic attempts showed the usefulness of having an embedded librarian in every AJPME seminar. First, the quality of research in students' papers improved significantly; second, instructors began to notice that students were not coming to the instructor with as many research related questions; and third, students almost universally reported (through both anecdotal comments and formal surveys) that having the embedded librarian in the course provided a significant benefit and made their research efforts both easier and more fruitful.

How the Distance Librarian Program Started at JFSC

In 2010, the situation improved dramatically when the Ike Skelton Library hired its first distance librarian (DL). The role and responsibilities of this librarian evolved over time, beginning as an AJPME reference librarian available during face-to-face sessions, moving towards a liaison to the department, and, ultimately, being embedded in the course. The evolution was facilitated by the willingness of the library staff to explore the options and possibilities for providing support to this unique group of students as well as the willingness of some instructors to allow the distance librarian to experiment to develop best practices.

While some of the instructors were enthusiastic about the use of the embedded librarian, others were more skeptical. The idea of someone outside the JFSC group of instructors, a non-military person at that, communicating directly with students through the Blackboard course and scheduling online sessions—acting more than a "support" person should—was overstepping bounds to some faculty. At JFSC, librarians are considered support staff rather than faculty, and some instructors could not see how an embedded librarian would benefit the distance students. For the first few classes, the DL was very careful to avoid "getting into the instructor's virtual way" in order to find a way to help the students. To do this, the DL sat down with each instructor and went over the plan for her involvement in the class, making sure scheduled sessions did not interfere with what was going on in the class that week.

Author (GN), who retired from JFSC as the library director after over 20 years of service, implemented . From the beginning, the library was committed to offering equal (or better) service to distance learners than in-person patrons; however, the early years were a time of learning and trial and error for the staff. Although the library reached out sporadically to the AJPME distance learners, a program specifically tailored to their requirements was not in place. During the early years, the librarians performed traditional reference services and waited for students to come to them with questions, rather than offering proactive assistance and support. This "status quo" continued until 2009, when, because of a staff retirement, the library director (GN) was able to convert a professional position within the library from another civil service career group to the librarian career group. At that time, the reader services chief and the library director wrote a position description for a DL and began the recruitment process. Because the DL position was new to the library and because the goal was to go through a "trial and error" period to find the optimal model of distance library services for students as well as for their faculty, the DL was given considerable freedom in program planning. From the library director's perspective (GN), the ultimate goal was to find a librarian who understood that the library's mission was to deliver equivalent or better reference, research, circulation, and interlibrary loan services to our distance learners. In a situation such as this—a fairly new program with somewhat receptive and flexible faculty members and students who were grateful for any type of assistance—the first step was to convince senior leadership and the faculty members that the DL could build an effective program and that they should allow time for this program to be built.

As it turned out, that was the easy part. The library had a solid reputation for excellence. Student surveys consistently revealed that the library staff was rated among the highest of the college's service elements. Library presentations to the institution's senior leaders clearly explained the goals and the steps needed to achieve these goals. Because the library's reputation preceded us, there was a degree of freedom and flexibility that might be considered unusual by other institutions.

It is important to note that the route from a nascent to a comprehensive distance library program was and is iterative. It began with a few ideas that were tested, accepted, refined, or discarded while constantly seeking better possibilities for great service. Feedback from students and faculty was gathered throughout program development. Whether formal, with the assistance of our Institutional Research, Accreditation, and Assessment Division, or informal, asking students "how are we doing" type questions on the spot, we were able to improve and refine the program.

The author (GN) noted that a colleague in another public higher-education institution made this comment: "We treat all of our students equally. They all get the same services." This philosophy was antithetical to the JFSC library goal, even though the words themselves reflected our intention of "equal or better" services to our distance learners. The JFSC library's staff strongly believed that they would have to do far more work, individually or in small groups, with AJPME students to achieve "equal or better."

With only a few exceptions, staff has always assisted students during official library working hours. It was very clear once the DL began that the limited schedule was only helpful to half the class. A student stationed at U.S. AFRICOM headquarters in Stuttgart, Germany would find it challenging to take full advantage of the library's "normal" reference hours of 7:00 a.m. to 5:00 p.m. (EST), Monday through Friday, which translates to 1:00 p.m. to 11:00 p.m. in Germany. Attempting to identify best service windows for students across the United States and overseas was not only challenging, but also conflicted with agency norms regulating limits of compensatory time per pay period. The DL received permission to assist AJPME students on a flexible schedule—before,

during, and after normal working hours. Thanks to an accommodating and forward thinking dean and a persuasive library staff, this particular problem was overcome until a new telework policy came into effect. As of this writing, the flexibility of telework scheduling has allowed many more options for serving distance students during times that are convenient for all.

The concept of an embedded librarian within a military distance education course is unique due in part to the nature of the AJPME course and the willingness of the faculty and staff of the college and the Ike Skelton Library to take a chance on the program. This is not to say it was an easy incorporation; at first, many instructors did not realize the scope and purpose of the embedded librarian, so there were some natural growing pains to the program. However, three years in to this academic experiment, the idea of a class with no embedded librarian is anathema to instructors and students alike.

Library Support for AJPME

As of 2013, there are five reference librarians assigned to students in three distinct programs. As previously discussed, two are certificate programs (JCWS and AJPME) and one master's degree program, the Joint Advanced Warfighting School (JAWS). The JCWS and JAWS programs use the liaison librarian format. Each librarian is assigned three JCWS seminars and one JAWS seminar. The short courses mentioned earlier in the chapter use traditional library reference services.

All faculty members receive library briefings as part of their initial orientation. The briefing consists of a general overview of library resources and services, an overview of the library portal, and an introduction to copyright law, including the process for reproduction of copyright-protected documents in JFSC course materials. The library issues new faculty packets, consisting of books recommended by the Chief of Faculty and

Staff Development to incoming instructors. The AJPME instructors also typically meet with the DL either in person or through Blackboard Collaborate. Military officers typically only spend two to four years assigned to a specific location so working at JFSC is a bit different from more traditional academic settings. Some instructors find it useful to have an in-depth brief similar to that given to the students with additional time allowing for discussion of questions that may be more specific to the learning management system (LMS) or about the librarian's perceptions of the students and the program.

The DL handles the majority of online synchronous sessions, informational e-mails, technical issues, evening and weekend sessions, and work with AJPME faculty. All the librarians answer information desk phone calls and questions sent to the reference e-mail and meet with students for individual face-to-face sessions. Several of the librarians have started meeting individually with students online for synchronous sessions on their research topic. One librarian who provides instructional classes on campus has also started presenting group sessions in the online forum for all programs.

The JFSC uses Blackboard as their LMS. The instructors use both asynchronous and synchronous discussions. Courses consist of mostly asynchronous lesson plans for students with occasional synchronous sessions and two face-to-face meetings. Due to security restrictions the JFSC library resources are held in Blackboard for distance students instead of an open webpage. The DL (CW) does not have a military background and realized that going through the online lessons in Blackboard gave her a better understanding of the questions students raised. The DL requested and was given a Blackboard role in each seminar. The DL has been invited to participate in online presentations and other types of training sessions for faculty. This improved the understanding of what a librarian could do for the program, and the faculty began to embrace the DL more as a member of their team than an external support entity.

During the first week of each course, the librarian posts a biography alongside the instructors and students and an announcement with information and synchronous session dates for upcoming weeks. Just as the students and faculty connected with each other through the online bios, the DL found her bio commented on by students who identified with her, which generated conversations with the students and better relationships developed.

In *The Embedded Librarian: Innovative Strategies for Taking Knowledge Where It's Needed*, Shumaker (2012) discusses that in "traditional reference that the operating assumption is that all librarians are interchangeable ... relationships can be formed but are not actively fostered. Embedded librarians deliberately build relationships—with faculty, with students" (p. 5). Shumaker also discusses degrees of embeddedness. When first starting at JFSC, the DL (CW) took several months to become familiar with the school and how military academic universities differ from civilian institutions. Maintaining the status quo of librarian services to distance students was necessary to better understand the institution as a whole. As much as the librarian might want to jump in head first, observation was the best course of action. Next, the DL started reviewing the AJPME course lessons in Blackboard. At first the DL received push back from the AJPME program, questioning why she needed course access. However, explaining that the better the librarian understands the program the better she can answer student's questions helped to address their concerns. Once the opportunity to embed a little more became possible, the librarian moved to a liaison model, which was also being used in two other JFSC programs. Instructors commented on the benefit of having a dedicated librarian in their distance courses. At the suggestion of several instructors, the librarian taught several hour-long online synchronous sessions in Blackboard. Another instructor suggested that the librarian should provide "office hours" similar to faculty, but this was found to be impractical when working with an internationally based population. Rather, the DL discovered that flexibility with appointments was a more efficient use of time.

The DL discovered that she worked with students of widely varying educational backgrounds and technological skill sets. There were those students who last attended school in the 1980s or early 1990s and others who finished graduate degrees in the past five years. The DL quickly realized that answering basic technology questions and helping students navigate Blackboard would be a focus during early sessions with students. When students began asking for resource assistance on short assignments, she created handouts and started e-mailing students before projects. The DL embedded further into the program when faculty formally added synchronous library sessions to the course roadmap.

Military and Civilian Program Differences and Student Demographics

The AJPME program is different from traditional degree programs. At typical civilian institutions, students are usually taking multiple classes for a degree. JFSC students all have bachelor's degrees; many have a master's degree, and several in each class hold doctorates. Yet all students are coming through for a JPME Phase II certification. Another difference from civilian programs is because of the military ranking system. During the first iterations of this course, the DL tried to address students by rank. However, she discovered that this practice had unintended consequences. Lower-ranking individuals began to defer to the higher-ranking students, and, conversely, the higher-ranking students felt uncomfortable showing their lack of knowledge regarding library resources and computer systems in front of lower-ranking officers. As a result of this and because of the academic nature of the course, instructors and the DL promote the use of first names during synchronous sessions.

Student demographics are unique as well; in any one class, the librarian will be working with officers from a wide variety of civilian backgrounds. Each student will write a persuasive research paper on a joint military topic of which the subject possibilities are endless. Often, the DL found it easier to work individually with students because of their diverse backgrounds and knowledge. From this author's (CW) perspective, this is one of the most enjoyable aspects of working at the military college. The diversity in topics keeps a librarian's search skills and knowledge of free and proprietary resources up to date. Research for this program is never boring or monotonous as during an hour-long session the librarian can show students how to find the best resources for cyber security deterrence, medical logistics, and the use of social media during disasters. Holloway (2011) noted that it is important to understand the student population. Although there are many library tools a student can use, due to differences in computer/electronic knowledge, the tools should fit the student. For one student, the suggestion might be e-books, while a print text might be the best option for another student. For some, screenshots work great; others need a recorded video of where to find material. Brown (2011) reviewed literature related to library anxiety. While Brown's article discussed the in-person reference desk, the suggestions are applicable to distance services. "Even with maturity and the development of critical thinking skills users may still find it very difficult to ask for help because they are vastly overwhelmed, either by the complexity of a single task or by the amount of available resources" (p. 312). The amount of available information is daunting in today's library world.

Many students have degrees and occupations that allow them to be very comfortable with research and writing whereas for others it is completely the opposite. Some students will need in-depth assistance on how to use the LMS, do topic research, and prepare citations. Just as in traditional reference where each librarian might be perceived as interchangeable, students may also be seen as having more similarities than differences. The embedded librarian is not easily interchangeable and knows neither are the students.

While there are many students in the AJPME program who have recently finished an upper-level education program, there are just as many who have not had the opportunity. Cooke (2010) discussed the needs of a "re-entry" student who may not be as technologically proficient and are often balancing family, work, and personal obligations. Holmes (2005) stated, "Instruction for re-entry students needs to be student-centered, life and situation based, beginning and ending in the experiences of the student, and connected to their real and immediate needs" (p. 135). Many students have not been in an academic environment in 20 years. Although it does take more time, developing a relationship with the student will give the librarian insight as to where the student is starting from, and he or she can then act appropriately for the student's current skill level.

Every student comes into the class with a different set of technical and information capabilities. The first library sessions for each cohort of students discuss library resources, but the main objective is for the student to have contact with a knowledgeable librarian and be reassured that he or she will not be on his own during the next 40 weeks. The librarian reviews the classroom structure and points out items that are useful to know, in particular, talking about the main research paper that will be due in 35 weeks and including a list of frequently asked questions.

During the first several weeks the DL offers over 20 synchronous classes since there may be as many as 80 or more students in all seminars. The library sessions cover the same material but vary somewhat due to student questions. Multiple classes accommodate family, work, and time differences; the variety of sessions provides the best return. The beauty of having a class online is that if no one shows up in the classroom, the librarian can always work on other computer related tasks. These first sessions are generally focused on small groups of students. The librarian will typi-

cally archive one to two sessions for those who are unable to attend. Again, because of the nature of the distance students' lives, there may be one person or six attending a session. It is important to remember that it is not a "waste" of the DL's time to only have one person in a session. Does the library quit providing reference desk hours because no one showed up each minute it is available? Each and every student is important, and it does not "waste" any time for a librarian to be available in case someone shows up in the session. As this author (CW) has stated earlier, the librarian always has something to do whether it is working on other student research, creating an instructional guide, or developing a collection. The fewer the people in the session, the more a relationship evolves between the embedded librarian and the student. Although it might be suggested that the session can be archived and multiple synchronous sessions are not needed, this DL (CW) strongly disagrees. What makes this library embedded service unique is the connection that is cultivated and developed with students.

The armed forces strongly encourages lifelong learning in their service members. The DL stresses the freely accessible resources and best research practices so students realize that the information learned can assist in future endeavors. Sometimes with a certification program students are only looking for a piece of paper showing they have completed the course for advancement. One entry point for the librarian is to look for all relevant information possibilities in the student's civilian and military life, and then show the student that search skills are relevant to other aspects of his or her personal and professional life. Each branch of the military has a "service portal" where service members can access a vast amount of information, which includes numerous library resources. These portals are behind a security wall and only accessible to designated individuals. Each branch of the military has separate funding for their library resources, and each academic military institution is under a different funding source so separate library pages and resources exist. The individual military services provide access to online paid resources through their portals. Information found on these portals is both useful and valuable but is also largely unknown to many users. Often librarians only discuss resources that are immediately available to the student and neglect to identify resources available post-graduation, especially since most colleges cannot afford alumni access to unique or major databases. Giving students a broad understanding of the variety of research platforms and databases as well as authoritative Internet sources can change their information awareness perspective and result in a more positive library experience.

Information Technology

The information technology dilemma in the academic military environment is widely known; security and access to a wide variety of information are often at odds. Working not just with but at a military institution produces a whole host of other problems. JFSC's information technology organization finds it challenging, if not impossible, to support many of the advancements in library service delivery. Although Blackboard Collaborate would be the software of choice for students, often the individual is located in a more secure environment and the DL must instead use an authorized government program called Defense Connect Online. Government computers are subject to many restrictions; users do not normally have permissions to download software. There is quite a lengthy process to receive approval to do so, and although Blackboard has a great instant messaging tool, many users cannot take advantage if they are working at a government location.

The use of tablets, e-readers, and smart phones as well as open source technology has revolutionized how students and faculty interact with a library. Unfortunately, the support deficit referred to above has been and continues to be a barrier to evolving library services. Although the library has subscriptions to many e-books, users are not allowed to download the software to view the e-books on government computers. Librarians find that they must use their own personal devices to better to explain certain processes to students.

These technology shortfalls specifically affect e-book download capability. E-books will account for a growing percentage of the library's available titles; library users are increasingly comfortable with the format due to the proliferation of e-books in public libraries and the variety of devices on which they can be read. Readers prefer to be able to download the entire book. Since military students travel regularly, both within the United States and overseas, access to electronic resources while in a travel status can make the difference between a good or excellent paper.

The future of library assistance will be mobile. Being able to move around the library and the college to help students, faculty, and staff, all while connected to a wireless network, is essential in the 21st century. Having these types of devices and a staff trained to use them will be essential for customer support. As the college follows the DoD into a "bring-your-own-device" environment, the library will have to be able to ensure that electronic resources work on a variety of devices and platforms.

The 40-Week AJPME Course

The DL provides scheduled group and individual instructional sessions as well as on-demand sessions as requested by students during the 40-week class. During the first 11 weeks there are numerous weekly group sessions scheduled during the day and evening as well on the weekend to accommodate various time zones, work, and personal life commitments. The sessions cover resources that support designated student assignments. Using Blackboard, the DL creates announcements and e-mails for each seminar, identifies synchronous session dates, and suggests resources that might be useful for their assignments if they are unable to attend a session.

During the first face-to-face session in week 12, students can schedule individual appointments with a reference librarian to begin or continue research for the major research paper, which is 10–12 pages. A 30-minute library overview for each seminar is presented during this session as well as the opportunity for students to sign up and meet individually with a librarian. During the second face-to-face session, just before graduation, the DL briefs students on alumni access to resources during the seminar-out processing.

The DL is available to AJPME students and faculty via Blackboard instant messaging, Blackboard Collaborate, e-mail, telephone, and in person for local students and faculty. Library staff members are available to assist distance students via e-mail, telephone, and in person; several of the reference librarians are also available through Blackboard instant messaging. The Ft. McNair "physical" library at NDU is also available to AJPME students living in the metropolitan Washington, DC area. This policy came about as the conversation and relationships developed between students and the DL. Many students expressed an interest in having check-out privileges at NDU's DC campus. Through discussions with the DL and the chief of research and information services at Ft. McNair, a standard operating procedure was written and approved.

AJPME Course Roadmap: Library Sessions

The AJPME course roadmap below presents an overview of library support to AJPME students.

Weeks 0–12: DL provides topic resources for students' joint research paper (JRP).

Week 0: DL adds biographical information to Blackboard course material.

Weeks 0–7: DL offers online welcome sessions as an introduction to library services.

Weeks 9–11: DL offers online sessions for country paper and strategic analysis.

Week 11: DL offers online sessions for JRP topics and JRP research. (These sessions are highly recommended and well attended, but not a course requirement.)

Week 11: Selected reference librarians offer students individual online appointments to discuss JRP topics and research.

Week 12: During the first face-to-face session, a reference librarian talks with each seminar about library services. In addition, five librarians (four reference librarians and the chief of reader services) offer individual instruction appointments.

Weeks 13–39: Librarians offer online and e-mail support at the request of students.

Week 40: DL briefs graduating students regarding alumni services.

The DL also assists students with rudimentary technology issues and forwards questions or requests to the IT staff when appropriate. Two reference librarians maintain the Blackboard JFSC library module. Electronic resources are shared with and maintained by the NDU library. The DL troubleshoots most database and proxy issues with the assistance of a systems librarian at NDU. The librarians are committed to making every effort to obtain research materials for AJPME students. Resources and materials unavailable online or through NDU libraries are provided through postal mail, fax, and interlibrary loan.

Reference librarians add content to the library's Blackboard page and create resource guides for patrons. The Blackboard page provides multiple points of access to library resources using both an alphabetical listing and topical groupings. Librarians annotate the portal entries to assist users in selecting the most appropriate resources for their needs. Reference librarians research and compile dynamic online bibliographic subject guides using the LibGuides platform. The library also creates tutorial videos, designed to enhance research skills that can be viewed by students online on their own schedule. As with all subject specialties, the JFSC librarians must know how to use specific databases. Due to the nature of the program and background of the students, the librarians need to be aware of both free and paid resources with military and national security content.

The JFSC emphasizes publishing for students' papers, and the reference staff aids students by providing a list of places to publish on the library's organization on Blackboard. The students also compete for a variety of writing awards that are announced at graduation. Award-winning papers are gathered by the library reference staff and stored on an internal document server where they can also be accessed by subsequent classes of students. AJPME students whose papers are determined by faculty to merit consideration for publication receive editorial assistance from the AJPME faculty to enhance their opportunity to have their papers published.

The military is fabulous about identifying "lessons learned," and we often find that new students and faculty pose lessons-learned type questions. A librarian is usually considered a non-threatening, neutral person in the academic arena. Faculty and students seem to feel more comfortable and less reluctant asking the librarian what they are afraid might be perceived as a stupid question rather than asking it of their counterparts. If the librarian does not know the answer, he or she can query one or more instructors for an answer while protecting the student's anonymity. Just as in the civilian world, there is a difficulty when working with instructors who see the value of the library and think it is great that "we" are there to provide assistance but don't really get what we do. Instructors see the necessity of the library but

not always the librarian. Librarians must repeatedly explain that today's librarian or information professional is the right person to help students with their research requirements and foster skills for lifelong learning.

At JFSC, the DL also assists the faculty members with lesson research and technology assistance. All copyright questions are referred to the two librarians that handle copyright issues. Instructors who are currently enrolled in a civilian-degree program often come to the librarian in a student capacity.

Assessment

In May 2013 two voluntary surveys were distributed to 378 AJPME students; 134 responded. Fourteen faculty members received the survey, and eight responded. The survey was produced from Blackboard, and, unfortunately, numerous students sent e-mails saying that they were unable to access from their government computer. When these students attempted to log on to the survey from home, Blackboard locked out the user due to the earlier but unsuccessful log-on attempts. Most of the AJPME students are very or extremely satisfied with the embedded DL experience: 117 rated the experience very good to excellent, four good, one fair, and 11 marked the question was not applicable to them. Sixty-eight individuals took the time to write specific comments on the usefulness of having an embedded librarian in their online program. Below are a few of the student survey comments on contact with the embedded DL:

- Accessibility, understanding our course and class. Being our advocate.
- Ability to understand my intent, formulate it into tangible research and resource questions, then assist in the search… patience and foresight is commendable.
- Willing to help me do research, offer ideas and resources, and teach me first hand (via Blackboard Collaborate) how to use the tools.

- Insight into assignments and enthusiasm to help or foster questions. Also a great ability to shift topics of discussion during sessions.
- Ready access to librarians who are responsive to my educational needs.
- The ability to interact and ask specific questions of someone who knew the system. It saved time which is a valuable commodity given the format.
- Time saver! Increase value to my output.

Six faculty members rated the DL experience as excellent and one marked non-applicable. Of the eight who completed the survey, seven felt that the AJPME program should maintain an embedded librarian in their program and one faculty member selected a liaison librarian. Below are a few faculty comments on contact with the embedded DL:

- The embedded DL is very supportive and informative.
- The DL is getting the students on the right track early.
- Personal attention given to student. DL functions as a faculty member specifically focused on research component.
- Embedded is necessary due to large amount of time students spend in distance learning mode.
- DL is very accessible and sync sessions are very useful.
- The DL has supported our students well beyond expectations and is consistently lauded by students each class as the most valuable educational asset at JFSC.
- When a student comes in with no idea where to start on a paper and after spending time with the librarian, the student comes away with a topic, thesis, and the start of research.
- Synchronous session and accessibility are key. The introduction of the synchronous session early in the program now has students working on and completing their JRPs early in the course schedule.

According to an informal discussion with the JFSC distance education Blackboard technology specialist, the presence of an embedded librarian has decreased helpdesk requests. The DL became a point of contact for library database issues and assisted students with minor technical issues. Additionally, the librarian now has a better understanding of Blackboard.

Conclusion

Although applicable to all educational courses, this precept is very much true for online programs: It's the relationship that matters! The world is overwhelmed by information sources, and the librarian's goal is to help users navigate the information waters. How does one develop a relationship when students are not required to contact the librarian? In this program, the librarian may be dealing with anyone from the age of 35 to 60 with varying degrees of computer abilities, research skills, and information literacy. Not all students or instructors realize that spending one hour with a librarian can save ten hours of time with research.

There are many variables regarding a student's understanding of the maze of information and identifying credible information sources. Everyone can Google, but Google in itself does not give a student academic level resources for a professional paper. Also, these students come from varied backgrounds. In the same class, the DL might have physicians, teachers, pilots, lawyers, business men or women, and a chaplain. The students are required to pick a topic that is "joint" in nature, but there is no formula or "cookie-cutter approach" to the appropriate research resources for each student. To do so would short change the student. Many students have not been in an online program before and need assistance navigating the Blackboard portal. One of the best ways to engage students and catch their attention is show them how Google and Google Scholar can be used for academic research, including how limiting the domain to .mil when searching Google can weed out many undesirable hits. Wowing students is always important, to get their interest and to show that you have skills to teach.

The embedded librarian needs to be a full-service librarian. Within the realm of responsibilities is to assist with technology and connect the student to the institutional research specialists or a subject specialist. The librarian's specialty is finding information, including acting as a sounding board for students on possible topics, helping them with research and searching the databases, giving information and resources for lifelong learning, and demonstrating practical uses for the databases in their civilian life. In today's world, it seems that many students as well as instructors hold the belief that they are research experts. However, "they don't know what they don't know," and if not partnered with a librarian or required to attend library classes, the unknown will remain.

Professional development has proved to be an indispensable tool for this distance librarian (CW). Attendance at the Distance Library Services conferences in 2010 and 2012 was an eye-opening experience. The rigid, organized structure of library land can be challenging for a distance/embedded librarian. It was invaluable to attend these conferences and speak with other like-minded professionals in an environment where one can gain tools, strategies, and understanding that slowly but surely times are changing. The DL became a member on numerous list-servs and spent time reading books and articles geared towards distance and or embedded librarianship. The DL also talked with other military librarians who worked with distance students to find best practices. In addition, as part of the JFSC faculty professional development that is paid through the college; faculty may enroll in a local certificate program on college teaching, and distance instructors may attend online the University Wisconsin-Madison's Professional Certificate in Online Education program. Although librarians at the university do not have faculty status, the DL was invited and elected to participate in both programs.

In closing, the DL (CW) feels that there are five main attributes that an embedded DL must have: flexibility, adaptability, resourcefulness, enthusiasm, and curiosity. Distance librarianship can be a challenge in and of itself; however, adding the military component can make it even trickier. Often students are in locations that will not allow Blackboard software. In many cases, the librarian must be flexible, adaptable, and resourceful while maintaining an enthusiastic demeanor. Too often students will comment that they do not want to cause problems and are embarrassed by the technical issues. It is the librarian's job to put them at ease and keep them connected while trying to fix or work around the technical issue. The DL might need to quickly login to a DoD website for synchronous sessions or explain via phone as the student clicks through resources on their end—not ideal but sometimes necessary. A curious librarian will be thinking outside the box to find the best answer for the student regardless if it is research, instruction or a technical issue. All the above is also mandatory because Murphy's Law seems to rule supreme in the online environment, which is also why librarian services to distance students are best complemented by having an embedded librarian in the program.

REFERENCES

Advanced Distributed Learning. (2013, October 26). *Overview: History.* Retrieved from http://www.adlnet.gov/overview/

Allen, I. E., & Seaman, J. (2013). *Changing course: Ten years of tracking online education in the United States.* Retrieved from http://www.onlinelearningsurvey.com/reports/changingcourse.pdf

Brown, L. J. (2011). Trending now—reference librarians: How reference librarians work to prevent library anxiety. *Journal of Library Administration, 51*(3), 309–317.

Cooke, N. A. (2010). Becoming an andragogical librarian: Using library instruction as a tool to combat library anxiety and empower adult learners. *New Review of Academic Librarianship, 16*(2), 208–227. doi:10.1080/13614533.2010.507388

Duncan, S. (2005). The U.S. Army's impact on the

history of distance education. Quarterly Review of Distance Education, 6 (4), 396-404.

Exec. Order No. 13111, 3 C.F.R. 42–46 (1999).

Holloway, K. (2011). Outreach to distance students: A case study of a new DL. *Journal of Library & Information Services in Distance Learning, 5*(1-2), 25–33.

Muhleman, D. (1994). The ABCs of JPME. *Joint Forces Quarterly, Spring*(4), 108–110.

Sheppard, Dennis K. (2004). *JPME for reserve component officers* [White paper]. Retrieved from http://www.dtic.mil/cgi-bin/GetTRDoc?Location=U2&doc=GetTRDoc.pdf&AD=ADA426003

Shumaker, D. (2012). *The embedded librarian: Innovative strategies for taking knowledge where it's needed.* Medford, NJ: Information Today.

Goldwater-Nichols Department of Defense Reorganization Act of 1986. 10 U.S.C. §§ 201–406 (1986). Retrieved from http://www.nsa.gov/about/cryptologic_heritage/60th/interactive_timeline/Content/1980s/documents/19861001_1980_Doc_NDU.pdf

National Defense Authorization Act for Fiscal Year 1999. 10 U.S.C. §§ 16131–16401 (1999). Retrieved from http://www.gpo.gov/fdsys/pkg/USCODE-1999-title10/pdf/USCODE-1999-title10-subtitleE-partIV.pdf

National Defense Authorization Act for Fiscal Year 2000. 10 U.S.C. §§ 16131–16401 (2000). Retrieved from http://www.gpo.gov/fdsys/pkg/USCODE-2000-title10/pdf/USCODE-2000-title10-subtitleE.pdf

U. S. Department of Defense. (2000). Implementation plan for Advanced Distributed Learning. Retrieved from https://www.hsdl.org/?view&did=480013

U. S. Department of Education, National Center for Education Statistics. (2013). *IPEDS, fall 2011, institutional characteristics component and 12-Month enrollment component* (NCES Publication No. 2013-172). Retrieved from http://nces.ed.gov/pubs2013/2013172.pdf

From the Antipodes: Embedded Librarians at the Open Polytechnic of New Zealand

Alison Fields and Philip Clarke

Introduction

As New Zealand's leading distance learning polytechnic, the Open Polytechnic of New Zealand provides tertiary education to over 30,000 students, largely within New Zealand but also in 40 other countries around the world. The majority of students are adults who are "combining work and study to upskill or broaden their knowledge base" (Open Polytechnic, 2012, p.34), with 93% studying "part-time, fitting vocational education around other commitments in their lives" (Open Polytechnic, 2012, p.34). They state "Our vision [is] a New Zealand that's continually learning to succeed. Our purpose [is] to inspire success through the most flexible, accessible and motivational learning experience in the world" (Open Polytechnic, 2012, p.4).

To support the purpose of the Open Polytechnic, embedded librarians have been available for inclusion in online classrooms since 2006. Faculty are able to opt into the embedded librarian service, which they are doing in increasing numbers as benefits become more visible and widely known. This case study examines the growth and use of embedded librarians in online and blended delivery courses within this institution using a Moodle platform, where the faculty opt-in system to enlisting embedded librarian services ensures that courses that are more likely to benefit from this added classroom service are the first to receive it. It also considers faculty and librarian attitudes and understandings of the embedded librarian programme as it currently operates.

In addition to describing the process of embedding librarians within these courses and how interactions are typically conducted within these classrooms, interactions outside of the classroom are also described, showing how library-faculty collaboration is developing from this new process and benefitting both groups. Attention is also turned to subject areas where the faculty uptake of the embedded librarian program is low, and possible reasons for this low uptake are suggested. Finally, a look is taken at how the embedded librarian programme at the Open Polytechnic has developed, and various issues associated with this programme are discussed.

The New Zealand Context

New Zealand is a small island nation in the southwest Pacific Ocean, generally comparable in land area and population to the state of Minnesota, with 4.4 million people distributed across its 1,600 km length. Large concentrations of the population live in the main urban centres, with around 32% of the country's population living in the main centre of Auckland (Auckland Council, 2012, p.13). Ethnicity is comprised of the indigenous Maori, New Zealand Europeans, Polynesians, and a growing mix of other cultures. Official languages are English, Maori, and New Zealand sign language. The education system is divided into three sectors: primary, which teaches children for the first eight years of school; secondary, which teaches a further five years; and tertiary, which covers both undergraduate and postgraduate education up to the doctoral level. At the tertiary level, New Zealand has eight universities and 18 polytechnics or institutes of technology alongside a range of industry training organisations to educate its population. The majority of these are based around physical campuses and face-to-face courses, but in recent years there has been an increasing amount of distance education being offered by many of these institutions. A very few institutions have been built on or include a large component of distance or extramural learning. This includes the Open Polytechnic and Massey University.

The Open Polytechnic has been in existence for over 50 years and was established as a distance education provider to train and educate New Zealanders unable to travel or leave employment or other commitments. It describes its history and development in these terms:

> Open Polytechnic began life as the Technical Correspondence School in 1946, providing resettlement training for returned servicemen and women following World War II. In 1963, it became the Technical Correspondence Institute (TCI) and began offering national training in trades subjects. As part of wider education reforms, the institution was renamed The Open Polytechnic of New Zealand in 1990, becoming the specialist national provider of open and distance learning at tertiary level. The following years were a period of profound transformation, with many new programmes and courses introduced in response to market demand. Open Polytechnic also adopted internationally proven models for distance learning course design, student support and quality control. In a new phase, Open Polytechnic is now developing an expanding range of online courses and services. (Open Polytechnic, 2013b)

The Open Polytechnic and Its Library Services

The library at the Open Polytechnic provides a range of services for students, faculty, and others. For students, services centre around circulation and reference. The Open Polytechnic Library

> lends recommended and additional resources listed in your course materials, with free courier delivery to your door and a pre-paid return courier envelope; provides access to books, e-books, DVDs and journal, magazine and newspaper articles that are relevant to your subject; provides access to online databases you can search to find resources about your subject; determines the best sources to search for information about your topic; and searches for information about your subject. (Open Polytechnic, 2013c)

Services to faculty include assistance with individual research and further study, assistance with course development, support for keeping teaching and learning materials up to date and, since 2006, the embedded librarian programme. Assistance with course development and course revision ensures that faculty are made aware of the current literature and resources available in any field and particularly of resources that are able to support new course content and be available to students studying these courses; it also ensures that liaison librarians who deal with particular disciplines and subjects are fully aware of the content and information resources needed for courses well before they are taught. In addition to creating subject guides to assist students in different subject areas, liaison librarians also assist faculty by monitoring new editions of key resources and new titles that may enhance or update existing courses and inform faculty as details of these become available. In the past seven years, liaison librarians have also acted as embedded librarians within online and blended courses where faculty have made library forums active. This extends the assistance librarians can offer and places it within the key learning environment for each course, allowing for course-specific assistance to be given at the students' point of need.

The Embedded Librarian Programme at the Open Polytechnic

The embedded librarian programme was an initiative of the library, not of the faculty. Self-service was a key concern of the library in 2006: Innovative's Millennium had been chosen as the new integrated library system, and it made student self-service much easier than the previous system, including the ability to create and incorporate subject guides into the webpages of the catalogue. The idea of having librarians in course forums was suggested at a brainstorming session in October 2005. The purpose of the session was to come up with ideas for self-service to be included in the 2006 Library Business Plan. At the initial session, a clear intention was to utilise Moodle forums to promote the self-service tools such as the catalogue and subject and assignment guides. In the 2006 Library Vision statement, which formed the basis of the business plan, the goal was to have a library presence in two online course forums. How this was to be achieved was left to the liaison librarians to determine.

Since this pilot project was experimental, the aim was to find willing members of faculty to be part of it. A key aspect of the approach was to base the new embedded librarianship project on the existing liaison librarian model as well as emphasize the need for a personal relationship between the librarian and faculty. The approach was not completely ad hoc; liaison librarians focused on NZQA level 5–7 (bachelor's degree) courses as they were seen to be the courses that could most benefit from having a library presence. A librarian's presence on discussion forums was seen as a natural extension of subject guides and the librarians' involvement in course revisions.

From the beginning, librarians did not want to be considered intruders in the online classroom: They needed to be there because faculty wanted them to be there. From the library's point of view, the primary aim of having a librarian in the online classroom was to promote the library, its resources, and librarians to students. A key driver was the difficulty in connecting students with the library and, specifically, the resources available to students in the online environment as many students appeared to focus only on their course pages in the learning management system (LMS) and did not venture to other areas of the Polytechnic's resources, including the library. The question was how could the library target students and connect with them. The librarians' hypothesized answer was that by being in the learning space where the students spend most of their time, there the library could point to targeted resources specific to the individual course the student was studying.

First on Board: Initial Courses Using the Embedded Librarian Programme

The first forum posts were made in March 2006, and the first courses to have embedded library services were a bridging course to tertiary study and four first-year undergraduate papers.

Two of these, courses 424 and 72142, were obvious first choices for library forums. Course 424 is a pre-degree tertiary study skills paper with the goal of preparing students for bachelor's degree studies. The course summary reads,

> This course covers the learning strategies, writing, information literacy, computer and numerical skills needed to support independent tertiary study. It is designed for people entering tertiary study for the first time or those who have been away from study for some years. Topic covered

include: Effective learning and study; information literacy; academic writing; working with numbers; and tables, spreadsheets and graphs. (Open Polytechnic, 2013d)

Likewise course 72142: Accessing Information deals with information literacy, and its course summary reads,

This course will provide learners from all disciplines with an introduction to information literacy and the skills required to fully participate in problem-based and applied learning. The course will take the learner through each facet of information literacy, allowing them time to practise and demonstrate understanding of these core skills. You will need an understanding of and familiarity with the enabling technology. (Open Polytechnic, 2013a)

Both these papers include library-related tasks and always generated student calls to the library. Faculty took little convincing that a library forum would be an excellent addition to the course.

Other courses such as 72175: Principles of Records Management; 74109: Art and Literature New Zealand; and 74111: Aotearoa New Zealand Society: Structure, Culture and Change were the other three papers that formed the first complement of courses at the beginning of the embedded librarian programme. These courses, like the other two, are part of the Departments of Information and Library Studies, Social Science, and Humanities, which were early adopters of the embedded librarian services.

The link between information and library studies and the embedded librarians was obvious, but for the social science and humanities, there were several contributing factors to this early adoption; the first was the was student need for library support in the subject area. The second was the existing professional relationship between the liaison librarian and the faculty, which the authors

believed was a particularly good working relationship with a good level of mutual understanding and trust. Faculty also felt they were able to allow liaison librarians into their courses without any great risk. During an interview with the authors, one faculty member described this close linking where the liaison librarians are the ones embedded within the courses where they advise faculty:

Embedded librarians have knowledge of the subject and prior to the course they've helped identify resources… The embedded librarian on my course has found lots of useful videos— online streaming YouTube videos. Again there was to-ing and fro-ing before the course.

The modest goal of a library forum in two courses in the Library Vision for 2006 was easily achieved. By the end of 2006 librarians were contributing to forums on 21 courses and a total of 61 posts had been made. Librarians were enthusiastic about the experiment, library managers were supportive, and subsequent library plans included the goal of adding more forums.

An analysis of posts within the library forums in these courses in the first year of the programme shows that courses 424 and 72142 accounted for 28 (46%) of the total of 61 posts. Surprisingly, the posts didn't lead to an immediate decrease of one-to-one reference work for those courses. In 2006, there were 43 one-to-one reference enquiries by 424 and 72142 students. These enquiries were very specific to a student's topic or addressed searching problems particular to each student.

An immediately apparent issue from the first year was that library forums in some courses generated further discussion, but other courses were very light on posts. In the first year, 14 (64%) of the 22 total courses with library forums consisted simply of the introductory post by the librarian. Despite this and because of the fact that the initial driver was making sure that students knew about the services the library could provide, this lack of interaction was not seen as a failure. Indeed, if the forum post raised awareness of the library and students used the self-service features to find relevant information, then the forum post could still be seen as a success.

Pattern of Uptake of Embedded Librarians in the Faculty Opt-in System

Over the seven years that the embedded librarian programme has been running to date, the number of faculty opting in to the system has steadily increased. Table 5.1 shows the increase in individual course occurrences using embedded librarians in each consecutive year, with the change per year.

At the end of 2012, the library was active in 112 courses, although in total 166 different individual courses have had library forums at one time or another since 2006. Courses have closed and new courses opened over that time, partially explaining the change. The drop in the number of courses in 2008 is partially accounted for by the discontinuation of nine courses, but another contributing factor was the need for the librarian to be added to the course by the tutor each time the course was taught; librarians had read-only rights within the LMS to view all course pages except forums. To create forum posts and view the forums, including library forums, the librarian had to be given read and write access by the tutor for each course with a library forum. Even with the best intentions by librarians and faculty, this confusion meant some courses were left off. After 2008, librarians were more proactive in reminding faculty members to add librarians to courses, and read and write forum access for librarians has now been automated.

There are a variety of other factors that may affect the number of courses choosing to include an embedded librarian: the level of the courses being taught, the influence of course designers, the fact that librarians could point to other courses with a library forum, and the benefits accruing to faculty of having a forum. Finally, with the migration to the latest version of the student management system, a library forum has been included as a default in the course template. This has made it very simple to add the librarian to the course and has further increased the number of courses with a library forum. The default is not without its problems: Sometimes it is activated without the librarians' knowledge, so suddenly there is a forum where there had not been one before, and, alternatively, faculty who do not want a library forum see it appearing as a default setting when the latest version of the course is being set up.

How Much Interaction and How Support Is Given

Over the last seven years a pattern has been established of few to frequent interactions; many courses have just a solitary post, while others are relatively active. Table 5.2 outlines this and shows the annual gains (or losses) in the number of posts made each year.

Interestingly, as the embedded librarian programme becomes more established and both faculty and librarians are becoming more comfortable with the information needed and the interactions being made, the number of interactions is rising disproportionately to the number of courses containing embedded librarians.

Table 5.1. Growth in Uptake of Embedded Librarians within Online Courses at the Open Polytechnic

Year	2006	2007	2008	2009	2010	2011	2012
Number of courses with library forums	21	51	45	53	63	90	112
Change per year	+21	+30	-6	+8	+10	+27	+22
% change	NA	+143%	-12%	+18%	+19%	+43%	+24%

Table 5.2. Growth in Forum Postings Made by Embedded Librarians within Online Courses at the Open Polytechnic

Year	2006	2007	2008	2009	2010	2011	2012
Number library Forum posts made per year	61	165	117	178	142	246	354
Change per year	+61	+104	-48	+61	-36	+104	+108
% change	NA	+170%	-29%	+52%	-20%	+73%	+44%

More interactions per course is an indication of the increasing value of embedded librarians within these courses over subsequent trimesters. It is taking some time for the embedded librarian programme to come to maturity, but as it is a new programme and needs to work as a partnership between faculty, librarians, and students, it is expected that gains will be shown over a number of years and not all at the inception of the programme.

Content of the Library Forum Postings

Forum postings made by embedded librarians generally follow the same types of learner support made in the mainstream library service. This encompasses making the library service known to students; detailing what types of assistance are available—some user education for catalogues, databases, and other resources; and answering specific reference questions asked by the students. Typical forum postings begin with an introduction by the embedded librarian, followed by a later post identifying key resources and searching techniques pertinent to upcoming assessments for the particular course they are posted in.

Following these proactive posts are usually reactive answers to directional and reference questions posted by the students, often about identifying and accessing information resources. Some questions may be directed to the embedded librarians by faculty, although most come directly from students, particularly around areas of referencing and the finer details of the APA referencing style. Moodle generates e-mail copies of forum posts and sends these to all participants who have subscribed to the forums one hour after the initial post was made in the forum. This enables embedded librarians to receive copies of forum questions and answer them within a short time frame without the need to be constantly checking the forums themselves. Large scale analyses of the content of library forum postings have not yet been made, although this may be considered in the future as it could help clarify the role of the embedded librarians in practice and may identify areas where this service can be refined or further developed.

Common Understandings on the Role of the Embedded Librarian

One of the issues involved in a working partnership between librarians and faculty is ensuring common understandings of what will be done, how it will be done, and how the two interact within the online classroom. It is important that common understandings exist between all players in the online classroom as differences in expectations may diminish the effectiveness of each role. Using liaison librarians as embedded librarians has gone a long way towards providing common understandings as these librarians are already working in partnership with faculty in course development, resource provision that supports course delivery, and other work, including support for the faculty research.

There appears to be a common understanding of the roles and assistance given by embedded librarians in those classrooms where there have been long periods of involvement, although that is expected. More data needs to be collected from

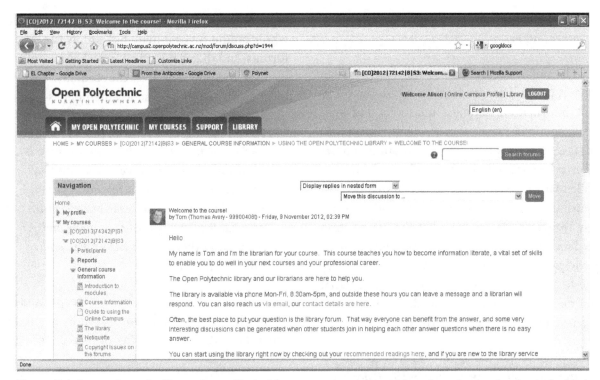

Figure 5.1. Screenshot of a library forum. Typical forum postings begin with an introduction by the embedded librarian.

those areas where involvement is new as it is suspected that in these areas that the highest benefits of working together can be gained quickly.

The Upsides and Downsides of Embedded Librarianship

When a number of faculty and librarians at the Open Polytechnic were interviewed in 2013 regarding the embedded librarian programme, they were asked what the upsides and downsides of embedded librarianship are to them, and several interesting points came to light. One is the feeling of support that faculty has within the online classroom, which was quite different from implications of intrusion that were first voiced when the programme was mooted. A comment from a faculty member stated,

[The best thing is] knowing that you've got back-up, especially for the technical questions. For example, APA and referencing questions, using the databases and helping the students find information.

In relation to the running of the online classroom, another faculty member remarked,

I was contacted by my embedded librarian who told me that holds on a particular book which was recommended reading for my course had suddenly increased and that he knew some students would not get a chance to view the book prior to the assessment it was being used for falling due. I had no idea! He suggested alternative texts and made online copies available, then gave the new list to me and I gave it to my class. It makes everyone look good!

On the downside, some other issues have been identified by faculty. One remarked,

I'd question the pedagogy of the forum process. There's a large class [around 140 students] and a lot of postings... The expert's post—i.e. librarian or tutor—gets lost in the

noise or comes in the middle of a whole lot of other postings.

The noise, or proliferation of postings, can make it difficult for students to locate the pertinent information amongst questions and ventured opinions from other students. Related to this is a secondary difficulty, where student posts often come from a small number of students while many others may be reading posts but not contributing or not reading posts at all. It is not easy to determine exactly what the information needs are for of many of these students as nonparticipation in these forums may mean they are able to access what they need or conversely that they do not know what they need. A faculty member described this phenomenon as—

a problem for the faculty as well as the embedded librarian in that we just don't know what the students don't know.

Another challenge is in using an asynchronous communication method rather than real-time interactions. There is no choice with regard to this as the Open Polytechnic is an asynchronous provider, with students able to study at their own pace and in their own time. In terms of embedded librarians working directly with students in their courses, it has been described as—

the lack of synchronicity [means] that incorrect or misleading information gets promulgated and even though it's corrected not everyone goes back to read the corrected information.

This is particularly true of discussions where students answer the questions of other students or venture ideas or opinions before faculty or embedded librarians are able to step in and give the definitive word. With so much information being offered on some of these forums it is difficult for some students to discern which information is of merit and which is not.

Another downside is one common to the whole online environment, not simply the library forums, and that is the way in which this communication method is used by the students. This has been described by one faculty member as—

[the] learning environment [is] too much like social media and social media isn't a great thing… it should be a learning space but the problem is the social media generation… in that they don't read or concentrate on what they're supposed to be doing and… in the way they talk to each other and to tutors on the forum.

Although this view has not been expressed by a majority, it is certainly one raised by faculty in other contexts and is worthy of further thought and investigation.

Non-Utilisation of Embedded Librarians

There are large areas of the Open Polytechnic where use of embedded librarians is very low. Many of these appear to cluster around subject areas that have low research requirements, typically vocational courses based in workplace experiences and some degree courses such as parts of the mathematical and IT areas where assessment questions are based on coursework without needing support from additional information resources. This is confirmed in the words of one faculty member:

As a numerically based course, students are not encouraged to use other resources… books often tackle topics in different ways and it is confusing for students if they move away from the materials provided. It's only in the last assignment that they may need to look at other literature, and then only in a minimal fashion.

For the library service, however, this represents little more than the status quo of service for these subject areas; generally speaking, it appears that the pattern of contact students have with the library roughly mirrors the pattern of contact made via forums within the online classrooms.

The full range of reasons for not utilising the embedded librarian services are more likely to encompass more than just these two factors and may also include attitudes, perceptions, and understandings of what embedded librarians can offer for each individual course. Anecdotal evidence suggests that some faculty who are not aware of the services embedded librarians are able to offer either see no need for granting access or are reluctant to let them enter into their own online classrooms for some other reason. Other faculty are highly supportive of the embedded librarians even if they do not feel they are a good fit for their particular courses. Indicative of this are the comments of one faculty member:

> *I don't see a library forum as being of great use, although would be happy to give it a try. Librarians may be able to help… but would need a very good grasp of what is required.*

This is certainly borne out in the pattern of uptake across the wide subject range at the Open Polytechnic where one or two courses using embedded librarians will result in others in the same subject area being picked up in subsequent years. It appears the good work is spreading.

As the embedded librarian programme becomes part of "business as usual," non-uptake is decreasing. This may be partly attributed to expectations of how courses should be run. One newer faculty member indicated that she was not asked if she wanted an embedded librarian in her course; it was just presented to her as part of the normal process of teaching at this institution, and she accepted it on this basis.

Impact of Embedded Librarianship beyond the Online Classroom

One of the key questions asked by the library services in providing an embedded librarian programme is "Do the services provided positively affect students?" This needs to be considered in terms of the provision of learner support, enhancement of the student experience, and effectiveness of delivery of service. The first of these is difficult to measure, as learners are not often able to determine how much various forms of support mean to them, and course results cannot be divided into discrete portions of course learning, own study, and support from other areas of the online campus. Enhancement of the student experience is again difficult to measure, although student satisfaction surveys may go part-way towards providing indicators for the embedded librarian programme, but none have been specifically performed to date. A measure of the effectiveness of delivery of service may be locatable through a combination of library usage statistics, although these have not yet been explored at the Open Polytechnic. The question of "Does it make a difference for faculty?" is more easily answered as faculty can communicate this for themselves.

The annual student satisfaction survey is an independent instrument that samples the student body on a range of topics, including their awareness and interactions with the library. This survey has shown small but statistically significant increases in student use and awareness of the library in recent years. The survey confirms the library's own increased usage statistics; however, it is not possible to link the increase directly to the embedding librarians in forums. There are too many other dependent variables, including the upgrade of the library OPAC and webpages and the upgrade of the LMS, all of which gave a more prominent place to the library links.

Faculty-librarian collaboration includes assistance with finding material for faculty research, and, in some instances, faculty and librarians have been working side by side on research topics dealing with student-learning and information-seeking preferences. Again, it is difficult to determine if any of this collaboration is a result of the embedded librarian programme or if the existing library services were enough of a link to promote the collaboration that currently exists. The embedded librarian programme can also be seen in some ways as working because it is a result of faculty-librarian collaboration as well as being an example of it.

Has the Embedded Librarian Programme Operated as Anticipated?

One of the key questions from the beginning of the experiment in 2006 was whether forum activity could be sustained over the long term. Experience in the first and subsequent years is that forum activity as it has been developed at the Open Polytechnic is sustainable. From the beginning, posts have stressed the availability of self-service resources, and, for a majority of the courses with library forums, that information is enough for the students to find the resources they need to support their work. Knowledge of past questions asked by students has enabled librarians to anticipate future questions. Since students can see the answers to all questions, which means answers to one question also answer other students' queries. Another phenomenon that has been emerging is peer support: students answering other students' questions in the forum. On these forums the librarian is more of a guide, affirming student posts rather than answering all posts individually.

Another concern has been managing student expectations of a reasonable response time to a query. Standard response times for faculty are a 48-hour turnaround for all student questions, although in practice it is often 24-hours or same-day, and students have come to expect quick answers within asynchronous online courses. There was initial concern that librarians would have to work extended hours, but in most cases student expectations have not been unmanageable. A combination of proactive anticipatory posts prior to assignments and a range of supporting material available online coupled with students helping each other on the forums has meant that posts could be dealt with during regular library hours.

A further question asked at the outset was whether this new embedded librarian service would replace or run complementary to existing reference services and student support from the library. The librarians worked from the premise that a key facet of the embedded librarian approach is to anticipate demand and manage it on a one-to-many basis. Well-timed and structured posts by embedded librarians should lead to a decrease in demand for time-consuming and relatively inefficient one-to-one reference enquiries. These ideas have yet to be explored in the light of the now seven years of operating the embedded librarian programme, and the next step is to look for any evidence that this is happening from the statistics generated from the library service. It is not yet known if a specific measure can be determined to answer these questions.

One last concern has been in regards to training: Initially training for the embedded librarians was in how to use the LMS, specifically how to post to forums rather than what to post. Since 2008, liaison librarians have been taking the Open Polytechnic's Certificate in Designing and Facilitating E-Learning papers prior to working in the online environment. This in itself has been incredibly beneficial as liaison librarians have become students in the Open Polytechnic's online environment at the same time as working alongside faculty to support students in their own learning. Undertaking these courses in e-learning also means that liaison librarians are learning more about their online environment alongside new faculty and learning centre staff who are also taking these papers. This encourages working collaboratively and developing closer ties with faculty and with their own peers and provides more credibility along with a wider range of skills for the embedded librarians in this online environment.

Conclusion

Looking back over the seven years of embedded librarians in online courses at the Open Polytechnic of New Zealand, there is little doubt that the high-use library forums within the online course pages have been a success. Students have appreciated the library presence embedded within the online course pages in which they spend the most of their time. Because Open Polytechnic students tend to study over long periods of time, taking one or two papers a year, it does take a long time for initiatives like library forums to bear fruit. A direct line into the virtual classroom has been a key feature of the library's vision for its services over the past seven years, and it will continue to be promoted to faculty as a service that can be easily incorporated into their online courses. The primary aim of the initiative was to increase the use of self-service resources available to students and that aim has not changed. The drive of all library forum work will continue to be helping students to help themselves.

There remains a question of what "embedded" librarians are, and the model used at the Open Polytechnic may not be the traditional or standard one. There is a library presence within the online course pages with user education and reference service provided at a tailored level within the online classroom running parallel to more traditional library services provided by the Open Polytechnic Library. Other aspects of involvement of "embeddedness" occur outside of the online classroom: There is involvement and advice in developing new courses with faculty, in revising and updating courses, and in locating research material for faculty and other material as requested. Faculty-librarian collaboration extends to include some joint research, and planning for new initiatives and other projects often include library staff as a key player within this dis-

tance education institution. When all of these are considered together, the library service is truly embedded within the life and work of the institution and now also being integrated within the teaching space of the online classroom brings a wider definition and example of embeddedness, which benefits all parties: the students, faculty, and the library service.

REFERENCES

Auckland Council (2012). *Long-term plan 2012– 2022*. Retrieved from http://www.aucklandcouncil.govt.nz/EN/planspoliciesprojects/plansstrategies/Long_term_plan/Documents/ltpvolume1.pdf

Open Polytechnic. (2012). *Annual report 2012*. Retrieved from http://www.openpolytechnic.ac.nz/about-us/corporate-publications/

Open Polytechnic. (2013a). Accessing information. Retrieved from http://www.openpolytechnic.ac.nz/subjects-and-courses/72142-accessing-information/

Open Polytechnic. (2013b). History of Open Polytechnic. Retrieved from http://www.openpolytechnic.ac.nz/about-us/who-we-are/history-of-open-polytechnic/

Open Polytechnic. (2013c). Open Polytechnic Library. Retrieved from http://www.openpolytechnic.ac.nz/study-with-us/services-for-students/library/

Open Polytechnic. (2013d). Tertiary study skills. Retrieved from http://www.openpolytechnic.ac.nz/subjects-and-courses/424-tertiary-study-skills/

Web 2.0 Toolkit: A Guide for Virtually Embedded Librarians

Chanitra Bishop and Christina Sheley

Virtually embedded librarians need to bridge distance and engage users in instruction, research assistance, and the use of library resources and services. In addition, librarians must proactively develop and deliver valuable tools and services that lead to learning, research, and teaching success. Effectively accomplishing these directives requires a deep understanding of users' needs and behaviors and the development of strong relationships with faculty and students. Web 2.0 tools and their inherent social features can be instrumental in growing a community and facilitating robust communication and participation, thus, creating strong connections to the library and librarian and providing feedback that can be used to enhance and direct initiatives.

This chapter begins with a historical review of Web 2.0 technologies and their use in academic libraries and then moves to a case study that details how the authors used two Web 2.0 tools, a blog and a wiki, in a library research component for an online business course. The chapter concludes with overviews and analyses for a variety of individual Web 2.0 tools, with special attention paid to the learning curve librarians will experience with these applications and the technical requirements for implementation. Additionally, the authors cite examples of current practice, demonstrating how Web 2.0 has been incorporated into many facets of embedded librarianship.

Introduction

The term Web 2.0 was popularized by O'Reilly to define the new, emerging web after the dot-com collapse (O'Reilly, 2005) and to "describe a group of emerging online technologies characterized by the opportunity for almost anyone to contribute and participate in their ongoing creation" (Bobish, 2010, p. 55). Web 2.0 came to embody many meanings, but its core revolves around user-generated and shared content; the development of the Web as a social platform; and activity characterized by collaboration, participation, and interactivity (Bowman, 2008; Click & Petit, 2010; Harris & Rea, 2009). Today its presence is universal—easily identifiable in the personal realm but also in the spheres of business, journalism, technology, education, etc.

Web 2.0 and Academic Libraries

The literature reveals Web 2.0 technologies and academic libraries have been associated since the early 2000s. Stephens (2006) noted he first heard the term "blog" at a library conference in 2002. Technical expertise and a focus on education and research resulted in quick adoption of Web 2.0 technologies in academic libraries since these first references (Xu, Ouyang, & Chu, 2009). Mahmood and Richardson's (2011) survey of 100 U.S. Association of Research Libraries (ARL) libraries' websites showed an "overwhelming acceptance" of Web 2.0 (p. 372), with all libraries using a variety of tools—particularly blogs, microblogs, Really Simple Syndication (RSS), instant messaging, social networking sites, mashups, and podcasts. Practical examples of Web 2.0 tools and social networking implementation can be found across the literature in all aspects related to library collections, services, and instruction (Chase, 2008; Hricko, 2010; Oxford, 2009; Wan, 2011).

Use in libraries has become so popular, the term "Library 2.0" developed (Click & Petit, 2010) to signify a library model that emphasized "user-centered change and participation in the creation of content and community-based services" (Peltier-Davis, 2009, p. 18). *Library 2.0: Initiatives in Academic Libraries* (Cohen, 2007) presents several case studies of the use of Web 2.0 and social networking tools in academic environments, illustrating the close relationship between these technologies and library collections and services.

Web 2.0 Usage Case Study

This case study illustrates how Web 2.0 tools were used to embed the authors in an online, internship course (X498) for undergraduate business students. The authors created a library component, comprised of a blog and a wiki, to provide information literacy instruction and technology practice, address research needs, and facilitate communication among course participants. Learning outcomes called for students to use these platforms to reflect on information use and behavior and practice skills related to information choice, evaluation, and recommendation in the workplace. Tool usage garnered positive student feedback and was deemed successful for instruction and course application by all involved.

X498 Course Overview

X498: Internship for Credit is a 12-week, two-credit hour course for juniors and seniors in the Kelley School of Business at Indiana University Bloomington. In recent years, the need for business students to complete an internship has risen as companies are increasingly using this experience as an extended job interview. X498 was developed in 2008 to provide an academic com-

ponent for the internship experience in hopes of further building upon knowledge gained and to enhance future outcomes. In addition, the course helps students develop a keener sense of self, inspiring them to explore, discover, and navigate the lifelong learning process—skills encouraged by Indiana University's General Education Curriculum (2008). In X498, students complete assignments that require deep examination of the overall internship, including journal reflections on training and learning opportunities, motivation, teamwork, and leadership styles, and a final portfolio project that encourages a comprehensive view of one's experience (Dayton & Sheley, 2012).

Approximately 120 students enroll in X498 each academic year, with a higher concentration during the summer semester. Students are nationally and internationally dispersed during their internship experience; therefore, assignment and course content is delivered online through Indiana University's course management system. No classroom instruction is conducted; however, e-mail is used to provide additional clarification and teaching when needed. Class participants meet face-to-face after the course's completion to debrief and provide feedback.

The authors became virtually embedded in X498 in Summer 2012. Their project stemmed from a small grant awarded to instill information fluency and research support in the course; there had been no library and/or librarian involvement in the class prior to this award. At the outset, the authors worked closely with the instructor of record, a business faculty member, to develop our library objectives.

X498 Library Objectives

Class reflection assignments as well as end of course evaluations from previous X498 iterations indicated that interns were required to navigate unfamiliar, specialized business resources or locate information that was not easily found via a Google search. Sometimes peers, co-workers, and supervisors could be relied on for assistance, but often interns were left to their own devices and reported feeling ill-equipped. No interns identified the library as a source of assistance. Consequently, one of the library objectives was to provide and heavily market research and resource assistance that interns could access on an "as needed" basis.

Feedback also suggested that many interns needed to be proficient in the use of Web 2.0 and social media technologies. For example, one intern was asked to oversee a company's blog and make regular content contributions. In addition, a large percentage of interns were required to maintain and update a company's Facebook and/or Twitter accounts. These responsibilities varied widely by position and industry, but given the high rate of inclusion, most employers assumed that the interns were comfortable with these tasks. Self-reporting indicated that this often was not the case. Therefore, the authors incorporated Web 2.0 training and practice into their library objectives.

Another objective was to integrate information literacy instruction into the overall course to augment workplace-specific critical thinking skills and enhance the interns' employability. Recent literature suggests that employers are increasingly interested in employees that have significant information literacy skills. Klusek and Bornstein's (2006) examination of business and finance job profiles in the Department of Labor's O*Net database revealed that four of the five Association of College and Research Libraries' (ACRL) Information Literacy Competency Standards for Higher Education (Standard Five, the ethical and legal use of information, was excluded from examination) were considered "important" or "very important" for a majority of the studied positions and thought to be a "core competency required in the career" (p. 18). Sokoloff (2012) studied the importance of information literacy skills in the workplace by interviewing supervisors and managers of entry-level staff. He found that employers highly-valued the ability to criti-

cally think about and use information in the decision-making process. Selingo (2012) stated that numerous employer surveys indicated future workplaces need individuals with a number of skills related to adaptability and those "who can come up with novel solutions to problems and better sort through information to filter out the most critical pieces" (para. 5).

While information literacy skills are highly desirable, there are some indications that college graduates do not meet expectations. The Project Information Literacy Research Report, "How College Graduates Solve Information Problems Once They Join the Workplace" (Head, 2012), shared findings from interviews with 23 employers and identified four often-cited, optimal information competencies that "employers said they needed from new college hires—but rarely found" (Head, 2012, p. 11). These include

"1. Engaging team members during the research process,

2. Retrieving information from a variety of formats,

3. Finding patterns and making connections,

4. Taking a deep dive into the 'information reservoir.'" (Head, p. 12, Figure 5)

Taking employer desires and the perceived gaps into account, the authors' pedagogy centered on having interns practice information choice, evaluation, use, and recommendation for concepts they were addressing in the workplace. In addition, the authors felt extensive information literacy knowledge and a better understanding of processes and required skills would come if interns reflected on information use and behavior in their particular working environment (Marcum, 2002). A thorough discussion of how Web 2.0 can be used to support and teach to the ACRL Information Literacy Competency Standards for Higher Education can be found in Bobish (2010).

Overarching the authors' objectives was the desire to obtain a deeper grasp of research needs and behavior in the workplace to help inform their activities while embedded in X498 and also to give them a broader perspective on preparing business students for the working world. Furthermore, course participants had requested to know what peers were encountering within their internship experiences. The authors packaged these needs and their objectives into a library component they called Information@Work.

Web 2.0 Rational and Tool Selection

As previously stated, Indiana University's course management system was being used in X498 to deliver content and instruction, but it did not allow for bringing the class participants together in a way that fully facilitated communication or allowed interns to interact and share experiences. Additionally, with the span and depth of their objectives, the authors needed an application that was customizable and adaptable enough to deliver instruction, research assistance, and other course activities. Given these drawbacks and the established need for many X498 interns to be familiar with Web 2.0 technologies, the authors decided to move forward with implementing Web 2.0 tools. After examining their objectives, their audience, and the various technologies available, they settled specifically on blog and wiki applications.

The blog provided a platform to share ideas and a collaborative space for librarians and interns to view and mentor best practices. Blogs encourage conversation, participation, and community (Stephens, 2007) and present a platform where "students are writing and interacting with each other in digital spaces beyond the boundaries of the classroom" (Hedge, 2013, para. 2). In addition, it gave the authors a chance to instruct students on the use of blogs as both a technology and an information source. Finally, it seemed the ideal "less formal" platform where interns could explore and understand the role that information use and behavior played in one's workplace.

The university's course management system had a blog add-in available, but it was in beta at the time of selection and limited in functionality. Additionally, the authors wanted to employ a platform that closely mimicked what interns might be using in a corporate environment. Finally, they had less than a month to implement the technology and create content, so an application that was familiar and easy-to-use was required. In the end, the authors settled on WordPress (http://wordpress.org) as their blogging platform.

The wiki was chosen because it helped the authors build an X498 community similar to what interns might be experiencing in the workplace. Additionally, it encouraged peers to interact with each other and with content and sources. The authors could also naturally discuss wikis as a source and the associated strengths and weaknesses of the technology. Finally, there was a hope that if interns picked similar topics or if this project spanned several iterations, the authors might develop a standalone "internship" collection—one that was curated and updated by the community. The authors applied the same considerations in selecting the wiki software as for the blog and chose PBworks for Education (http://pbworks.com/education) as their platform.

Implementation and Execution

Information@Work Blog. The Information@Work blog used a premium theme (Linen), which featured a clean, uncluttered design and enhancements like custom typography, background images, and colors and a featured post slider. The blog was not locally installed on IU's servers but hosted on WordPress.com. Access was restricted, requiring a username and password to post, to ensure privacy for both the students and to protect any company and industry information relayed while completing assignments. Invitation notices were sent via e-mail to all those enrolled at the start of the course, and users were removed from the profile when dropping or exiting the class. Announcements sent via the course management system stated that the blog should only be used for X498. Other topics were not allowed. These messages also prompted students to be considerate in post content and comments, advising that any inappropriate material would be reviewed for removal.

Figure 6.1. The X498 Information@Work blog. A screenshot of a sample reflection post submitted to the X498 Information@Work blog in Summer 2012.

On the blog's landing page (see Figure 6.1), a search box, list of recent posts, an archival list, and rotating poll questions sourced from Polldaddy (e.g., "How many times a day must you locate information?") were featured. The authors created an "About" page that provided librarian contact information and a short summary of purpose. An "Instructions" page included detailed assignment requirements and grading guidelines. The "Resources" page housed research guides promoting various subject-specific and/or topical resources for use during the internship. For example, the "Internship Success" guide, posted at the beginning of the semester, included links to e-book chapters, database articles, and websites with information about making the most of an internship position and taking advantage of opportunities while in the workplace.

The authors created a welcome post that familiarized students with the blog's purpose and assignment parameters and then periodically added content on topics related to information literacy and blogging (e.g., writing effective blog posts, how to create posts, copyright and blogs, locating sources, and evaluation) for the duration of the course. Interns were asked to read all librarian-generated content and make comments.

In addition, as an outcome for the information literacy instruction, interns were assigned two 250-word reflection pieces, requiring them to describe information use and behavior within their particular company, industry, and/or internship. The assignment also allowed the authors to proactively provide research assistance as they learned about what interns were encountering in their workplace. Prompts for this assignment were guided by the open-ended questions Sokoloff (2012) used when interviewing employers, and included

- What research or information guides your internship activities?
- Who provides needed/required information? How much is provided? In what way?
- What types of information sources (e.g., books, journals, websites, databases, raw data, etc.) are you using in your internship?
- What research skills are required in your internship and workplace?
- Are there specific information creation and/or management tools that you use (e.g., spreadsheets, wikis, blogs, intranets, social media sites, apps, etc.)?

Each reflection assignment was worth 50 points and due in the third and ninth week of the course. Full-credit was given for completion. The authors read and commented on each reflection entry, giving research guidance and resource suggestions where appropriate. Peers were also encouraged to read and comment on posts so strategies and ideas could be shared.

Information@Work Wiki. The Information@Work wiki was created using the freely-available version of PbWorks for Education. Similar to the Information@Work blog, access was restricted, requiring a username and password to add or change content to ensure privacy for both students and corporate employers. Invitation notices were e-mailed midway through the course to avoid confusion with the Information@Work blog invitation e-mails sent at the beginning of the class. The same announcements regarding appropriate use were posted in the course management system.

The wiki's landing page (see Figure 6.2) contained a welcome message with links to the author's contact information and the wiki bibliography assignment. A folder was created to house students' contributions, with each person creating a wiki page to be placed there. Since technology training and practice were one of the objectives, interns could only receive full credit if the page was filed in the correct location.

The assignment completed in the wiki platform was in two parts: an annotated bibliography and a wiki entry. Interns were first required to complete an annotated bibliography comprised of 10 sources on a research topic related to his or her internship. The audience and/or purpose for the bibliography were to educate one's peers on the topic. Prior to completing the bibliography, interns read content (housed in librarian-created modules in the course management system) that provided a definition and overview of an annotated bibliography, how to find sources, how to evaluate found information, and guidance on citation development. The annotation guidelines asked students to interact with chosen sources beyond a surface or summary level and answer questions related to purpose, audience, author, and relevance.

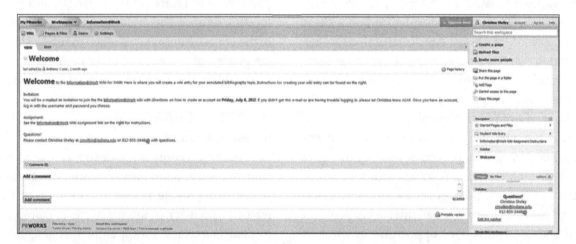

Figure 6.2. The X498 Information@Work wiki. A screenshot of the "Welcome" message of the X498 Information@Work wiki seen by students in Summer 2012.

Once complete, interns used the annotated bibliography to create a wiki entry. Each entry included a 500-word summary providing context and an overview of the topic's use in the workplace. In addition, interns were asked to carefully examine the 10 sources from their annotated bibliography assignment and pick the "top" five to include in the wiki entry. A justification for inclusion was also required.

The annotated bibliography and wiki entry were each worth 100 points and due in the seventh and 11th week of the course, respectively. The authors graded each assignment based on several criteria, including quality of cited sources, appropriateness for audience, thoroughness of evaluation, and choice rationale.

Assessment and Reflection on Web 2.0 Use

Assessment of Information@Work and Web 2.0. At the conclusion of X498, interns met with the authors and the business faculty member of record to provide qualitative feedback about the overall X498 experience, including the Information@Work component. During this meeting, interns were asked to complete an end of course survey generated and distributed via SurveyMonkey (www.surveymonkey.com), to obtain quantitative feedback. Several survey questions specifically addressed Information@Work:

- If you needed research help during your internship, would you consult the librarian?
- What could be done to improve the Information@Work assignments?
- What could be done to improve the overall Information@Work portion of X498?
- What is the best way to communicate Information@Work assignment details and instructions?

Intern Feedback. The blog and reflection assignment overwhelmingly garnered positive intern feedback. For many, the reflection helped make a connection and develop an understanding of the role research and information literacy played in an internship. Numerous posts indicated that research and the skills needed to execute it well were highly valuable in one's position and/or company. As for blog use, many stated that it made the reflection more enjoyable and that the short posts did not feel like the "typical" paper assignment. In addition, interns liked seeing what peers contributed and encountered in their own experiences. Negative feedback centered on assignment parameters and gaining access via e-mail invitation.

The wiki garnered more negative feedback, mostly because of the related assignments. Many interns found them to be too long, time consuming, and/or not applicable to their experience. This presented an interesting dichotomy given the importance placed on research and information literacy skills in the reflection posts. While interns indicated value in the blog, they did not think it was important or applicable to spend time practicing these skills using the annotated bibliography and wiki.

Faculty Feedback. Overall, the business faculty member of record was pleased with the Information@Work experience, stating that he felt "the addition of this component to the course enhanced the experience of the students in their internships and added significant value to the course." As for the Web 2.0 technologies themselves, "This use of the blog and wiki with X498 has been the result of both student demand to share information about their experiences and the creative use of technology to deliver this pedagogy" (K. Dayton, personal communication, August 20, 2013). In addition, the faculty member felt that both platforms allowed for relatively seamless integration into the curriculum without disrupting the existing course structure.

Librarian Feedback and Next Steps. Both the blog and wiki proved to be excellent vehicles for building a bridge to interns in the distance environment and engaging them in instruction and activity. The social nature of the blog let the authors quickly adapt posts and provide research assistance at the interns' points of need. Comments, feedback, and suggestions could be personalized and made in real time, providing interns with individualized and meaningful service. Implementation of Web 2.0, however, was labor-intensive, as the authors devoted significant time to set-up, development of assignment parameters, content creation, and intern interaction.

The library objectives for Information@Work were to provide research assistance, help interns become more Web 2.0 proficient, integrate information literacy instruction into the course (particularly addressing concepts of information choice, evaluation, usage, and recommendation), and develop a deeper understanding of workplace research needs and skills. The authors feel they were successful in incorporating all of these objectives and achieved moderate results in outcome.

The authors were able to provide unsolicited research assistance at the point of need; however, a majority of interns revealed in feedback that they would not actively consult a librarian for research assistance during the internship experience. Additional probing is needed to determine why this is the case. A change for the next Information@Work iteration will be to incorporate a chat widget into the Web 2.0 environment to provide interns with another communication channel. Further marketing of this service will also take place.

All interns were able to complete the Information@Work assignments using the desired Web 2.0 tool in the desired way, demonstrating success for this outcome. If interns continue to indicate that the ability to use Web 2.0 is important and/or desirable in the corporate environment, then the authors may try to define outcomes for various levels of proficiency beyond basic exposure and execution.

The authors were able to successfully integrate information literacy concepts into the X498 course. We did not conduct a formal assessment of this instruction to assess learning but are planning to do so next time. The authors are working to redefine the existing assignments to try and correct some of the disconnect interns displayed in addition to making them more manageable and applicable.

Finally, the authors gained a deeper understanding of workplace research and information needs at the intern level. This knowledge is now being used to inform future iterations of the course and their instruction and teaching activities within the academy.

Web 2.0 Technologies Overview

The authors chose to incorporate a blog and a wiki into the X498 course based on their library objectives and the collaborative nature of these tools. However, there are a variety of Web 2.0 technologies—ranging from more traditional tools like blogs, podcasting, RSS, and wikis to a growing list of social media like Facebook, Twitter, and Pinterest—available for virtually embedded librarians' use. What follows is an overview of several Web 2.0 tools with emphasis on technical requirements (for both librarians and library) and pros and cons of usage. In addition, the authors cite examples of how embedded librarians have integrated Web 2.0 and more recently social media into instruction, reference, outreach, and other library services. Finally, the "Is Web 2.0 Right for You?" section provides a series of questions to ask when contemplating the use of Web 2.0 in a project.

While our overview focuses on the required librarian's skills for Web 2.0 integration, the technical knowledge of students is also worth noting. Millennials are typically social media savvy and are also thought to be adept with new technology usage. However, they can be unfamiliar with less popular Web 2.0 tools such as wikis, podcasts, RSS, or even "newer" technologies like Twitter. Therefore, it is imperative that time be allotted for tool explanation and familiarization with features and functionality. For example, if students are required to post to a wiki, a Jing screencast (http://www.techsmith.com/jing.html) can be created to demonstrate and explain the tool. In addition, class time can be used for practice exercises related to features and function. This preparation allows students to become more comfortable and can minimize the number of questions later during assignment implementation and execution.

Traditional Web 2.0

Traditional Web 2.0 tools have existed for some time and have become a staple in the library technology toolkit. Increasingly, stand-alone applications are being used in conjunction with these tools, integrating older more established platforms with newer technologies (Stephens, 2007). Some examples include an instant message widget on a library blog or sending out links to blog posts via Twitter. These new uses and the resulting functionality make it important to define and include traditional platforms in our discussion. Furthermore, project or classroom objectives might dictate the use of something more conventional.

Table 6.1 highlights frequently used traditional Web 2.0 tools. Technical requirements are addressed, including librarian learning curve and library implementation and maintenance needs in addition to pros and cons of usage.

Table 6.1. Traditional Web 2.0 Tools Overview

Technology	Technical Requirements	Pros and Cons
Blogs: Blogger www.blogger.com WordPress www.wordpress.com www.wordpress.org	Hosted blogs are easy to create and update and have a low librarian learning curve. Non-hosted blogs have a higher learning curve and require more advanced IT skills, including programming knowledge for installation and institutional server space for housing.	*Pros:* • Participants can easily publish and share links and content online. • Widgets can be added to increase functionality and incorporate polls, images, slideshows, chat widgets, etc. • Blogs encourage community communication, discussion, and interaction and can help remove the sense of isolation that sometimes comes in a virtual environment. • Blogs provide an excellent platform for embedded librarians to provide research assistance and updates on services, programs, and collections. *Cons:* • Blogs can take a great deal of staff time to generate content and provide regular, relevant updates. • Management and maintenance of non-hosted blogs can be particularly time consuming. • Developing a community where users read and interact through commenting can be a challenge.
Wikis: Google Sites http://sites.google.com MediaWiki www.mediawiki.org PBworks http://pbworks.com Wikispaces Classroom www.wikispaces.com	Overall, wiki software can be less intuitive and have a medium librarian learning curve. It is best to have some prior experience editing wikis or a similar tool. Using vendor-provided tutorials can ease the process. Most popular wiki platforms like Google Talk are hosted and easy to create and update. The MediaWiki platform is the least intuitive of the popular applications mentioned. Non-hosted wikis require more advanced IT skills, including programming knowledge for installation and institutional server space for housing.	*Pros:* • Participants can easily publish and share links and content online. • Wikis can be used to create a website that can be edited without prior HTML knowledge. • Widgets or plugins can be added to increase functionality and incorporate video, images, calendars, etc. • Wikis are ideal for projects requiring collaboration or group editing. Discussion features can help develop a sense of community. *Cons:* • Wiki software has unique features that may be unfamiliar to users such as the discussion boards and built-in tracking mechanics. • Wikis provide a blank slate for users to create links to other content in a nonlinear form. This requires more thought about organizational structure to ensure easy site navigation.

Examples of traditional Web 2.0 tools being used by embedded librarians are numerous. Glass and Spiegelman (2007) implemented a blog to teach research skills in math and computer science courses. Students explored and posted on topics related to the history of math or the origin of an algorithm and were also asked to comment on classmates' posts to encourage reciprocal learning. The blog resulted in increased class interaction and online discussion. In one instance, a student created a new blog thread, which led to several comments from both the students and the instructor.

Niedbala and Fogleman (2010) incorporated a wiki into an education course where the assignment called for a description of a school dis-

Table 6.1. Traditional Web 2.0 Tools Overview

Technology	Technical Requirements	Pros and Cons
Virtual Reference: Google Hangouts www.google.com/hangouts LibAnswers with LibChat http://springshare.com LibraryH3lp http://libraryh3lp.com Mosio for Libraries www.textalibrarian.com Skype www.skype.com	IM or chat software setup and administration for virtual reference can have a medium to high librarian learning curve. Chat widget customization requires HTML knowledge. More skill is required if creating multiple queues to allow librarians in various locations to participate in one system or when integrating instant messaging clients such as Google Talk. IM or chat software usage has a low librarian learning curve after implementation.	*Pros:* • Virtual reference allows virtually embedded librarians to provide assistance at the point of need, including providing office hours or research consultations. • The audio and video functionality of platforms, like Skype and Google Hangouts, can be used by virtually embedded librarians to simulate a more traditional face-to-face interaction. *Cons:* • Interacting with users through chat does not allow for physical cues, such as body language, to help determine if a user is satisfied with the interaction. This could require a more extensive reference interview and additional points of clarification. • Chats can be mistakenly dropped in mid-session due to a poor Internet connection or mistakenly closed browsers. This could lead to confusion or dissatisfaction for the patron. • Establishing a regular chat schedule with several hours of availability is optimal to produce high levels of usage. This can present a challenge for institutions with a small staff.
RSS (Really Simple Syndication/Rich Site Summary): Bloglines Reader www.bloglines.com Feedly http://cloud.feedly.com Flipboard www.flipboard.com	RSS readers have a low librarian learning curve and require little to no knowledge of the tool prior to first use.	*Pros:* • Web content is automatically delivered to the reader platform. • Where available, users can subscribe and receive updates for an entire website or section of a website. • Some RSS readers provide a magazine-like experience, which can make browsing easier and more desirable. Feedly and Flipboard offer mobile applications. • Virtually embedded librarians can use this platform to easily share content with students. *Cons:* • Finding content to populate a RSS reader can be time consuming. • Both librarians and students have to access content from a secondary site, which may be a barrier for use. • Social media like Facebook and Twitter have almost replaced the need for RSS readers since their very nature is to automatically provide organizational and individual updates to followers.

trict and community using public data. Students worked in small groups to analyze this data and used library resources to learn more about their assigned area. Each research task had a corresponding, customized wiki page for working with the needed sources. In addition, the wiki included prompts students used to craft a statements reflecting on the project's purpose and source inclusion.

Social tagging has been used at Boston University's Alumni Medical Library to explain Medical Subject Headings (MeSH). Students completed an online assignment that required tagging of an article, a video, and an image. After completion, the class discussed the accuracy of the selected tags and issues associated with use of natural language versus subject headings (Maggio et al., 2009).

Table 6.1. Traditional Web 2.0 Tools Overview

Technology	Technical Requirements	Pros and Cons
Podcasting/Vodcasting: Audacity http://audacity.sourceforge.net Camtasia www.techsmith.com/camtasia.html Adobe Captivate www.adobe.com/products/captivate.html ePodcast Producer www.industrialaudiosoftware.com/products/epodcastproducer.html iTunes www.apple.com/itunes LAME (MP3 encoder) http://lame.sourceforge.net Windows Media Player http://windows.microsoft.com/en-us/windows/windows-media-player WinSCP (SFTP client) http://winscp.net Filezilla https://filezilla-project.org	Creating a podcast or vodcast has a high librarian learning curve because it requires the ability to create and edit audio and video as well as work within file storage and sharing sites. For novices, it is important to learn the process and tools prior to creation. In most cases, one will need supplementary equipment like headphones and a high-quality microphone. Adequate server space will be needed for any internal storage of these large files.	*Pros:* • Virtually embedded librarians can use podcasts or vodcasts to provide a series of research tips or tutorials. • The ability to hear and see content helps mimic a traditional classroom experience and may better address student learning in some instances. *Con:* • The planning, development, and creation of a podcast or vodcast requires several steps (e.g., creating an outline, writing a script, recording voiceover, finding/generating graphics, etc.) and can be a complicated and lengthy process.
Social Bookmarking, Annotations & Tagging: Delicious www.delicious.com Diigo www.diigo.com Tumblr www.tumblr.com Pinterest https://pinterest.com	Social bookmarking sites have a very low librarian learning curve and require little to no knowledge of the tool prior to first use.	*Pros:* • Bookmarks can be public or private and tags can be used to share a sub collection of saved websites with students. • Easy for virtual librarians incorporate into pedagogy and to generate course-specific resources with student participation. • Some sites allow for social annotation, which can facilitate reciprocal learning and student reflection. *Con:* • Consistent tagging methods are necessary to increase the likelihood of discovering tagged or bookmarked material at a later point.

Social Media

Within the last five years, more cloud-based Web 2.0 tools have developed. One area of rapid increase and growth is in social media or web-based applications that enable social networking, where users connect and share messages, photos, videos, and websites online. There is an ever-growing list of social media sites, including the established Facebook and Twitter and niche resources such as Foursquare and Vine.

Table 6.2 highlights popular social media tools and includes both established technologies such as Facebook and YouTube and newer applications like Instagram. Technical requirements are presented, including librarian learning curve and library implementation and maintenance needs as well as pros and cons of usage.

The usage of numerous social media tools by librarians is being cited in the literature. Currently, one of the most popular is Twitter, which is frequently used to encourage classroom participation and community. Ellen Hampton Filgo, a librarian at Baylor University, used Twitter to embed herself in a first-year honors seminar. The course required students to make use of the microblogging site to ask questions and post comments with a hashtag, thus creating a backchannel for classroom conversations. Filgo then took this opportunity to follow and interact with the class and provide services, research assistance, and resource suggestions at the point of need (Hamilton, 2012).

Librarians have also explored Facebook as a means for embedding themselves into courses. Haycock and Howe (2011) used a Facebook group to give feedback and suggestions related to the library and its collections and services for a College of Education and Human Development course at the University of Minnesota. The Facebook group provided a private space and allowed for participation outside of having to "friend" all the participants. Student feedback indicated they found the interaction helpful and Facebook was an effective means of sharing this information.

Table 6.2. Social Media Tools Overview

Technology	Technical Requirements	Pros and Cons
Edmodo www.edmodo.com Facebook www.facebook.com Flickr www.flickr.com Foursquare www.foursquare.com Google+ http://plus.google.com Instagram http://instagram.com Pinterest https://pinterest.com Twitter www.twitter.com Vine https://vine.co YouTube http://www.youtube.com	Use of social media tools have a low to medium librarian learning curve. They can be easy for those already familiar with Web 2.0 technologies. Each social media site has its own features and functionality that will need to be learned by new users. In addition, constant changes make it necessary to stay abreast of new developments. More advanced skills (e.g., video/audio editing and file sharing capabilities) will be required if creating videos for YouTube and Vine. Photographs and images being posted to photo sharing sites might require the ability to use graphics software like Adobe Photoshop or Adobe Illustrator.	*Pro:* • Virtually embedded librarians can share content and connect with students to provide research assistance and instruction at the point of need. *Cons:* • Social media can require a high-level of interaction to maintain user engagement, which can be time consuming. • Privacy is difficult to manage on social media as much of the content is open by default. • Newer tools such as Instagram require the use of a mobile device.

Other Web 2.0 Tools

There are a host of newer tools built upon Web 2.0 principles that allow users to create and share information. Examples of these latest tools include Animoto (http://www.animoto.com/), Poll Everywhere (http://www.polleverywhere.com/), and VoiceThread (http://www.voicethread.com/). Animoto, an application that allows users to create videos from images, can assist in making short library videos or tutorials. In the "Individual in the Information Age" course at Indiana University Bloomington, students used Animoto to create an online video as a replacement for the traditional library tour (Bishop, 2010). Poll Everywhere and a similar website Socrative (http://www.socrative.com) allow for surveying or polling of users online, which can be beneficial for assessment. VoiceThread allows for discussion thorough audio, video, and text and can be used to facilitate interaction and communication in distance environments.

Is Web 2.0 Right for You?

Below are prompts to help you determine whether to use Web 2.0 in a given project. These were guided by questions Kim (2012) outlines in his blog post "Tech Project Questions to Ask: Why? Who? What? When? How?"

Defining Your Objectives and Environment

- Why are you developing this project, creating this service, incorporating instruction, etc.?
- What are your learning objectives or project or service goals?
- Why would you use Web 2.0 technologies (e.g., improve collaboration, increase efficiency, build relationships, etc.)?
- How do Web 2.0 technologies align with your goals and/or objectives? Which tool(s) are most appropriate?
- What is your experience with the chosen Web 2.0 tool(s)?

- Will other individuals/departments be involved with the Web 2.0 tool(s) integration? What other support will you need?
- Is there a cost associated with implementing your chosen Web 2.0 tool(s)?
- How much time do you have for implementation, including creation and assessment?
- Do you have the required equipment to create and/or work with the chosen Web 2.0 tool(s)?
- Are there any constraints within your technical environment (e.g., Does your institution have any guidelines or policies that need to be followed?; Do you have enough server space?)?
- How would you incorporate your chosen Web 2.0 tool(s) in your existing technical environment?

Identifying the Audience

- Who is your audience (e.g., traditional vs. non-traditional students)?
- Where is the audience located?
- What type of technology access does your audience have (e.g., How much bandwidth?)?
- What devices might your audience use to interact with your Web 2.0 tool(s)?
- What Web 2.0 tool(s) does your audience typically use? What tool(s) do they like?
- Is your audience knowledgeable about the chosen Web 2.0 tool(s)? Will they be comfortable? Will you need to instruct them on use?
- Do you need to account for any disabilities (e.g., learning, developmental, visual/audio impairments, etc.)?

Making the decision to use Web 2.0 to embed in virtual environments may seemingly appear to be an easy question to answer, particularly since the tools are ubiquitous in nature. In addition, the proliferation of new technologies has made it tempting to use the "latest and greatest" when opportunities arise, even if not always the most appropriate option. However, it is important to have a clear purpose before incorporation. Knowing how a particular application will assist you in meeting your learning or programming objectives and best serve your audience will help ensure smooth integration and positive outcomes.

REFERENCES

Bishop, C. (2011). *L161: Library skills and resources: Wells Library video tour* (Unpublished assignment sheet). Indiana University, Department of Information and Library Science, Bloomington, IN.

Bobish, G. (2010). Participation and pedagogy: Connecting the social web to ACRL learning outcomes. *The Journal of Academic Librarianship, 37*(1), 54–63.

Bowman, J. (2008). Communities of practice: Web 2.0 principles for service in art libraries. *Art Documentation, 1*(27), 4–12.

Chase, D. (2008). Using online social networks, podcasting, and a blog to enhance access to Stony Brook University Health Sciences Library resources and services. *Journal of Electronic Resources in Medical Libraries, 5*(2), 123–132.

Click, A., & Petit, J. (2010). Social networking and Web 2.0 in information literacy. *The International Information & Library Review, 42*(2), 137–142.

Cohen, L.B. (Ed.). (2007). *Library 2.0: Initiatives in academic libraries*. Chicago, IL: Association of College and Research Libraries.

Dayton, K., & Sheley, C. (2012). *X498: Internship for credit* (Unpublished course syllabus). Indiana University, Kelley School of Business, Bloomington, IN.

Glass, R., & Spiegelman, M. (2007). Incorporating blogs into the syllabus: Making their space a learning space. *Journal of Educational Technology Systems, 36*(2), 145–155.

Hamilton, B.J. (2012). Case profile: Ellen Hampton Filgo. *Library Technology Reports, 48*(2), 16–20.

Harris, A.L., & Rea, A. (2009). Web 2.0 and virtual world technologies: A growing impact on IS education. *Journal of Information Systems Education, 20*(2), 137–144.

Haycock, L., & Howe, A. (2011). Collaborating with library course pages and Facebook: Exploring new opportunities. *Collaborative Librarianship, 3*(3), 157–162.

Head, A.J. (2012, October 16*). How college graduates solve information problems once they join the workplace*. Retrieved from http://projectinfolit.org/pdfs/PIL_fall2012_workplaceStudy_FullReport.pdf

Hedge, S. (2013, January 15). Teaching with blogs. *Inside Higher Ed*. Retrieved from http://www.insidehighered.com/blogs/gradhacker/teaching-blogs

Hricko, M. (2010). Using microblogging tools for library services. *Journal of Library Administration, 50*(5-6), 684–692.

Indiana University Bloomington. (2008). Why general education? *In General Education at Indiana University Bloomington*. Retrieved from http://gened.iub.edu/whygened.html

Kim, J. (2012, December 18). Tech project questions to ask: Why? Who? What? When? How? *Inside Higher Ed*. Retrieved from http://www.inside-highered.com/blogs/technology-and-learning/tech-project-questions-ask-why-who-what-when-and-how

Klusek, L., & Bornstein, J. (2006). Information literacy skills for business careers. *Journal of Business & Finance Librarianship, 11*(4), 3–21.

Maggio, L.A., Bresnahan, M., Flynn, D.B., Harzbecker, J., Blanchard, M., & Ginn, D. (2009). A case study: Using social tagging to engage students in learning Medical Subject Headings. *Journal of the Medical Library Association, 97*(2), 77–83.

Mahmood, K., & Richardson, J.V., Jr. (2011). Adoption of Web 2.0 in US academic libraries: A survey of ARL library websites. *Program: Electronic Library and Information Systems, 45*(4), 365–375.

Marcum, J. (2002). Rethinking information literacy. *Library Quarterly, 72*(1), 1–26.

Niedbala, M., & Fogleman, J. (2010). Taking Library 2.0 to the next level: Using a course wiki for teaching information literacy to honors students. *Journal of Library Administration, 50*(7-8), 867–882.

O'Reilly, T. (2005, September 30). What is Web 2.0? *O'Reilly*. Retrieved from http://oreilly.com/pub/a/web2/archive/what-is-web-20.html?page=1

Oxford, S. (2009). Being creative with Web 2.0 in academic liaison. *Library & Information Update, 8*(5), 40–41.

Peltier-Davis, C. (2009). Web 2.0, Library 2.0, Library user 2.0, Librarian 2.0: Innovative services. *Computers in Libraries, 29*(10), 16–21.

Selingo, J. (2012, September 12). Skills gap? Employers and colleges point fingers at each other. *Chronicle of Higher Education*. Retrieved from http://chronicle.com/blogs/next/2012/09/12/skills-gap-employers-and-colleges-point-fingers-at-each-other/

Sokoloff, J. (2012). Information literacy in the workplace: Employer expectations. *Journal of Business & Finance Librarianship, 17*(1), 1–17.

Stephens, M. (2006). Exploring Web 2.0 and libraries. *Library Technology Reports, 42*(4), 8–14.

Stephens, M. (2007). Tools from "Web 2.0 & libraries: Best practices for social software" revisited. *Library Technology Reports, 43*(5), 15–29.

Wan, G. (2011). How academic libraries reach users on Facebook. *College & Undergraduate Libraries, 18*(4), 307–318.

Xu, C., Ouyang, F., & Chu, H. (2009). The academic library meets Web 2.0: Applications and implications. *The Journal of Academic Librarianship, 35*(4), 324–331.

part three:
online embedded librarian—outside the classroom

Avoiding Curricular Combat Fatigue: Embedding Librarians in E-Learning to Teach the Teacher

Kathleen A. Langan

As information literacy (IL) becomes more accepted as a core mission for a comprehensive post-secondary education, efforts on many campuses to universally integrate it into the curriculum are thwarted by logistical and pedagogical obstacles. Using the embedded librarian model in the e-learning environment can remove many of the hurdles that present themselves in the academic library. Librarians can use e-learning to "teach the teacher" on how to provide IL education. This frees up time, manpower, and classroom space. The following chapter looks at many aspects of an embedded teach-the-teacher program, including theoretical advantages to an e-learning environment for training particularly when many faculty are actually part-time instructors. This chapter will also provide examples of teaching content and assessments for teacher training.

In 1999, anthropologist Bonnie Nardi introduced the concept of information ecologies, an analogy that describes the inter-relational networkings of a given learning community. Nardi defines information ecologies as "system(s) of people, practices, values, and technologies in a particular environment" (1999, p. 49). With many variations of information ecologies, Nardi emphasizes that a successful information ecology is one that is diverse and dynamic, has clearly defined purposes, and is willing to adapt as elements evolve. For example, one such information

ecology is that of the time-honored concept of the brick-and-mortar classroom with its established tradition of purpose and relationships among its members. All ecologies have an identified keystone species, a member who is essential to the survival of all others. Nardi identifies librarians as the keystone species to any information ecology whether a traditional brick-and-mortar classroom or a virtual one. In Nardi's schema, the librarian (a seemingly auxiliary constituent in many other schemas) shifts to a more central role, essential to the identified teaching and learning goals in higher education.

Currently, as course offerings and classes are partially or fully migrating into the e-learning environment, the established, traditional roles of all members in the learning ecology are changing, including librarians. This chapter presents why librarians need to redefine their role in the learning ecology and shift their role towards an embedded librarian model at the programmatic level. In doing so, the embedded model will help the ecology thrive by supporting library instruction services. Librarians will be able to avoid curricular combat fatigue, being overextended and overcommitted to teaching one-shot IL sessions for large-scale programmatic research and writing-intensive courses. Given the constraints of time, space, and manpower, embedding librarians virtually at the programmatic level and recruiting the instructor to teach IL concepts addresses these constraints that often hinder the success of an IL program.

The Problem

The digital shift from brick-and-mortar classrooms into the virtual domain provides a new arena for IL initiatives in post-secondary education. Rather than targeting individual classes or course sections and embedding oneself into a single course for the duration of a semester, librarians need to concentrate their efforts at the programmatic level, using e-learning as a platform to "teach the teacher" about IL. The potential impact is great with a chance of reaching more students. "A 'teach the teacher' approach provides a realistic way of graduating more students who can find, evaluate, and use information to solve problems, make decisions, and continue to learn" (Smith & Mundt, 1997, "Conclusion," para. 3). Librarians can opt to "teach the teacher" about IL. The most effective approach is for librarians to target those courses whose curricula match well with introductory IL standards and also have high student enrollment. In doing so, librarians circumvent many of the common constraints such as time, space, and manpower that hinder a successful IL program. Rather than teaching individual sections of a class in one-shot IL sessions, librarians

should focus on teaching faculty how to integrate IL learning outcomes into their classes.

In 2012, librarians at Western Michigan University (WMU) surveyed faculty on their perceptions of IL. Faculty were asked to rate their students' ability to find and evaluate information through WMU Libraries search interfaces. They were also asked to rank their expectations according to student class standing. There were 118 valid responses. Faculty overwhelmingly rated both underclassmen and upperclassmen as "marginal" when using WMU libraries to find and evaluate information. Faculty were asked to rate students on certain IL learning outcomes such as develop a workable research question, select appropriate search tools, evaluate information sources, correctly cite sources, and avoid plagiarism (Perez-Stable, Sachs, & Vander Meer, 2013).

Faculty overwhelmingly rated both underclassmen and upperclassmen as "marginal" when using WMU libraries to find and evaluate information.

Faculty overwhelmingly communicated that it was "very important" for undergraduate and graduate students to possess IL skills. It seems faculty witness an improvement in IL skills that develops over time, with freshmen and sophomores perceived to be performing with the lowest ability (Perez-Stable et al., 2013).

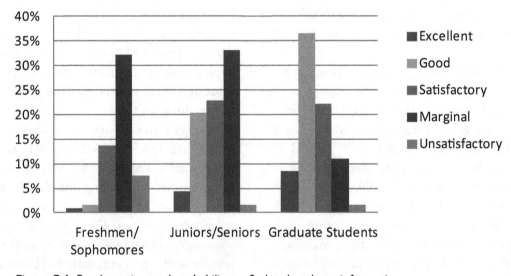

Figure 7.1. Faculty rating students' ability to find and evaluate information.

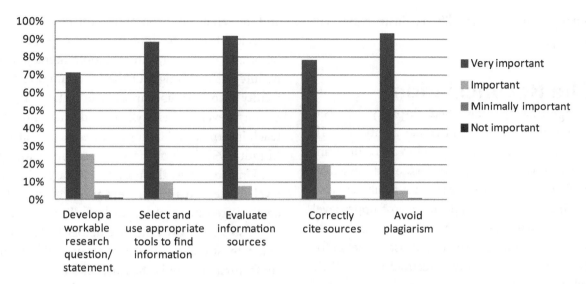

Figure 7.2. Faculty rating the importance of IL skills.

Faculty overwhelmingly communicated that it was "very important" for undergraduate and graduate students to possess IL skills.

Why does such an extreme disconnect exist between faculty perceptions and the number of IL sessions being taught? With this obvious discrepancy in expectations and deficits, why are faculty not reaching out to the university libraries to help students attain these skills? When asked these questions, 52% were not aware of the service despite WMU libraries' best efforts to promote the IL program. The second most common reason (33%) why they did not come in to the library for IL instruction is that they did not want to give up class time.

Many faculty members were not aware of WMU's libraries' services, and those who were aware of the services did not use them because they did not want to give up class time.

If faculty are not aware of IL programs through the university library for traditional face-to-face instruction, then how can librarians realistically promote embedded IL services to be successful? It is also important to keep in mind that faculty prefer online resources and minimal time commitment, "30 minutes or less" (Perez-Stable et al., 2013, p. 338). It might be helpful to identify why faculty deem IL to be an important component in the undergraduate experience. Perhaps if librarians can identify the pedagogical hook,

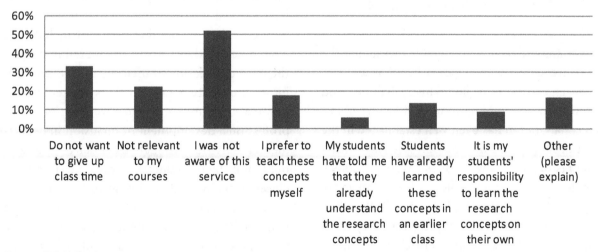

Figure 7.3. Why faculty have not used librarian-led IL instruction.

better recruitment for library instruction will develop.

The Reconciliation

Recognizing the identified disparity between desired performance and actual ability with IL skills, the challenge is to develop an IL program that addresses these very real issues addressed by the faculty. As the survey reflects, faculty are also disappointed in the performance of upper-level undergraduate students. Yet, they themselves do not take the initiative to bring those classes in for IL instruction nor do they scaffold IL into their syllabus. While faculty recognize the importance of teaching IL, many do not take responsibility for it. Many assume that the lower-division classes such as college-level writing courses are where students should get this sort of instruction. Information literacy instruction must start at the beginning of students' academic career so that they can become more and more capable in IL as they progress through their studies. This means that teaching librarians need to target not only the students in the lower-level classes but also the instructors. "Ultimately, information literacy programs succeed when they are no longer the sole responsibility of the library but reach across departmental boundaries through faculty-librarian collaboration" (Miller et. al., 2010, p. 831).

Who the Librarian Should Really Be Teaching

Librarians and faculty are equally invested in the IL conversation as it shapes collections and services and structures librarian availability and physical space. The importance of faculty-librarian collaboration has been well established in the field of library and information sciences, with a long history spanning decades (Mounce, 2009). Faculty are the target audience for the majority of the liaison programs. More specifically, when libraries think about liaison programs, they think about outreach that supports teaching, learning,

and research. In promoting instructional services, it is typical to think of promoting teaching librarians. However, "information literacy will be integrated throughout the curriculum only if faculty recognize its importance, make it a goal as they develop their syllabi, and know how to teach information literacy themselves" (Smith & Mundt, 1997, "A Problem—A Solution," para. 5).

Unfortunately, the proposal to target lower-level classes presents a new problem as these courses are often not taught by full-time faculty but instead by part-time instructors (PTIs) and graduate students. The author uses the word "unfortunately" only because there are many more institutional obstacles that hinder or do not promote a positive working environment for PTIs than for full-time board-appointed faculty. Whether you call them PTIs, adjunct faculty, or contingent instructional staff, this group of classroom instructors, dubbed the "invisible faculty" by Gappa and Leslie (1993), are often well qualified with years of teaching experience shouldering heavy teaching loads of lower-level service classes and thereby reaching thousands of students. "By 2001, the number of part-timers… was closing relentlessly on the total count of full-timers" (Schuster & Finkelstein, 2006, p. 40). In 2003, there were 630,000 full-time faculty and 543,000 part-time faculty (Schuster & Finkelstein, 2006). According to the National Center for Education Statistics (NCES) 2004 National Study of Post-Secondary Faculty, 56.3% of all faculty and instructional staff were not tenured or not on the tenure track. This number does not include the 8.8% of respondents who were not tenured or on the tenure track due to their institution not having a tenure system. Even so, PTIs frequently have minimal institutional support for such things as professional development or inclusion in departmental activities. Though essential to the core mission of higher education, they are disenfranchised, teaching without job security or a chance for substantial advancement. Often they struggle with logistics such as obtaining a functioning workspace or office. Many are only on campus for teaching related activities (NCES, 2005) and are isolated from professional networking opportunities or producing scholarly output (NCES, 2004). There is also a chance for high turnover rate and short notice on class assignments along with some PTIs juggling work for multiple institutions. If one thinks tenured and tenure-track faculty are struggling for time and resources, one can assume that PTIs are struggling that much more.

There is no shortage of current scholarship addressing the role of PTIs in higher education, but in the library literature, there seems to be a genuine lack of attention. Libraries are just as guilty at neglecting PTIs in most areas, and PTIs are minimally treated in the library and information sciences literature (Sult & Mills, 2006). The relationship between academic librarians and PTIs is proving to be pivotal in moving the IL initiative forward on campus as they are the gatekeepers to the majority of lower division courses. Like faculty, the other hurdle for librarians is effectively promoting the importance of integrating IL into the curriculum. Inspiring PTIs to collaborate with librarians proves difficult as there is little motivation or leverage for PTIs to take on additional work. Librarians do not often think of liaison services or outreach services with PTIs in mind. Librarians need to reconsider outreach efforts for this population if librarians are going to ask instructors to shoulder some of the IL responsibility. Librarians can do so by providing teaching resources. Creating an "information literacy toolkit" that maps out how to integrate IL into the curriculum is one way that academic libraries can support the professional integration of PTIs into the larger university-wide initiative while also alleviating the stress for both parties. Librarians can help PTIs overcome the barriers of the academic gestalt and can augment their agency in the machine of higher education. Outreach and liaison librarians can be campus leaders by developing strong partnerships, accommodating both the university strategic plan for improving IL and the constraints that face PTIs.

What Should the Content Be?

WMU is a mid-sized, midwestern, doctoral-granting public university with an FTE of approximately 21,000 undergraduates. As of 2010, there are nearly 900 full-time, board-appointed faculty and just under 550 part-time instructors. In light of WMU's Academic Affairs Strategic Plan 2010, which included IL as a skill students needed to be highly successful in their lives and career, the author targeted the introductory writing courses as the most beneficial for promoting IL ("Goals and Strategies," para. 2). All students are required to take a college-level writing course. Industrial Management Engineering (IME) 1020: Technical Communication and English (ENGL) 1050: Thought and Writing fulfill the college-level writing requirement. This chapter specifically looks at ENGL 1050 as the pilot for the future study.

There are approximately 113 sections of ENGL 1050 offered each academic year with a capacity of 22 students per section. Approximately 2,300 freshmen enrolled in ENGL 1050 during the 2012–2013 academic year. This represents nearly 55% of the entire freshmen class (4,200 freshmen enrolled in Fall 2012). The potential to integrate IL into the curriculum and effectively reach many students is evident. Of this total number of sections, there were 43–44 PTIs teaching one or more sections, 27 graduate students teaching one or more sections, and three faculty, each teaching only one section. The English department hires PTIs on a semester-by-semester basis. Some appointments are not renewed for the spring semester, but a person's teaching contract could be reinstated for the following fall semester, skipping the spring appointment.

In the past, WMU libraries extensively marketed one-shot IL sessions to this course. Even so, not all sections of ENGL 1050 come into the library for instruction. During the heaviest semester, the fall semester, 35 sections on average come into the library for instruction. Librarians often joke that they would be victims of their own success if all sections of ENGL 1050 requested instruction. With 18 full-time public services librarians, seven are typically in rotation to teach the approximate 113 sections of ENGL 1050, of which approximately 35–40 request a librarian to teach IL. The libraries struggle to accommodate the requests with limited access to classroom space while also balancing additional IL teaching loads and other professional duties such as reference desk rotation and committee work. The problems that hamper a large IL program when limited to one-shot sessions such as scheduling, classroom space, and manpower can be resolved in part via a by-proxy librarian approach. For example, numerous sections are taught on a M/W or T/Th schedule, and many of these sections are taught simultaneously at 8 a.m., making it physically impossible to staff or offer a classroom for all sections or find enough librarians to teach.

Librarians also need to take into consideration the prior student research experience. During AY 2012–2013, the author polled 179 students in 11 different ENGL 1050 sections to find out if these students have ever engaged in academic research prior to their experience at the university. Approximately 18–20% of students had never written a research paper in high school nor had they used the high school library-media center for academic purposes. Nevertheless, most of these students are digital natives. Therefore, it may be more meaningful for these younger scholars to focus more on the conceptual aspects of research since these digitally literate natives can likely figure out how to navigate the resources once they are identified. Most likely, their weaknesses lie in that they do not know how to match the research process with the written work. Conceptually, do they understand that they as researchers are conversing and opening up a dialog? And do they know how to identify what the topic of the dialog is or know what information needs to be found to support it? Further, do their instructors know this? Is it possible that these PTIs have no real idea of how to identify, teach, or assess IL? If not, then librarians need to teach them.

Currently, when an instructor for ENGL1050 schedules a session with a librarian, the librarian asks for a list of learning outcomes. It is possible that these instructors do not know how to identify information-literacy specific learning outcomes. They may be very much ensconced in the expectation of the traditionally passive "dog and pony show" mindset rather than focused on teaching threshold concepts that will promote more success in students during their undergraduate experience and beyond. Librarians do not need to emphasize the technical skill set of information seeking. Librarians need to emphasize the foundational concepts of IL such as the commodity of information and the process of creating information and identifying authority (Townsend, Brunetti, & Hofer, 2011).

The IL Venn Diagram: Embedded Librarianship, Teaching the Teacher, and E-learning

Having identified the lack of fluency (faculty perception), the target audience (ENGL 1050), the campus partnership (PTIs), logistical constraints (time and manpower), and the learning preferences (social, à la carte, online), it is possible to address all of these issues simultaneously. The e-learning platform provides a flexible environment where the librarian can facilitate the *en masse* integration of IL into the ENGL 1050 curriculum by providing PTIs instruction on IL and instructional materials to use in the classroom.

By using e-learning platforms to embed IL outreach services into the program, librarians are promoting a professional network for learning where ideas and experiences can be shared. This e-learning environment also adds a social dimension that can potentially break down any professional isolation that might occur. Lev Vygotsky, a cognitive development theorist, says that learning occurs best when people can learn from each other. In social constructivist learning theory, the instructor, in this case the librarian, is the guide, promoting ideas and concepts, ultimately allowing the student (the PTI) to arrive at his or her own conclusion on how to best implement the teaching strategies in his or her own classroom, i.e. pedagogical agency. Vygotsky calls this the *zone of proximal development*—the potential to problem-solve with the guidance of a teacher or collaboration of peers; "human learning presupposes a specific social nature and a process by which children grow into the intellectual life of those around them" (1978, p. 8). E-learning offers many tools for communicating online that promote a socially engaged environment where ideas can be shared.

If a PTI is isolated from his or her colleagues, then institutions of higher education are denying them the opportunity to construct a personal learning network. Using an online platform where one can share knowledge among peers who can on their own develop an otherwise nonexistent personal learning network is a chance for the instructors to connect to each other once they are separated after their initial contact at pre-semester training.

The development of an accessible training program that provides instructional support materials for IL is the first step in developing a collaborative work environment. By creating a digital repository of IL concepts or an IL toolkit of timelines, assignments, assessments, and resources in e-learning, librarians can reasonably pass the responsibility of teaching onto PTIs. The theory of connectivism embraces the role of technology in the learning process, emphasizing the importance of creating contacts with others in the network and the diversity of those "nodes." These nodes can be the content, the teaching skills, the library faculty, etc.—something outside of the PTIs original network, offering a more diverse way of thinking about research that they can then pass on to their students (Siemens, 2005).

Creating an electronic repository of information gives PTIs techniques and tools to best scaffold IL at their own pace, disseminating it into the curriculum throughout the semester at

key moments. Many emphasize a community of learning among faculty, and the same can be said for PTIs (Arp, Woodard, Lindstrom, & Shonrock, 2006; Miller & Bell, 2005). "Instead of treating faculty as invisible agents or catalysts who have no real role in information literacy training, we should be facilitating faculty efforts… which make it easy for faculty to integrate such instruction into their teaching."(Arp et al., 2005, p. 1) Librarian's "assistance," as Smith and Mundt (1997) said, should be framed more globally, thinking beyond the individual student and looking at the programmatic impact: "Teaching the students ourselves is usually *not* appropriate assistance if our goal is the integration of information literacy" ("Librarian Commitment to Faculty Development and Collaboration," para. 3). Creating an online repository is also an efficient use of the teaching librarian's "assistance." Rather than scattering librarian "assistance" throughout the semesters into one-shot IL sessions, it needs to shift to the beginning of the semester and focus on training teachers how to teach IL content. This approach is very much a professional development opportunity. The training can include orientation to IL, actual lesson plans, and materials in e-learning.

The Pilot Program
Current Training for Part-Time Instructors

Currently, a week before the semester starts, only new ENGL 1050 PTIs have a week-long training session developed by the course coordinator, introducing topics such as the sequence of assignments, overall learning outcomes, where the course fits in the larger scope of the university-wide curriculum, and university support services. The liaison librarian is invited to present for 20–30 minutes on the IL program and services. At that point, many instructors sign their classes up for instruction. Unfortunately, this is not the best time as instructors are not familiar with the syllabus or the intricacies of the four standardized assignments and not all of the assignments match up well with library instruction. As the numbers previously discussed reflect, many PTIs do not take advantage of this opportunity, or if they do, it may not be at the right point in the scope of a specific research project. Further complicating the matter, professional development is only offered once, at the beginning of a teaching contract, to new instructors. There is no on-going professional development thereafter, and it is difficult to reconnect with the PTIs after the initial contact. Therefore, librarians do not have the luxury of meeting with returning ENGL 1050 instructors each fall to remind them of IL instructional services. One also wonders how effective e-mailing is at this time of year; considering the onslaught of e-mails typical of the beginning of a semester, one risks getting lost in the void.

In looking at the past five years of data for ENGL 1050 IL sessions at the library, it appears that if instructors come once with their classes, they are more likely to come again during subsequent semesters. In the past five years, there were 293 unique instruction sessions with 97 different instructors, only six were full-time board-appointed faculty. Sixty-one instructors came in two or more times, averaging 2.5 library instruction sessions per instructor. Unfortunately, 37 individuals decided not to come back to the library. Of this number, four were faculty, 16 were grad students, and 17 were PTIs. It is unknown how many of the PTIs had more than one semester-long contract as the English department does not keep track of past instructors. In looking at the statistics kept on IL sessions per instructor, there are some PTIs who have had their contract renewed though have decided not to come into the library for a repeat IL session. There are many reasons why instructors decided not to return to the library for instruction. Some said that they found the IL instruction to be material that they already covered in class or could cover in class or that the session was irrelevant to the writing

assignment. These two comments reveal that PTIs see themselves as competent to teach IL concepts and that PTIs are in need of more effective training as to what a successful writing assignment would be for specific IL concepts.

Logistics

The e-learning environment for teach-the-teacher instruction is set up as a series of modules that are hosted on Desire2Learn, WMU's e-learning platform branded as "Elearning." The architecture of this course has two pillars of content. The first pillar is a series of modules that function as the pedagogical instruction for the PTIs. These modules contain introductory content and links to other resources on IL, instructing the faculty on what IL is, why it is important, student learning outcomes (SLOs), and a bibliography of selected readings on IL. The programmatic approach standardizes specific SLOs that have been mapped to the particular writing assignments for the course.

There are also other logistical modules that are used to introduce the instructors to the teaching librarians and library resources available to them. Whether the PTI uses the library instructional services or teaches IL concepts on his or her own, this series of modules prepares all instructors as to why certain concepts are important and what the best practices are for teaching them. It also provides them with a vocabulary that can be adapted as they personalize a syllabus or identify a pre-defined set of SLOs so that the PTI may confidently converse with librarians when scheduling instruction.

Since many of these instructors may not be that familiar with the culture at the university, it is important to connect them to others on campus. The section on introducing the librarians provides an opportunity for librarians to present their teaching philosophies as well as put a face to a name. By including photographs and biographies, librarians are more approachable, and this may reduce the phenomenon of library anxiety,

---

Student Learning Outcomes

After integrating information literacy into your class, your students should be able to reach some, if not all of the following:

Students will:

- develop a refined research topic that is neither too broad nor too narrow in scope.
- read and discuss the differences between articles from scholarly and popular resources.
- be able to describe/summarize (or compare and contrast) the differences between scholarly peer-reviewed articles, popular, and web sources based on salient characteristics of the articles themselves
- through a search of background information sources, be able to identify and appropriately focus a topic to research for their paper.
- find 2–3 relevant background sources of information on their topic (encyclopedias, books from collections, quality websites, general articles from popular magazines).
- find or identify 5–10 relevant search terms or keywords (including relevant synonyms) on their topics.
- identify and justify the selection of 3 possible subject databases for their writing assignment
- conduct searches in online databases (including the online library catalog), using Boolean operators, subject headings and date limiters to effectively and efficiently find relevant articles.
- evaluate articles obtained in their online searching, making appropriate changes to their search terms, topics, database limiters, or database selection etc, to obtain more relevant articles.
- find and choose 3 relevant scholarly journal articles on their topic.
- be able to effectively access full text articles either online or in print copies from the library's collection.

Figure 7.4. Suggested SLOs for information literacy for instructors.

---

which, it is presumed, could affect instructors, not just students. Library anxiety "manifests itself in negative emotions [toward the library], including tension, fear, feelings of uncertainty and help-lessness, negative self-defeating thoughts, and mental disorganization, all of which have the propensity to debilitate information literacy" (Jiao & Onwuegbuzie, 2002, p. 71).

The second pillar of content in the WMU Elearning course is a series of modules that include classroom instructional materials. These modules are directly linked to the four required writing assignments for the ENGL 1050 course, which all instructors must teach. For each writing assignment, the module includes a set of identified student SLOs, a timeline of when to introduce certain IL concepts, lesson plans for teaching different SLOs, assessments for those lessons, and links to other resources such as videos and class research guides to enhance instruction. With the wealth of web-based tutorials and instructional materials available, this section provides a variety of links to both WMU-created content and content created elsewhere. Since all classrooms are fitted with

digital projectors and access to WiFi, it is useful to include support materials that the instructors can show in class to stem discussion or launch a teaching point followed by a hands-on assignment.

Structuring the e-learning content in direct relation to the standardized writing tasks for ENGL 1050 actually alleviates several critical problems for librarians. First, the instructional services team and teaching librarians might not become over extended in teaching too many IL sessions if the instructor knows that there is a specific set of SLOs and accompanying plans and assessments tailored to each writing assignment. Secondly, the librarians might see a reprieve in the number of requests for instruction for assignments that are not best suited to library instruction. There exists one assignment that trips librarians up every year; nevertheless, librarians diplomatically take on the teaching challenge. The assignment is an "unknown genre" exercise where the students need to imitate and write about a specific genre, which could range anywhere from a how-to manual to writing a hip-hop song. The assignment does not match well with an introductory IL session in the library. Additionally, as part of this assignment, instructors frequently request librarians to teach students how to identify scholarly articles, even though this assignment does require them. Most of the teaching librarians are of the mindset to not refuse any IL request, citing dedication to service as the prime motivation. Embedding IL into e-learning and making accompanying teaching materials accessible to the instructors is a solution to this puzzle. Rather than systematically refusing to teach an IL session due to the inappropriate match of the assignment, librarians can steer instructors to teaching materials that match their learning outcomes. Empowering the instructor with adequate pedagogical support and structure allows the instructor to teach specific IL concepts related to this or any assignment.

Embedding teaching materials for PTIs also helps them realize that there are effective and ineffective uses of library instruction. Many, by no fault of their own, do not realize that a specific writing assignment might not be well matched with library instruction. It is assumed that many feel it is important to come into the library for instruction, but they are unaware that librarians have their own pedagogical agenda to fulfill. It is hoped that the use of e-learning to embed the librarian at the programmatic level and focusing on teaching the teacher will help alleviate any misunderstandings.

Putting It into Practice

An example of materials for the research writing assignment follows. It is important to note that the entire semester is mapped out for the instructor. Therefore, in reading the details below, keep in mind that it fits into a suite of SLOs for the entire semester and that the concepts are scaffolded not just into the one particular assignment but throughout the semester and in relationship to the other assignments. The SLOs are not isolated but build on each other. (The overview of all SLOs mapped to the semester long sequence for all four assignments is found in Appendix 7.A.)

For each writing assignment, there is a week-by-week entry on the timeline. Also, the majority of sections are offered only in the traditional classroom. On average, there are only five sections that are offered via online instruction. Even though the instructor is trained to teach online, the content and materials are developed with the face-to-face instruction in mind, though most of the material can be adapted to be used in e-learning.

By mapping the IL standards to the specific writing assignments, there are 12 instances of IL teaching opportunities with mini-lectures, class activities, and assessments. There are a total of 130 minutes of teaching and student activity/assessment time that range from one to 15 minutes for each activity. Normally, the librarian would cover these topics in the 100 minutes if they were to come the library for a one-shot session. The one-shot would have less assessment built in. However, this can be remedied by developing assignments that require students to consult with someone in the reference department. For example, the first IL assignment, developing a research question, is a great opportunity to ask the student to come into the library. In teaching the concept-mapping exercise and then writing a preliminary research question, the student is required to go to the central reference desk and consult with a librarian (5–10 minutes max) to talk about ways to broaden or narrow down the topic. The student then gets the librarian's signature and returns the assignment to the instructor. Students can also opt to use the e-mail or chat reference service and print out the electronic communication for proof of consultation. This requirement helps to break down barriers and get the student thinking about research and engaging with academic support on campus.

As an example, below are the expanded details for the first week of the fourth writing assignment, which falls during the 11th week of the semester (see Appendix 7.B for the assignment sheet). In addition to the actual lesson plan, which includes projected time, there are links to videos and other sources to be used in the mini-lecture such as handouts and assessments. There is also additional material taken from the library literature intended for the instructors to give them underpinnings to the pedagogical validity of the IL concept being taught.

The fourth project is the course's culminating research and writing project. Students address a community issue by researching the issue and producing an essay and multimodal presentation that raises awareness. Students need to write a minimum of six to eight pages with at least five scholarly sources, cited correctly. Identified SLOs proposed by librarians for this assignment are taken from the Association of College and Research Libraries' (ACRL) Information Literacy Competency Standards for Higher Education, particularly Standard 3, which focuses on higher order concepts such as synthesizing information (2000). The lesson that follows introduces students to the difference between scholarly and popular sources as well as provides an activity that walks them through how to interpret citation information as well as evaluate a source. This meta-analysis of information asks students to review the other types of materials that have already been presented in the semester such as websites (Sult & Mills 2006).

Week 11:

First week for the fourth assignment, the research assignment. The following mini-lecture and assessments can be done in one class or divided up into two class sessions, taking no longer than 30 minutes to complete.

Scholarly vs. Popular Articles Lesson Plan and Activities

25–30 minutes

- Introduce writing assignment.

  Link research to writing. Emphasize that clarifying a thesis prior to doing research will save them a lot of time. You may or may not want to do another concept mapping exercise with the students so they can identify a research question. This could be given as a homework assignment to be turned in the next class session.

- Mini-Lecture 1: Define the concept of a research assignment.

  Introduce why a research project requires more specific types of resources, particularly credible and authoritative sources. Have them compare and contrast information needs to the other writing assignments.

- Mini-Lecture 2: Define the scholarly articles and the peer-review process.

  Ask the class if they know how to define a scholarly article. Ask if they know what the review or peer process is. If they are stumped, ask them to think about what they look for when identifying a credible website. 5 minutes

  Show video from Vanderbilt that talks about how to distinguish scholarly from popular magazines. 5 minutes

  Review idea of editorial process. Point to mention: Reviews from specialists in the field confirm that information is accurate, unbiased, and thorough (not the same as copy-editing, checking grammar, etc.).

  Show video on how to search the library website using PowerSearch and how to narrow down to scholarly resources. 5 minutes

- Exercise:

  In groups of three or four, have students use smartphones, tablets, or laptops to do an on-the-fly search in PowerSearch [WMU's discovery service] on the topic of your choice. Have each group identify one article and present to the class why it is scholarly. 7–10 minutes

  Use the handout "Scholarly vs. Popular Article Checklist" for students to fill in while scanning the results. This sheet can be turned in as a group assignment and also as notes for their mini-presentation. This handout also helps the students identify the necessary information for a complete citation. [See Appendix 7.C.]

- Suggested reading on evaluating information sources:

Whitmire, E. (2002). Epistemological beliefs and the information-seeking behavior of undergraduates. *Library and Information Science Research*, 25(2): 127–142.

- Additional resources (videos, links to class/research guide). You can either use these as follow-up discussion points or as homework assignments:

Vanderbilt tutorial on popular and scholarly periodical http://www.library.vanderbilt.edu/peabody/tutorials/scholarlyfree/

WMU guide to different types of periodicals http://libguides.wmich.edu/content.php?pid=312307&sid=2556131

Setting up Google Scholar from off campus http://www.screencast.com/t/Z1DVKb-gOtNz

Since most instructors will be following roughly the same timeline, they could take advantage of the e-learning social tools to discuss with others best practices, tips, or tricks for the IL lessons. Librarians could also make use of them by mentoring conversations about teaching IL concepts.

Logistics of Running an E-Learning Class

The librarian functions as the instructor in the e-learning teach-the-teacher class. The librarian gets a roster of PTIs from the department prior to the start of the semester and manually enrolls them as the students. During the orientation session for the new instructors, the librarian can spend time presenting how to use the toolkit and walk them through how to integrate IL concepts into the syllabus. Depending on the e-learning platform, there is a suite of tools that can be used by the librarian, ranging from class e-mail to a blog to survey tools. During the course of the semester, the librarian can use the system tools to maintain communication with the PTIs and ask questions, introduce new teaching tools and/or resources, and use surveys to elicit end-of-the-year feedback. An e-learning class can be adapted from semester to semester and altered as writing assignments evolve.

There should be an index or guide to the materials that serve as a map to the content. Assignments, learning outcomes, and teaching materials should be hyperlinked and cross-referenced when possible. For example, when introducing the different learning outcomes for the individual writing assignments, refer back to the earlier learning points as well as link back to the ACRL webpage of IL standards and learning outcomes. Including the two main sections of the e-learning class, there should also be a section dedicated to listing and organizing the different library materials and resources that will be helpful to the instructor for teaching and to the student for researching. This can include links to online tutorials, library class and research guides, or specific databases.

Why Not a Research Guide or Help Page for PTIs?

The idea is to build a web presence for the exchange of pedagogical tools has previously been explored (Sult & Mills, 2006). Websites or library research guides may lack the social dynamic that builds a thriving learning ecology. In e-learning platforms, however, there are many built-in networking features that create a more desirable platform to house the IL toolkit. For example, there are communication functions like e-mail, discussion boards, blogs, and surveys that can help the librarian stay in contact with PTIs. It is also a secure site requiring a login and password so private and copyrighted materials can be protected.

The Reality

This electronic toolkit has existed for 18 months. It is possible to see who has accessed the Elearning class for ENGL 1050 PTIs. The metrics of Desire-

2Learn allow the instructor to see which modules were accessed by whom and how long students spent in one module. Based on this information, there is little evidence indicating that instructors are effectively using it. Aside from apparent lack of incentives and it being a selective instructional resource, one other reason may be that there is resistance to using e-learning because it is not easy to use. It presents new ways of teaching and learning for students, instructors, and librarians alike. To facilitate engagement with materials, the content must be well planned and delivered in a deliberate manner (Burd & Buchanan, 2004). Out of the 45 instructors who were enrolled in the Elearning class, only 12 visited the class site. The average length of time spent on the site was 24 minutes. The most popular content area in the class was the section for handouts to use in class. Essential to the future of this IL toolkit is assessing the efficacy of the learning tools used by those instructors who choose to use them.

Looking Forward

In 1992, the Association of English Departments adopted a Statement on the Use of Part-Time and Full-Time Adjunct Faculty (later adopted by the Modern Languages Association Executive Council in 1994) in which they state that PTIs "should be eligible for incentives that foster professional development, including merit raises and funds for research and travel" (1992, "Guidelines," para. 2). In attempting to professionalize their experience, PTIs expect financial compensation. However, is the university willing to invest appropriate time, money, and resources? If not, the question remains whether librarians have any leverage to entice PTIs to take responsibility for IL. A follow-up survey could prove useful in asking PTIs about their perception of library services. For example, questions could include—What do you think librarians do? What do you think IL is? How would you go about teaching it? Or assessing it? One could project how PTIs would answer this by looking at what they indicate as desired SLOs for their one-

shot session, which would be for students to be able to use a reputable website, identify a scholarly article, and be able to properly cite sources.

Going forward, this project will be looking at a larger scope of university programs. A wide-scale data collection will take place in the upcoming academic year (2013–2014), adding to the earlier survey by Perez-Stable et al. in 2011, which measured faculty attitudes and perceptions of IL. In the fall of 2013, the next phase will also look at PTIs' attitudes and perceptions of IL. In the spring of 2014, a final survey will elicit responses from WMU administration as to what they identify as appropriate support for PTIs and the role of IL. Finally, an assessment will take place a year later to look at how other institutions are supporting PTIs.

There may be other allies on campus that can help foster participation. Currently at WMU, the library instructional support team is collaborating with the Office of Faculty Development. The benefit of this is that the library has gained the attention of the associate vice provost who is now helping the library gain access to the dean's council to promote IL services. Since IL is now mentioned in the undergraduate affairs strategic plan, this term is starting to be noticed on campus. By hitting higher on the administrative food chain, librarians may be able to implement a more systematic campaign across campus, effectively and efficiently reaching many more teaching faculty. This is a top-down approach. Nevertheless, it is still helpful to work from the bottom up and maintain outreach and liaison services for teaching faculty and staff. For example, the WMU Office of Faculty Development has offered to let librarians meet with the new faculty during their yearlong new-faculty seminar. The office has also offered to host librarian-led workshops and seminars for faculty and instructors. These are typically three to four hour seminar/work sessions offered the week before the semester starts; however, there is still the problem of not accommodating the time constraints of PTIs. There is already an attempt by the Office of Faculty Development to support newly hired PTIs. The office has created a face-to-face orientation as well as electronic resources for PTIs, which presents information on resources and services available on campus. This is a self-selective course in Elearning but does not address IL or offer pedagogical tools specifically tailored to learning outcomes. In the spirit of collaboration, this would be an effective place to market the toolkit.

Another potential use for the e-learning environment is to create a MOOC-like environment where the faculty or instructor can self-register for a course on how to teach IL. This could be a self-paced à la carte program. Potential weaknesses in this model include having to develop an IL program that is both meaningful and generic enough to be adaptable to several different disciplines. This could be avoided by having several subject librarians collaborate to create subject-specific teaching content and recommendations.

Recommendations

Keeping in mind the main objectives of disseminating IL concepts in larger college-level writing courses, alleviating teaching loads for librarians, and facilitating the training and professional development of PTIS, the following recommendations should be considered.

Training: Contact the liaison department to determine how many PTIs there are and what sort of orientation program exists for them. Try to piggyback off of existing programming. If not, try to get contact information and host your own orientation program either in person or virtually and introduce PTIs to the toolkit.

Teaching Materials: Scaffold the IL concepts to the actual writing assignments if there is a programmatic curriculum available. If not, recommend writing assignments and/or research assignments for the PTIs with IL concepts mapped to librarian-developed assessments.

It is also important to work with the different departments and their undergraduate curriculum committees. It is necessary for librarians to be a part of that conversation: Faculty may be pleasantly surprised by what librarians have to offer and that there are shared IL goals when developing strategic plans or mapping curricula.

A teach-the-teacher approach is not to be seen as method that minimizes the importance of research instruction gained when taught by expert librarians. A teach-the-teacher approach is a thoughtful approach to managing time, space, and people in the ever-changing learning ecology of higher education. By carefully training PTIs on manageable, introductory IL concepts and how to implement them meaningfully into courses with high-student enrollment, librarians will successfully alleviate those time and space logistics that hinder a successful IL program. Thought absent from the classroom, teaching librarians will have virtually, pedagogically, and programmatically embedded themselves into the IL learning process.

Appendix 7.A. English 1050 Semester Schedule. Writing SLOs developed by Staci Perryman-Clark
Information Literacy SLOs identified by Author

Week	M or T	W or TH	Information Literacy Topic	ACRL Standard
Week 1 START	Introduction to course policies and syllabus; writing sample; genre	Reading Assignment Introduce Invention, Arrangement, Revision (IAR) Introduce Project #1	What is information? How does information change based on who wrote it and why they wrote it? **15 minutes**	**ACRL Standard 2:** The information literate student identifies a variety of types and formats of potential sources for information.
Week 2	Reading Assignment Invention Exercises Practice with Summary and Analysis	Work with IAR Work on Summarizing, Paraphrasing, and Quoting **Short Writing Assignment Due**	Scholarly research as dialog: Linking the writing and research process 15 minutes	
Week 3	Grammar Mini-lesson Reading Assignment Creating a Focus for Project 1 Invention exercises for Project #`	**Rough Draft of Project 1 Due Peer Review Day**	Information as a commodity **15 minutes**	**ACRL Standard 1.3:** The information literate student considers the costs and benefits of acquiring the needed information. **ACRL Standard 5:** The information literate student understands many of the economic, legal, and social issues surrounding the use of information and accesses and uses information ethically and legally.
Week 4 EDITORIAL WRITING PROJECT	Conferences and Revision Workshop with Project #1	**Project # 1 Due** Introduce Project # 2 Preliminary Invention exercises with Project #2 Reviewing Sample Whitepapers or Editorials	Defining and refining a research question / Concept mapping **20 minutes**	**ACRL** Standard 1.1: The information literate student determines the nature and extent of the information needed.
Week 5	Reading Assignment Brainstorming Topics **Short Writing Assignment Due**	Choosing and Proposing topics Reading Assignment Grammar Mini-lesson Project 1 notes and comments	Introduction to the library website **15 minutes**	**ACRL Standard 2:** The information literate student accesses needed information effectively and efficiently.
Week 6	Reading Assignment Ethos, Pathos, Logos Evaluating Arguments	Evaluating Uses of Evidence **Short Writing Assignment Due**	Searching sample editorials in PowerSearch **10 minutes**	**ACRL Standard 2.2:** The information literate student constructs and implements effectively-designed search strategies.
Week 7	Creating a Focus for Project 2 Project 2 writing exercises and drafting	Reading Assignment IAR Analysis	[blank]	[blank]
Week 8	**Rough Draft of Project #2 Due Peer Review Day**	Conferences and Revision Workshops with Project #2	[blank]	[blank]

Appendix 7.A. English 1050 Semester Schedule. Writing SLOs developed by Staci Perryman-Clark Information Literacy SLOs identified by Author

Week	M or T	W or TH	Information Literacy Topic	ACRL Standard
Week 9 START GENRE WRITING PROJECT	**Project #2 Due** Introduce Project #3 Preliminary work with sample genres Invention work with genre studies		How to analyze a website, how to look for authority in other types of documents **10 minutes**	**ACRL Standard 3.2:** The information literate student articulates and applies initial criteria for evaluating both the information and its sources.
Week 10	Reading Assignment IAR Analysis Citation Practice Exercises	Reading Assignment **Annotated Bibliography Due**	Catalog searching for books Keyword brainstorming exercise 15 minutes	**ACRL Standard 2.2, 2.3, 2.4:** The information literate student refines the search strategy if necessary.
Week 11	Reading Assignment Analysis of Genres and Conventions Group Conferences on Genres	**Rough Draft of Project #3 Due** **Peer Review Day**	Copyright/Image searching 15 minutes	[blank]
Week 12 START RESEARCH BASED PROJECT	**Project #3 Due** Introduce Project #4 Determine Communities/ Research Topics	**Thanksgiving Recess/ No Class**	If you would prefer to visit the library for instruction, do so sometime in the next few weeks For scheduling purposes, you will need to sign up for instruction no later than September 30.	[blank]
Week 13	Reading Assignment Ballenger Double-entry notes Grammar Mini-lessons	Reading Assignment IAR Analysis Citation Review	Difference between popular and scholarly materials 30 minutes	[blank]
Week 14	Reading Assignment Invention Exercises: Writing Up Research **Writing Assignment Due**	Ballenger Research Activities Project #4 Check-in Lab time for research and composition	Synthesis/Citations 20 minutes	**ACRL Standard 5:** The information literate student understands many of the economic, legal, and social issues surrounding the use of information and accesses and uses information ethically and legally.
Week 15	**Rough Draft of Project #4 Due Peer Review Day**	Conferences and Revision Workshops with Project 4	Ethical use of information 15 minutes	**ACRL Standard 5** cont.
Week 16	Conferences and Revision Workshop with Project 1	**Project #4 Due Project Presentations**	[blank]	[blank]

Appendix 7.B.
Assignment Four (Staci Perryman-Clark)
Inquiry-Based Research Essay

Basic Requirements
Formatting: Double-spaced, 1-inch margins, Times New Roman 12 pt. font
Length: At least 6–8 pages double-spaced
Bibliographic Documentation: Parenthetical in-text citations and works cited pages are required. MLA, APA, or Chicago citations systems are considered appropriate.
(See below for additional requirements.)

Assigned Readings to Be Referenced with this Assignment
Malcolm Gladwell: "None of the Above: What I.Q. Doesn't Tell You about Race"
Linda Kulman: "Food News Can Get You Dizzy, So Know What to Swallow"
Steven Pinker: "The Blank Slate"
Janet Raloff: "Researchers Probe Cell Phones Effects"
MyWritingLab Research Tutorials
Bruce Ballenger: "Writing the Research Essay" in *The Curious Researcher*

Overview
Over the course of the semester, we've explored a rich diversity of cultural communities. For the final unit, you will be provided with your own chosen community to explore. This inquiry-based essay requires that you engage in research, both with primary and secondary sources. As Ballenger puts it, the inquiry-based essay is "an essay that is less an opportunity to prove something than an attempt to find out." You will focus on your community observations and work with the connections you've observed within it. To develop this essay, you will research your chosen subject by consulting secondary sources in the Waldo Library, engaging primary sources in consultation with field notes, and conducting a personal interview with a member of your community. In preparation for writing this essay, we will also read examples of different types of research performed by various contributors in *Reading and Writing in the Age of Cultural Diversity*.

The Task
Your task will be to explore a community on campus that you believe to address issues of diversity, a community that you're interested in learning more about. The most important part of the inquiry-based essay is developing the question you want to answer about this community.

This essay should answer these questions:
- What is your chosen community/topic, and how does it address issues of diversity?
- Why is this community and diversity issue important to you?
- What have you learned through your research?
- How/to whom is what you've learned important?

You'll also need to collect, analyze, and provide evidence using these research methods:
1. A personal interview from an expert relating to the topic I've identified (we'll work on specific questions).

2. A minimum of five scholarly sources: You'll need to reference evidence from outside sources that highlight the significance of your chosen community. Appropriate bibliographic references are required.

3. Field observation notes: You'll devote 1–2 hours per week to observing this community for the next three weeks.

Processes

In addition to the reflection, rough drafts, and final drafts that you submit for each process portfolio, you'll also need to include the following:

1. Topic proposal on your gender issue and why you've chosen it (Date Due:)
2. Interview scripts from the person interviewed
3. An annotated bibliography of sources consulted

Date Assigned/Date Due:

Appendix 7.C.
Scholarly vs. Popular Article Checklist

What is the title of the journal?

What is the title of the article?

When was it published?

Who is the author of the article?

Is the author's affiliation identified? A university? A company? What is it?

Is the author's contact information provided?

Is there an abstract for the article?

Are keywords provided?

Are there a lot of unnecessary images in the article? If there are any images, what are they and do they provide essential information?

Is there a list of cited sources or a reference list at the end of the article?

REFERENCES

Association of College and Research Libraries. (2000). *Information literacy competency standards for higher education*. Retrieved from http://www.ala.org/acrl/sites/ala.org.acrl/files/content/standards/standards.pdf

Association of Departments of English. (1992). Statement on the use of part-time and full-time adjunct faculty. Retrieved from http://www.ade.org/policy/policy_faculty.htm

Arp, L., Woodard, B.S., Lindstrom, J., & Shonrock, D.D. (2006). Faculty-librarian collaboration to achieve integration of information literacy. *Reference & User Services Quarterly, 46*(1), 18–23. doi:10.5860/rusq.46n1.18

Burd, B.A., & Buchanan, L.E. (2004). Teaching the teachers: Teaching and learning online. *Reference Services Review, 32*(4), 404–412. Retrieved from http://www.academia.edu/936663/Teaching_the_teachers_teaching_and_learning_online

Gappa, J. M., & Leslie, D. W. (1993). *The invisible faculty: Improving the status of part-timers in higher education*. San Francisco, CA: Jossey-Bass.

Jiao, Q. G., & Onwuegbuzie, A. J. (2002). Dimensions of library anxiety and social interdependence: Implications for library services. *Library Review, 5,* 71–78.

Miller, R., O'Donnell, E., Pomea, N., Rawson, J., Shepard, R., & Thomes, C. (2010). Library-led faculty workshops: Helping distance educators meet information literacy goals in the online classroom. *Journal of Library Administration, 50*(7-8), 830–856. doi:10.1080/01930826.2010.488977

Miller, W., & Bell, S. (2005). A new strategy for enhancing library use: Faculty-led information literacy instruction. *Library Issues, 25*(5), 1–4.

Modern Language Association Executive Council. (1994). MLA statement on the use of part-time and full-time adjunct faculty members. Retrieved from http://www.mla.org/statement_faculty

Mounce, M. (2009). Academic librarian and English composition instructor collaboration: A selective annotated bibliography 1998–2007. *Reference Services Review, 37*(1), 44–53. doi:10.1108/00907320910934986

Nardi, B. (1999). *Information ecologies: Using technology with a heart*. Cambridge, MA. : MIT P.

Perez-Stable, M.A., Sachs, D. E., & Vander Meer, P.F. (2013). Inspiring results: Designing innovative instruction using faculty feedback on technology use and attitudes toward library research instruction. *Proceedings of the ACRL 2013 Conference.* Retrieved from http://www.ala.org/acrl/sites/ala.org.acrl/files/content/conferences/confsandpreconfs/2013/papers/Perez-Stable_etal_Inspiring.pdf

Schuster, J. H., & Finkelstein, M. J. (2006). *The American faculty: The restructuring of academic work and careers*. Baltimore, MD: Johns Hopkins University Press.

Siemens, G. (2005). Connectivism: A learning theory for the digital age. *International Journal of Instructional Technology and Distance Learning, 2*(1). Retrieved from http://itdl.org/journal/jan_05/article01.htm

Smith, R. L., & Mundt, K.E. (1997, April). Philosophical shift: Teach the faculty to teach information literacy. Paper presented at the meeting of ACRL 8th National Conference, Nashville, TN. Retrieved from http://www.ala.org/acrl/publications/whitepapers/nashville/smith

Sult, L., & Mills, V. (2006). A blended method for integrating information literacy instruction into English composition classes. *Reference Services Review, 34*(3), 368–88. doi:0.1108/00907320610685328

Townsend, L., Brunetti, K., & Hofer, A.R. (2011). Threshold concepts and information literacy. *portal: Libraries and the Academy, 11*(3), 853–869.

U.S. Department of Education, National Center for Educational Statistics. (2004). *Background characteristics, work activities, and compensation of instructional faculty and staff: Fall 2003*. (NCES Publication No. 2006176). Retrieved from http://nces.ed.gov/pubsearch/pubsinfo.asp?pubid=2006176

U.S. Department of Education, National Center for Educational Statistics. (2005). *2004 national study of postsecondary faculty (NSOPF:04): Report on faculty and instructional staff in Fall 2003.* (NCES Publication No. 2005172). Retrieved from http://nces.ed.gov/pubsearch/pubsinfo.asp?pubid=2005172

Vygotsky, L.S. (1978). *Mind in Society: The development of higher psychological processes*. Cambridge, MA: Harvard UP.

Western Michigan University. (2010). Academic affairs strategic plan 2010. Retrieved from http://www.wmich.edu/provost/AAPlanning/Academic%20affairs%20strategic%20plan%20final%202010.pdf

Not Just an Afterthought: Involving Librarians in the Instructional Design Process

Alex Mudd, Terri Pedersen Summey, and Matt Upson

Academic libraries and librarians are changing. Historically, libraries and librarians have provided reactive and inflexible services as they acted as custodians or gatekeepers of information. Now, libraries and librarians are becoming user-centered, which help them remain relevant in this time of technological innovation and information overabundance. Because of these changes, academic libraries are transforming into active, social, and collaborative facilities that can meet the terms and needs of 21st century learners. Librarians must become proactive and move out of the library building, taking services to the campus community, both in-person and online (Dewey, 2004). The passive reference librarian and departmental liaison is evolving into the active, embedded librarian who is more directly involved in the teaching, learning, and research activities of various academic departments.

In the past, academic librarians have had instructional responsibilities, but that instruction was often limited to a one-shot presentation in a course. In the online course environment, greater challenges exist for offering library instruction to students. Often, library instruction or faculty-librarian collaboration is an afterthought, initiated after the faculty member has developed the course and realizes that library research and access to library resources may be necessary. Ignoring or forgetting to include librarians and library instruction until the last phase of course development can cause frustration on the part of librarians, faculty members, and, eventually, stu-

dents in the course. This frustration is often the result of a misbelief that students are adept at conducting research and locating the information necessary to complete course assignments and projects. Students become frustrated when they encounter difficulties during research and cannot locate items that they need. Librarians experience a sense of frustration when they believe that they could provide help to students before the students encounter difficulties. A solution is to involve the librarian in course development from the beginning, adding them as a core member to the instructional design team.

Librarians and Instructional Design

In recent years, instructional design (ID) has played an increasingly important role for many librarians, especially for those in embedded or blended roles. Over the past decade or so, the library world has seen the emergence of the blended or ID librarians (see Shank, 2006), whose primary duties include building sound instruction within the library as well as collaborative efforts with teaching faculty outside the library, often using online delivery mechanisms. Despite the fact that librarians are in a prime position to integrate their services into the curriculum and serve as partners in developing instruction (Shank & Bell, 2011), many libraries still do not have an ID librarian on their staff, although there may be non-library instructional designers employed at the institution.

The "problem" with general, non-library ID positions is twofold. First, if a librarian is fortunate enough to have ID staff at his or her institution, the designer(s) must support the entirety of the teaching faculty. Second, the ID staff may or may not have specific content experience relevant to a particular department or course, which may cause a potential gap between the final design and intended function on the part of faculty. Librarians are in an excellent position to either fill in the knowledge gap or take on ID responsibilities if provided the right circumstances. Because faculty members often overlook librarians during the ID process, academic librarians must proactively work to become an integral part of an ID team. As a member of the ID team, librarians have an opportunity to be involved in the course design process and can ensure that library and information literacy skills are included.

Taking on ID responsibilities or becoming involved in course design may seem daunting, but it is vital for the future of academic librarianship. To continue to be an essential player on academic campuses, librarians must move outside of the library and become more involved throughout the campus, especially in the area of instruction. Academic librarians can play an important role as they are concerned with designing engaging instruction. They know how to use their resources to provide opportunities for critical thinking, evidence-based practice, and performance-based assessment. If librarians are to play a fundamental role in the design of courses, they need to be proactive and work with faculty to identify outcomes; fold in the appropriate resource; and develop relevant, engaging instruction (especially in the increasingly ubiquitous online or blended course). Teaching faculty are often so busy with their courses that they may not have time to stay up-to-speed with the latest instructional trends and may have little or no design experience. Again, librarians can fill that gap. Working closely with faculty members, librarians can more effectively ensure that faculty members and students feel their presence as a vital part of the curriculum, rather than an outside force desperately acting when and where they can. Librarians are early adopters, trendsetters, and creative risk-takers. So what are you waiting for?

Instructional Design Process and Models

Where to Begin?

First, it is important to provide a brief overview of what the ID process looks like. There are many different models and approaches to ID, including a few specifically adapted for librarians. The authors will examine several of these within the greater context of the ADDIE model, including the ADDIE model itself; Booth's (2011) USER (Understand, Structure, Engage, and Reflect) method; and Bell and Shank's (2007) BLAAM (Blended Librarians Adapted ADDIE Model) model along with examining the Dick and Carey model as it aligns with Association of College and Research Libraries (ACRL) standards for information literacy within course design.

The basic underlying schema for most ID models in use today is ADDIE (Branch & Merrill, 2012). The acronym stands for *Analyze, Design, Develop, Implement,* and *Evaluate.* You may realize that you already integrate one or more of the phases into your instruction but have yet to recognize it as a part of an overall process. Once the authors provide an overview of the model and how the librarian-specific models fit within ADDIE, it may be useful to take a step back and look at your instructional approach using the ADDIE framework. You may immediately notice a gap in your approach or an opportunity for potential improvement. Most importantly, you should begin to think about how this model or any of its derivations can provide a means to initiate discussion and develop a course or assignment(s) alongside teaching faculty.

Whereas ADDIE acts as a general framework for ID, Bell and Shank (2007) and Booth (2011) provide models adapted specifically for academic librarians in need of practical, scalable solutions to instructional problems. Bell and Shank's BLAAM model and Booth's USER model both recognize that many academic librarians have not had formal coursework on ID and that, due to the nature of their positions, they need fast and flexible models to work with. Both models compress or abbreviate components of ADDIE that are more dependent on extended periods of development or relatively high-resource demands in favor of practicality.

In addition to the ADDIE system model, BLAAM and USER models, the Dick and Carey model is also well suited for use by librarians as part of an ID team. It is a model for "identifying what is to be taught, determining how it will be taught, and evaluating the instruction to find out whether it is effective" (Dick, Carey, & Carey, 2009, p. 9).

Analyze

The initial phase of the ADDIE model focuses on identifying a gap in student learning or performance. Branch (2009) challenges the instructional designer to identify why that gap exists and how that gap could be closed through instructional means. The various components of the full model can be overwhelming and unrealistic for many librarians who have additional tasks on top of their instructional responsibilities. Therefore, it may be useful to examine library-specific ID models within the context of ADDIE to provide a less burdensome introduction as these models approach the ID process from the standpoint of a busy librarian who may not possess professionally acquired ID skills. Booth's (2011) USER model essentially breaks the *analyze* phase down into two components under her heading of *understand*: Identify the problem and analyze the scenario. Booth (2011) points out that identifying the problem can be relatively uncomplicated "when requests for instruction originate externally, a problem has already been somewhat defined for you—the requestor has identified an

issue library instruction can help solve" (p. 104). Still, it is important for the librarian to not be reactive but proactive in the attempt to ascertain any potential gaps. If you are completely reliant on the teaching faculty to provide a request for involvement, you may miss out on noticing another potential area in which library instruction would be appropriate. One approach may be to examine past syllabi and note if there are any opportunities to embed instruction. Just because there is no readily apparent problem or gap, that does not mean that intentional and focused instruction on the part of the librarian will not improve student learning.

Booth (2011) addresses the importance of analyzing "the four elements of instruction: *learner, content, context* and *educator*" (p. 107). She asks designers to take a closer look at the needs and motivations of learners; the instructional environment; and the necessary and desired knowledge, skills, and attitudes of both the instructor and the student. Similarly, Bell and Shank (2007) note as part of BLAAM the importance of not only working alongside a faculty member in identifying potential gaps, but performing a needs assessment of students as well. The authors of this chapter believe this is a crucial step in determining need, even if the assessment is very informal. The teaching faculty may have one idea of what student need is, but that assessment may only be partially correct. Providing students with the opportunity to voice their own individual gaps can lead to better design focus.

Design

The design phase focuses on figuring out the best, most efficient way for students to cross the gap identified during the analyze phase. "The purpose of the design phase is to verify the desired performances and appropriate testing methods ... you should be able to prepare a set of functional specifications for closing the performance gap due to a lack of knowledge and skills" (Branch, 2009, p. 59). In their work, Bell and Shank (2007) note that it is essential that academic librarians establish clearly defined and measurable objectives for instructional sessions as part of the design phase. Without clearly identifying where you want your students to end up, you will have no real way of knowing how to get there. Booth (2011) provides an excellent differentiation between multiple instructional endpoints by defining three types of "targets:" *goals, objectives,* and *outcomes.* She writes, "*goals* focus you on your instructional role; *objectives* organize content into activities and content units; and *outcomes* describe how participants are substantively different because of the knowledge they have gained" (p. 118). Creating these targets early in the ID process will allow for a more structured approach to establishing the right mode of delivery. In essence, you now know where you are headed, so you can appropriately determine the best vehicle and route for the trip. At this point, you are ready to determine the pedagogical methods and learning activities that you will utilize to deliver the instruction. As you move through the design phase, you will want to utilize formative assessment techniques to make sure that your instruction is meeting the defined learning objectives.

Develop

Once you have provided a design that is structured to hit a set of intended targets, you will need to actually develop or determine what resources you plan to utilize in your instruction. While it is reasonable to generate primary content and supporting media and even prepare lessons plans, it may be difficult or unnecessary to perform a formative evaluation and revision of materials *before* they are even utilized in instruction (Bell & Shank, 2007; Branch, 2009). This rapid prototyping process *can* be useful, though, and Booth (2011) notes that even quick informal feedback from colleagues or students can have an immediately beneficial impact, even though it is not supported by formal data.

Implement

The implementation phase is where the rubber meets the road. This is where the learners encounter the materials that you or your collaborative group has designed. Part of the initial process involves the creation of an implementation plan that ensures the maximum diffusion and potential adoption of the instructional product. For example, you created a video tutorial on how to locate online journal articles for a history course. Is the tutorial difficult to use or overly complicated? Does it function correctly within the confines of your learning management system (LMS) or website? Can students easily locate the resource? How did you inform users of the resource? Or do they not even know of its existence? All of these factors play into the success of the instruction (Bell & Shank, 2007; Booth, 2011).

Our library-specific models note that the library instruction cycle is likely to be more compressed and have fewer human and budgetary resources than a professional ID firm or department on campus. Bell and Shank (2007) note,

> The intent of ADDIE's implementation phase is to create the conditions for the instruction product's success. It is easy to understand the importance of going to great lengths to achieve diffusion when the product has taken months, many hours of labor, and thousands of dollars to produce. Under such conditions, every precaution to eliminate the chance of failure should be taken. But in a library instruction setting, the stakes are far lower. Granted, we want our instruction products or services to succeed, but if they fail to accomplish what they were designed for, the loss in time and resources is minimal, and we have opportunities to try again. (p. 57)

One word of caution: While the authors do understand that librarians often rapidly create and implement library instruction, if the instruction fails dramatically you may not get the opportunity to revamp the lesson and try again. The librarian should do their best to communicate with the faculty member and students ahead of time to ensure that they understand and know the instructional needs in order to put a collaborative plan of instruction in place. Developing outcomes to guide the instructional session(s) is imperative. Communication throughout the process is vital and cannot be overstated. If you are working in a vacuum, devoid of any real instructional context, your instruction will reflect that. It will be disjointed, lack relevance, and be boring for students, faculty, and librarians.

Evaluate

Did your students reach their destination? Has their knowledge gap been closed as a result of your instruction? The evaluation step should not only allow you to assess what your students learned but also the effectiveness of your instruction and materials. There are two types of assessment: formative and summative. You can generally utilize formative assessment during the design process to continually adjust your instruction to meet user needs and expectations. The evaluation phase is better suited to summative assessment. Instructors, including librarians, can use summative assessment to evaluate "effectiveness, efficiency, and benefits" (Bell & Shank, 2007, p. 54). Focusing on the instruction, the concept of effectiveness questions if the instructional objectives were met. Efficiency is concerned with the process utilized to develop and implement the instruction. Finally, you want to consider the instructional benefits or return on the time invested in designing the instruction. Were the objectives achieved at a reasonable and justifiable cost (Bell & Shank, 2007)?

It is useful to note that evaluation does not just attempt to assess whether students met the assigned targets. It also helps you, as both designer and/or instructor, to determine appropriate adjustments for future instruction. Booth's

(2011) focus on reflective teaching emphasizes "that to educate effectively you must be responsive to your learners, meaning that when summative feedback has been gathered, it should be used to adjust your approach" (p. 146).

Finding Support

This information presented on ID concepts and models may seem overwhelming, especially if a librarian lacks a background in course development or ID. However, a librarian does not have to accomplish this alone; interested constituencies can form a team for course design. Becoming involved with an ID team may require a librarian to be proactive in communicating with faculty in the areas in which they are embedded or partnered. If there is an instructional designer on campus, a librarian can become acquainted with that individual and utilize that person as a springboard to involvement in course design. Often the instructional designer works with individual faculty members and can recommend the assistance of a librarian for research, course assignments, or content.

Team Approach to Instructional Design

Using a team approach to ID has a variety of benefits. It facilitates the efficient design of a quality course because the creation process utilizes the strengths of the team members. It is often difficult for faculty to utilize a team approach to course design as they are used to individually designing their own courses. Some might even think that their academic freedom is being taken away as they need to consult others for help with the technology. Often faculty and even librarians do not have the technological expertise to create online modules, videos, and other elements present in an online course. Online courses require a change in pedagogy. Because of this and the use of LMS tools, online courses are best designed through collaborative teamwork.

An ID team may consist of a variety of individuals. At a minimum, it is best to include a faculty member, an instructional designer, someone from the computing or IT staff, and a librarian.

The faculty member serves as the subject matter expert (SME). This individual provides the subject or discipline specific content for the course. Usually this person would also provide the outcomes along with the various activities and assignments that make up the course. However, using a team approach, the faculty member and the librarian may be able to work collaboratively to develop the outcomes and assignments. An instructional designer can serve as the project manager guiding the team through the design steps. This individual possesses the pedagogical tools and expertise needed to ensure the course meets the learning outcomes. At some institutions, the instructional designer and the computer staff member may be the same individual (Laverty & Stockley, 2006). A computing or IT staff member provides the technical support as needed with the technology. It is helpful if this person is familiar with or an administrator of the LMS or course management system (CMS). Finally, the last individual is the librarian. Laverty and Stockley (2006) advocate for the inclusion of a librarian in the design process and emphasize the richness and depth that librarians add to online courses. In their article, they state "librarians encourage a resource-rich environment that may not develop without their direct involvement in the planning and development of online courses" (Laverty & Stockley, 2006, p. 53). Librarians enrich courses by providing resources and links to relevant sources beyond those found on the open web. They have the expertise to teach students information literacy skills such as how to use resources to locate information and methods used to evaluate sources critically. Through their understanding of the research process, librarians can facilitate the development of pedagogically sound research assignments.

Collaborating with a team to incorporate information literacy into online courses can help eliminate barriers that librarians face. Creating a library presence in online courses or the LMS facilitates student learning and enhances the educational experience by providing students with not only resources needed to complete course requirements but also additional sources adding to their overall knowledge. Online students are often DIY learners; they are highly motivated and independent. Nevertheless, distance learners do not always seek out scholarly resources on their own and perceive the distance from the library as a barrier. They have busy schedules and do not think to ask librarians for assistance. As the LMS is a self-contained learning environment, students, depending upon the information and resources provided to them by their instructor, often will not venture outside of the course shell, unless it is required. With their skill in locating information, librarians are the perfect candidates to assist faculty in locating resources that they may utilize as content or learning objects in courses such as readings, videos, and other instructional tools (Shell, Crawford, & Harris, 2013; York & Vance, 2009).

Benefits to Including Librarians on the Instructional Design Team

Including a librarian as a full member of the ID team and not waiting until after the faculty member designs the course has a variety of benefits. A librarian's information literacy expertise not only supports student learning but also helps the faculty member teaching the course. When librarians collaborate with faculty on course design, outcomes, and assignments, it results in more effective library or research-based assignments. By collaborating to create customized instructional materials, the materials will meet the course outcomes and needs of the learner better. As a result, the quality of resources utilized by the students in papers and projects should increase while the research anxiety of the students will diminish. In the 21st century, higher education is placing a greater emphasis on critical thinking and research skills to develop lifelong learners. Engaging with information resources has become a part of learning, and, as a result, information literacy skills are necessary for future success in an information-rich world. Librarians have the expertise to provide pathways to key resources, enhancing the learning environment. Edwards, Kumar, and Ochoa (2010) discovered that collaborating to include information literacy content in a course not only increased the comfort level of students in using information sources for research but also improved their self-confidence. Faculty support was essential to the success of the project. Other key factors in making the partnership work were communication, collaboration, and integration of the materials into the course. The collaboration during the design phase produced content that was "integral to the fabric of the course" and not as a separate afterthought (Edwards et al., 2010, p. 279).

Challenges Faced by Librarians

As with any course-related instruction, academic librarians face a variety of challenges in not only becoming embedded in online courses but also specifically becoming an equal partner in the design of courses. Faculty members often do not think about research assignments or information literacy skills until after they design the course and present the assignments to the students. For the most part, they do not consider contacting a librarian for assistance until the students begin asking questions about a particular assignment or course activity. More often than not, collaborating on library instruction for courses involves the librarian trying to squeeze content into a course that the faculty member has already designed. Getting faculty on board with including a librarian during the early stages of the course design process can have numerous benefits. Fully integrating information literacy instruction in the

course design legitimatizes the instructional content and sends a message to the students that these skills are useful and vital to success in the course. Communicating with a design team or, at least, with the faculty member during the initial phases of course design can help ensure that research or information literacy skills relating to the course are included in the course outcomes, content, activities, or assignments.

Assessment is another challenge faced by academic librarians in offering library instruction, not only in the online classroom but also face to face. How does one measure whether students grasp the content? In the online environment, are the students actually utilizing the content or modules presented by the librarian? As a member of the design team, the librarian can facilitate the development of assessment measures, such as activities, assignments, quizzes, or other assessment techniques, to gauge student learning.

The ACRL Standards and Embedded Librarianship

The ACRL's Information Literacy Competency Standards for Higher Education (2000) notes that "faculty, librarians, and others will find that discussing assessment methods collaboratively is a very productive exercise in planning a systematic, comprehensive information literacy program" (p. 7). Due to an increase in the number of students learning at a distance, whether wholly or partially online, the need for systematic planning for these students is especially important with regards to "direct communication with the appropriate personnel" (Association of College and Research Libraries, 2008, p. 1). Thanks to this increased enrollment, institutions are paying closer attention to how to improve delivery of distance education.

Early inclusion of librarians in the ID process provides the added benefit of allowing learning objectives and classroom activities to align with the standards for information literacy. This alignment is particularly helpful in ensuring that the role of the librarian is more than a teaching assistant (or, worse yet, a passive observer of the course) and that the lessons or activities meet the goals and outcomes of library instruction. This is crucial in ensuring learning outcomes for distance students. ACRL's *Standards for Distance Learning Library Services* (2008) states,

> The library must provide information literacy instruction programs to the distance learning community in accordance with the ACRL Information Literacy Competency Standards for Higher Education, as cited below under Services. The attainment of lifelong learning skills through general bibliographic and information literacy instruction in academic libraries is a primary outcome of higher education, and as such, must be provided to all distance learning students. (p. 1)

Given the technological changes that are taking place on college campuses, emerging technologies have presented an opportunity to provide more robust information literacy instruction. Whether it is in the LMS; on the library website; in an online, for-credit course offered by the library; or as a component of a faculty member's class, these rapid technological changes have also complicated the relationship librarians have with the information literacy standards. As a result, librarians operating in a virtual environment need to be particularly mindful of the ACRL standards and consider how to best adapt them for the modern information landscape. Individuals cannot separate information technology skills from information literacy as both are interconnected and lend support to each other (Association of College and Research Libraries, 2000). While information literacy at its core is independent of information technology skills, in the virtual world, it is wholly on information technology skills. Because of this dependency, a team of instructional designers is critical for understanding the necessary technological requirements to deliver instruction mod-

ules efficiently using available technologies, support sound pedagogy, and create information literate students who, in this instance, are dependent on technologies to achieve this literacy. However, research suggests that delivery has no impact on student retention of information literacy skills and that when used appropriately, most instructional methods are effective (Anderson & May, 2010). Due to the technological fluency required of online or blended courses, thoughtful design of online learning will help facilitate an even playing field, which is particularly important for higher education stakeholders.

Because the ACRL's *Standards for Distance Learning Library Services* include outcomes for each information literacy standard, it is far easier to implement the ACRL standards into distance education. As mentioned earlier, the Dick and Carey model is appropriate for use by librarians. Dick, Carey, and Carey (2009) describe their model as "a powerful tool for planning successful standards-based education because of the tight alignment among learning outcomes, student characteristics, instructional activities, and assessments" (p. 8). Because librarians may work with multiple faculty members across campuses, the systems approach also allows a design team to formulate a template that they can replicate or duplicate for multiple occasions and that can handle larger and smaller scales of enrollment. The systems approach is an "outcomes-based approach to instruction because it begins with a clear understanding of the new knowledge and skills that students will learn" (Dick et al., 2009, p. 9).

In outcomes-based instruction, instructional goals and objectives are key elements. Instructional goals are broader and generally define what the instruction is intended to teach to the students. Objectives are more specific and describe the actions or competencies that students will be able to demonstrate at the conclusion of the instruction (Brown & Green, 2006). Instructional objectives are specific, measurable, and observable behaviors of the students. Instructors or course designers use these objectives as the building blocks or foundation upon which they construct instructional activities or lessons to meet the broader instructional goals (Martin, 2010). The important aspect for librarians as part of a design team is to make sure that the outcomes of the ACRL standards are in alignment with the goals of a course that is not necessarily your own. Through collaboration with faculty members who are part of a design team, the outcomes outlined by ACRL can be included and assessed through all activities in the course.

Assessment

By using a team approach to the ID of courses, outcomes related to information literacy learning tie directly into the course design, resulting in greater assurance that students learn what they need to learn. Reeves (2006) outlines meta-outcomes that cut across learning domains and that are useful for thinking about what specifically instructional designers should be assessing. For librarians familiar with information literacy, these outcomes are cut from the same cloth as the ACRL standards. For Reeves, these include "accessing and using information," which parallels Standard Two, communicating using multiple media, which is analogous to Standard Four, thinking critically/make sound judgments/solve problems, which is similar to Standards Three and Four, among others (p. 299).

Because of the standards, librarians have a framework for broad outcomes. To assess and evaluate student learning, instructors should utilize the instructional goals and objectives as the guide to measure student learning (Brown & Green, 2006). The specific ways students demonstrate these outcomes may vary because of the technologies used by distance and blended courses in which the librarian is embedded. Matthew and Schroeder (2006), in an example of an embedded librarian program, illustrate activities such as answering forum questions and posting tips about creating a research topic and citing

sources, which are more akin to reference services than to information literacy instruction, though are still valuable to contributing to learning outcomes. Other examples of embedded librarianship define the role similarly, including posting in a library specific discussion board within a LMS (Hoffman & Ramin, 2010). By forming a team that incorporates one of any number of models for ID or components of several, embedded librarianship shifts from reference to instruction. This allows it to meet the instructional goals in ACRL's *Standards for Distance Learning Library Services*, which libraries and their parent institutions must provide to all distance-learning students (2008)

The Dick and Carey (2009) model states that all instruction materials should have some form of assessment component; pretests, post-tests, and/or a performance context are all described as ways to assess student learning in a course. Assessments used by librarians in face-to-face contexts are typically easy to adapt to online environments, including surveys, multimedia, tests, and questionnaires (Dewald, Scholz-Crane, Booth, & Levine, 2000). A large community of practice exists around the assessment of library instruction; techniques outlined by various researchers and practitioners are useful for developing the assessment needed in particular instances (Burkhardt, MacDonald, & Rathemacher, 2010; Radcliff, Jensen, Salem, Burhanna, & Gedeon, 2007). Information literacy is demonstrable; tests and surveys can be useful for abstract knowledge, but case studies and simulations provide an opportunity to see information literacy in action (Dewald et al., 2000). Electronic portfolios that demonstrate processes have been used effectively in the authors' courses, and annotated bibliographies are another potential assessment tool (Burkhardt et al., 2010).

While design team members share responsibility in designing the course and aligning assessment with outcomes, individual team members have unique areas of expertise that may be called on in some instances. The Dick and Carey (2009) model dictates that a SME is responsible for making sure that the information and instruction is accurate and current. As such, when designing and then executing a course, it is in the interest of both student and instructors that the assessments utilized are reviewed on a regular basis. In assessing information literacy outcomes, librarians should be wholly responsible for designing appropriate assessment materials to measure student learning, just as other members of a design team (faculty, for instance) should be responsible for assessment in areas where they are the SME. This is in contrast to one-shot library instruction sessions where it is difficult for librarians to assess student learning.

Examples of Embedding Librarians in the Design Process

Librarians may be already involved in the courses design process, including collaboration on the content of library instructional modules and the use of the LMS to present information on research and information literacy skills. One such project involved creating a library orientation program within the shell of a LMS for students in a nursing program. The librarian worked with the faculty members in the department to determine needed skills and content. Collaboration between the librarian and the faculty members facilitated the design of relevant modules, tutorials, and learning activities, leading to a successful partnership. Because of this collaboration in designing the orientation course, faculty noticed an improvement in student learning and higher quality assignments (Xiao, 2010).

A nursing informatics course was the subject of another partnership between a librarian and a faculty member (Schulte, 2008). Because of the nature of the course, the faculty member was interested in adding an information literacy component. The faculty member developed the final project in collaboration with the librarian. As a result, to complete the project, students utilized skills learned in the course, including informatics and information literacy competencies. To design the course, the librarian and the faculty member collaborated on the content and then the librarian designed the information literacy unit. The librarian became a co-teacher of the course and participated in all aspects of design. Through this project, the librarian discovered that involvement in course design and teaching required a significant time commitment to create the modules and presentations. Added to that is more time interacting with and connecting to students in the course. A challenge encountered by the librarian was creating content that actively engaged the student learners. The author identified several key factors in making this project a success: the librarian worked with the faculty member as an instructional and design partner; students perceived the importance of the module because it was an integral part of the course and graded; and finally, the librarian and faculty member had adequate time to collaborate, design, and present the content.

Many times faculty may not know the best way to incorporate content on research or information literacy skills. One of this chapter's authors (TS) worked with Emporia State's departmental faculty in Health, Physical Education, and Recreation (HPER) to identify research elements in the course in order to design course specific instructional guides and modules. When the faculty member began to conceptualize the course, the librarian and faculty member brainstormed ways that the librarian could participate in the course and how to best present the content. Through conversation, the faculty member and the librarian determined the learning outcomes for the students and developed the various assignments, especially those relating to information seeking, retrieval, and evaluation. Together, the faculty member and the librarian decided the content and topics of the library instruction portion of the course. At the same time, they delineated the role of the librarian and the extent of her participation in the course. More in-depth assessment and analysis of the experience still needs to occur, but the librarian believes that this collaboration was successful and will lead to future opportunities to work as a team with this faculty member. Potentially, the word will spread so that others will become interested in working with a librarian from the beginning. In addition, one of the goals for this particular librarian is to contact faculty and show up at their office door to let them know that she can help during the course design phase.

Tips for Creating Successful Partnerships

Various examples of best practices exist to guide librarians in the promotion of embedded librarian services. Jackson (2007) recommends that a liaison be dedicated to the campus LMS and encourages librarian training of LMS functions, being an active participant in discussions and packaging supplemental content for students that can be used in multiple courses. York and Vance (2009) echo some of these sentiments and add a few of their own. They suggest building relationships with individuals in charge of the CMS/LMS to help facilitate easier integration of library resources and the inclusion of library links and modules into whatever software is used. Hoffman and Ramin (2010) also promote follow-ups with the instructor and suggest going outside a subject specialty to promote the service.

These strategies are useful once a librarian is embedded, but developing a design team requires some additional time and energy to get the project off the ground and presents unique challenges in finding collaborators. While the strategies suggested are neither comprehensive nor a list of requirements, they have been useful in promoting the concept to faculty on the authors' campus.

Creating Partnerships

Because librarians are often either the forgotten element in course design or an afterthought, they need to be in charge of their own destiny. Instead of bemoaning the fact that librarians and library instruction are often not included in online courses, librarians need to take action and seek out partners. As mentioned earlier, this may be as simple as creating a partnership with the instructional designers or those who manage the LMS at a particular institution. Often faculty, when embarking on developing a new online course, may ask the instructional designers on campus for assistance. If a librarian establishes a good relationship with the learning technologies staff or instructional designers, the latter can mention to individual faculty members that working with a librarian would be useful for particular parts of the course or assignments. Alternatively, advocating for a library presence in the LMS that links to webpages, library guides, or even course-specific documents is a simple place to start and may lead students to utilizing the library and its resources.

Getting out of the library and moving into the environment of the faculty to form partnerships and build relationships with subject discipline faculty is important. Creating a good working relationship can help subject faculty perceive the librarian as an equal partner in creating quality courses, but it also takes promoting the benefits that librarians can add to the process. Librarians can work with faculty members to determine course outcomes, especially those that relate to research or information literacy skills. As a result, the librarian in collaboration with the faculty member can customize the library instructional materials or content to meet the learning outcomes of the course. By working closely with the faculty member, the librarian can not only assess the needs of the course but also discover the characteristics of the learners enrolled in the course.

Communication, Communication, Communication

In creating a working partnership, communication between the parties involved in course design is essential. One of the first steps for the librarian to take is to work with the faculty member to clarify the role of the librarian and state the expectations of each party. This way, there are no misunderstandings as the project progresses. Communicating and working closely with the faculty member allows both or all parties to collaborate in determining which content to present and crafting relevant assignments to help meet the outcomes of the course. As Love and Norwood (2008) state, "We found that clear communication between the instructor and librarians plays an important part in communicating accurate and timely information to the students" (p. 92).

Promote Library Instruction Accomplishments

Libraries are meticulous in keeping records of their instruction sessions, and librarians often have positive interactions with an existing course or department. Composition courses are a frequent visitor to the library at many institutions, and the instruction activities that take place in these courses, either online or face-to-face, are a major part of student learning. These examples demonstrate the capabilities of the library in instruction and, in the case of composition, illustrate the scaffolding that is done, allowing for more focused, discipline-specific instruction in an embedded course. Because of the volume of students that come in for instruction during composition, many libraries may already employ an ad-hoc design team for implementing this instruction and can use these experiences to bring in faculty from other departments.

Marketing the benefits of including a librarian in the design process is another best practice. Librarians need to advocate for themselves and proactively disseminate information through many channels on the services they can provide to an instructor designing a course. Ways to communicate include e-mailing faculty, visiting department meetings, creating informative links in the LMS, offering campus workshops, and having face-to-face conversations. All of these are ways that librarians can clearly describe the role they can play in planning and designing a course, along with presenting the benefits (York & Vance, 2009).

Recruit New Faculty

New faculty members provide an opportunity to promote and build library services. While this may require a librarian to go outside his or her subject expertise (Hoffman & Ramin, 2010), new faculty have a number of demands on them to develop new courses, publish, and teach a full course load. At the same time, they are still familiarizing themselves with the resources unique to the institution. Due to this convergence, new faculty are prime recruits for an ID team as it eases some of the responsibilities they have in developing a new syllabus or taking over a required course in the department. Many are willing to ask for and accept help. As universities develop and refine distance education plans, many general education courses are taking place online and collaborating with new faculty allows the team to harness the energy that brand new faculty members often possess.

Ask for Help When Needed

It is okay to ask for help when needed, and a variety of circumstances may require librarians to seek assistance when embedded or attempting to become embedded in online courses. Because librarians want to share knowledge on and expertise with information literacy skills, they often take on more than they can effectively complete. One of the tips provided by York and Vance (2009) is for librarians not to overextend themselves. Be willing to seek out assistance as needed. When librarians are embedded in a course, and especially in the design of the course, it is time consuming and the time that it will take to create the material for the course needs to be considered when selecting courses or determining an appropriate course load.

Some may be hesitant to approach faculty about working on a course together because of technological barriers. Librarians may perceive that they do not have the production or design expertise to create online modules. In a team approach to ID, this is something that can be resolved within the team. Team members who have the technical expertise, such as the instructional designer or IT specialist, can assist in overcoming technological barriers.

Conclusion

The trends of blended and embedded librarianship describe a role of academic librarianship that is not only challenging but also stimulating and empowering (Held, 2010). Becoming embedded in the design process can be demanding, but any challenges are outweighed by the benefits. Librarians need to assume a proactive stance in promoting their services and the benefits of including them in the design process. Learning about instructional pedagogy and technologies are also important. To remain relevant in this changing technological environment and avoid marginalization, academic librarians need to redefine their roles by assuming different responsibilities and becoming more involved in the design of instruction and teaching at universities. Librarians have a unique position in academic institutions to collaborate and cross-disciplinary lines, resulting in a redefinition of what it means to be an academic librarian.

REFERENCES

Anderson, K., & May, F. A. (2010). Does the method of instruction matter? An experimental examination of information literacy instruction in the online, blended, and face-to-face classrooms. *Journal of Academic Librarianship, 36*(6), 495–500.

Association of College and Research Libraries. (2000). *Information literacy competency standards for higher education.* Retrieved from http://www.ala.org/acrl/sites/ala.org.acrl/files/content/standards/standards.pdf

Association of College and Research Libraries. (2008). *Standards for distance learning library services.* Retrieved from http://www.ala.org/acrl/standards/guidelinesdistancelearning

Bell, S. J., & Shank, J. D. (2007). *Academic librarianship by design: A blended librarian's guide to the tools and techniques.* Chicago, IL: American Library Association.

Booth, C. (2011). *Reflective teaching, effective learning: Instructional literacy for library educators.* Chicago, IL: American Library Association.

Branch, R. M. (2009). *Instructional design: The ADDIE approach.* New York, NY: Springer.

Branch, R. M., & Merrill, M. D. (2012). Characteristics of instructional design models. In R. A. Reiser & J. V. Dempsey (Eds.), *Trends and issues in instructional design and technology* (pp. 8–16). Boston, MA: Pearson.

Brown, A., & Green, T. D. (2006). *The essentials of instructional design.* Upper Saddle River, NJ: Pearson.

Burkhardt, J. M., MacDonald, M. C., & Rathemacher, A. J. (2010). *Teaching information literacy: 50 standards-based exercises for college students* (2nd ed.). Chicago, IL: American Library Association.

Dewald, N., Scholz-Crane, A., Booth, A., & Levine, C. (2000). Information literacy at a distance: Instructional design issues. *The Journal of Academic Librarianship, 26*(1), 33–44.

Dewey, B. I. (2004). The embedded librarian: Strategic campus collaborations. *Resource Sharing & Information Networks, 17*(1-2), 5–7.

Dick, W., Carey, L., & Carey, J. O. (2009). *The systematic design of instruction* (7th ed.). Upper Saddle River, N.J.: Pearson.

Edwards, M., Kumar, S., & Ochoa, M. (2010). Assessing the value of embedded librarians in an online graduate educational technology course. *Pubic Services Quarterly, 6,* 271–291. doi:10.1080/15228959.2010.497447

Held, T. (2010). Blending in: Collaborating with an instructor in an online course. *Journal of Library & Information Services in Distance Learning, 4*(4), 153–165.

Hoffman, S., & Ramin, L. (2010). Best practices for librarians embedded in online courses. *Public Services Quarterly, 6*(2), 292–305. doi:10.1080/15228959.2010.497743

Jackson, P. (2007). Integrating information literacy into Blackboard: Building campus partnerships for successful student learning. *The Journal of Academic Librarianship, 33*(4), 454–461.

Laverty, C., & Stockley, D. (2006). How librarians shape online courses. *Journal of Library and Infor-*

mation Services in Distance Learning, 2(4), 41–55.

Love, M., & Norwood, S. (2008). Finding our way as "embedded librarians." *College & Undergraduate Libraries, 14*(4), 87–93.

Martin, F. (2010). Instructional design and the importance of instructional alignment. *Community College Journal of Research and Practice, 35,* 955–972. doi:10.1080/10668920802466483

Matthew, V., & Schroeder, A. (2006). The embedded librarian program. *EDUCAUSE Quarterly, 29*(4), 61–65. Retrieved from http://www.educause.edu/ir/library/pdf/EQM06410.pdf

Radcliff, C. J., Jensen, M. L., Salem, J. A., Jr., Burhanna, K. J., & Gedeon, J. A. (2007). *A practical guide to information literacy assessment for academic librarians.* Westport, CT: Libraries Unlimited.

Reeves, T.C. (2006). How do you know they are learning? The importance of alignment in higher education. *International Journal of Learning Technology, 2*(4) 294–309.

Schulte, S. (2008). Integrating information literacy into an online undergraduate nursing informatics course: The librarian's role in the design and teaching of the course. *Medical Reference Services Quarterly, 27*(2), 158–172.

Shank, J. D. (2006). The blended librarian: A job announcement analysis of the newly emerging position of Instructional Design Librarian. *College & Research Libraries, 67*(6), 515–524. Retrieved from http://crl.acrl.org/content/67/6/514.full.pdf+html

Shank, J. D., & Bell, S. (2011). Blended librarianship: [Re]envisioning the role of librarian as educator in the digital information age. *Reference & User Services Quarterly, 51*(2), 105–110.

Shell, L., Crawford, S., & Harris, P. (2013). Aided and embedded: The team approach to instructional design. *Journal of Library & Information Services in Distance Learning, 7*(1-2), 143–155. doi:10.1080/1533290X.2012.705627

Xiao, J. (2010). Integrating information literacy into Blackboard: Librarian-faculty collaboration for successful student learning. Paper presented at the meeting of ALSR 2010: Conference towards Future Possibilities, Hong Kong, China.

York, A., & Vance, J. (2009). Taking library instruction into the online classroom: Best practices for embedded librarians. *Journal of Library Administration, 49*(1), 197–209.

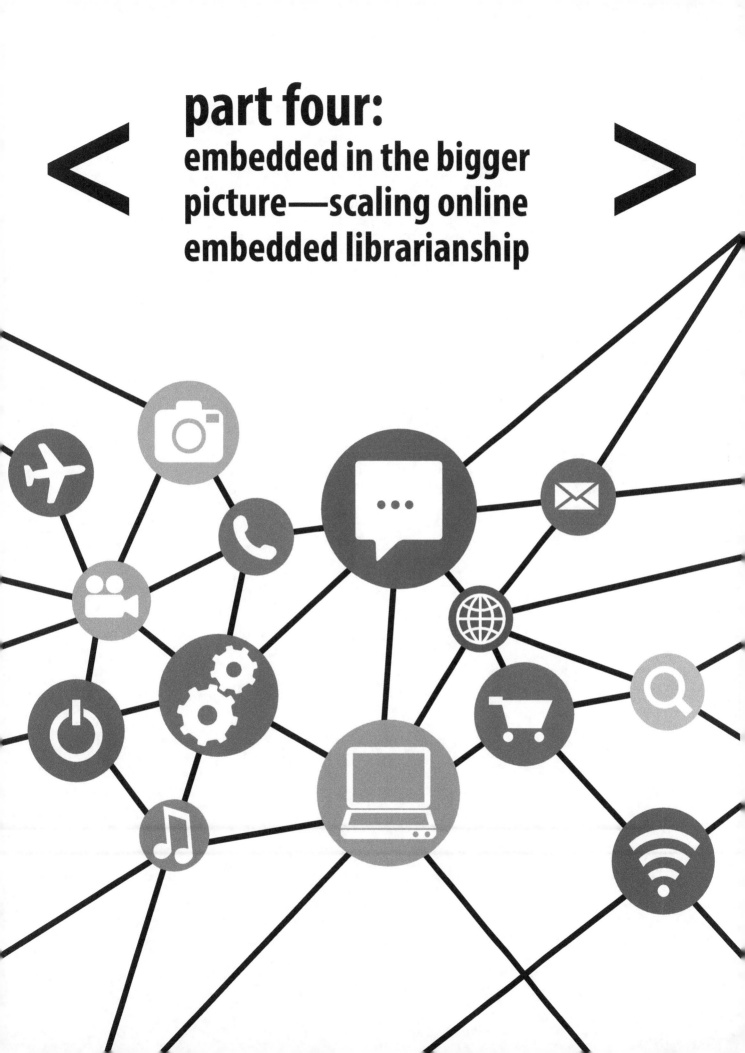

part four:
embedded in the bigger picture—scaling online embedded librarianship

Win-Win: Embedding Future Librarians to Extend Service to Online Classes

Timothy Peters and Julie LaDell-Thomas

The rise of online classes in higher education during the last 10 years has been prolific. According to the report *Going the Distance: Online Education in the United States, 2011*, the average annual growth rate of online classes between the fall of 2003 and the fall of 2010 was 18.55 %. During this same period, enrollment in online classes at institutions of higher education as a percentage of total enrollment grew from 11.7 to 31.3 % (Allen & Seaman, 2011, p. 11). It has become apparent to administrators at institutions of all sizes that online classes and degree programs will drive institutional enrollments and success in the coming years, and, because of this growth, colleges and universities have begun shifting substantial amounts of resources to creating, administering, and supporting online learning. This increasing emphasis on online learning has given rise to a variety of concerns on the part of both university administrators and faculty.

Some of the concerns expressed include the efficacy of student learning in online classes when compared to face-to-face instruction, a lack of engagement on the part of both students and instructors when participating in online classes, the ability to maintain instructional effectiveness when retooling a face-to-face class for the online environment, and the impact online classes will have on the traditional classroom model of education (Angelino, Williams, & Natvig, 2007; Merisotis & Phipps, 1999; Schachar & Neumann, 2010; Schaeffer & Konetes, 2010). Of particular relevance to this chapter is the notice-

ably elevated drop-out and attrition rates seen by many experts in online classes (Lee & Choi, 2011; Nistor & Neubauer, 2010). By one estimation, attrition rates in online classes run 15–50% higher than the rates for the face-to-face counterparts of these same classes (Bambara, Harbour, Davies, & Athey, 2009). In an age when institutions of higher education are being asked by their funding agencies to justify their expenditures and when those same institutions are compelled to focus their energies on retaining a declining pool of potential students through completion of a degree, this noticeable rise in course attrition rates is an alarming development.

In the spring of 2011, the Global Campus Library Services (GCLS) department at Central Michigan University (CMU) was challenged by the vice president of Global Campus Programs (the division within the university that develops and administers online courses and programs) to find new ways to better support online students. After having seen a 275% increase in the numbers of online classes offered by the university between the 2005–06 and 2010–11 academic years (M. Roestel, personal communication, March 13, 2013), Global Campus Programs also noticed attrition rates in a number of classes running well above the average for the university's face-to-face classes. In response to this development, the vice president identified three goals the Global Campus Programs personnel would pursue immediately in an effort to reverse this trend: (1) increase proactive support to online students in hopes of preventing them from becoming frustrated and dropping the class, (2) reduce attrition in online classes, and (3) increase student retention within online classes and the university's growing number of online programs. The vice president then approached GCLS, a department with a history of and a national reputation for providing library resources and services to non-traditional student populations (including both off-campus and online populations), with a specific charge to begin library support initiatives that would help Global Campus meet the goals outlined above. This chapter will detail one initiative undertaken by the GCLS librarians to meet the challenge presented to them and to assist the university in making its online instruction as effective and successful as possible.

The Project

As the GCLS librarians were thinking about ways to meet the challenge posed to them by the vice president of Global Campus Programs, one of the GCLS librarians attended the Distance Learning Administration Conference held in Savannah, Georgia in May of 2011. At a presentation by Linda Lillard, associate professor in the Department of Library Sciences at Clarion University and adjunct professor in San Jose State University's School of Library and Information Science, the CMU librarian heard about a past project that involved embedding library school graduate students from one institution (Emporia State University) into online nursing classes at a second institution (Central Missouri University). At the end of the presentation, Lillard suggested that she was open to collaborating with other institutions, so the CMU librarian brought the idea of embedding San Jose State University (SJSU) student librarians into CMU classes back to her colleagues.

The other CMU librarians learned more about the project through an article that explained that although the nursing students did not utilize the embedded student librarians as much as was

hoped by the project organizers, the overall the project was judged to be valuable and a very good learning experience for the Emporia State University students. There were plans to duplicate the project in the following semester (Lillard, Norwood, Wise, Brooks, & Kitts, 2009). After some discussion, the GCLS librarians concluded that embedding student librarians to enhance research support for online students seemed a good fit for the library's distance services model. The librarians were excited by the idea of collaborating with Dr. Lillard in her capacity as an instructor SJSU, and she was approached with the idea of collaboration between CMU and the SJSU students. Although the student librarians in her past special topics course at Emporia State University actually negotiated their level of involvement directly with the faculty at the University of Central Missouri, Lillard thought that her SJSU students would benefit from working with CMU, even though the GCLS librarians would be playing a more active role in facilitating embedded service to CMU students.

After more specific discussions of the logistics and processes necessary to actually make this happen, the GCLS librarians agreed to undertake this project as a pilot. Additional discussions with Lillard helped fill in the details, so the partnership was formed and project planning began.

Lillard was scheduled to teach LIBR 220, a special topics course at SJSU, during the Fall 2011 semester. It was decided that the CMU embedded student librarian project would be incorporated into the structure of the LIBR 220 class. Under the auspices of this project, Lillard would provide the SJSU students with both a theoretical introduction to distance library services as well as an opportunity to gain real-world professional experience by embedding within CMU classes. The first eight weeks of LIBR 220 would consist of lectures and learning about the topic of distance librarianship while the second eight weeks would offer students the opportunity to apply what they learned through their embedded "internship" in the CMU classes.

The GCLS librarians decided to utilize two graduate-level master of science in administration (MSA) classes at CMU for this pilot project. The two courses were MSA 600: Foundations of Research Methods in Administration and MSA 601: Organizational Dynamics and Human Behavior. These courses were chosen because the MSA program requires their students to perform library research, and GCLS has a long history of working closely with the MSA program at CMU, thereby having established solid collaborative relationships with a number of the instructors within the program. It was felt that the existing relationship with this particular program and its instructors would help GCLS attract and engage participants for the new embedded library student idea.

The librarians felt MSA 600 would be the best course in which to embed because it provided an introduction to research methods and required a literature review as its primary assignment. This course also served as a prerequisite for the MSA 699 capstone course, which completes the requirements for the degree. Unfortunately, only two of the three faculty teaching MSA 600 online agreed to participate, so an alternate course, MSA 601, was chosen. MSA 601 involved less research, but the instructor was an enthusiastic proponent of library services and eager to join the project.

Project Objectives

The GCLS librarians determined three primary objectives for the embedded librarian pilot:

1. To provide point-of-need library support for online students. This reflected the charge given by the vice president of Global Campus Programs. It was hoped that being embedded within the online class would allow MSA students to have more immediate access to the library's resources and services that would help them complete their assignments.
2. To expand GCLS services without increasing the GCLS librarian workload.

As the number of online classes at CMU increased, so did the workload of the GCLS librarians. Between 2005–06 and 2010–11, the number of questions asked of the GCLS librarians increased 27%. At times, especially during the busy fall semester, librarians found themselves dealing with an almost overwhelming workload. By increasing the capacity of GCLS' online reference and leveraging the skills of the SJSU students, it was hoped that GCLS could extend its reach and give even more attention to the students it serves.
3. To offer real-world professional experience to the SJSU students. Both the GCLS librarians and Lillard considered this a significant part of the project. It would provide the library school students with an opportunity to interact with real-world patrons that they might not otherwise have, and it would also introduce them to distance librarianship, which the GCLS librarians and Lillard feel is becoming an increasingly important part of the future of our profession.

Project Planning

Once the project objectives and timeframe were determined, GCLS began to work on addressing the logistical challenges associated with connecting the SJSU student librarians (who had no formal affiliation with CMU and its systems) to the CMU students they would be assisting. To enable access, the librarian designated as the project coordinator worked with the library's director of information services and CMU's Office of Information Technology (OIT) staff to arrange access to the various systems that would be used for the project. It was determined that the SJSU students would need access to four systems during the pilot:

1. They would need a temporary CMU guest login similar to the Global ID and password that allows CMU students, faculty, and staff to authenticate as valid users.

2. They would need access to Blackboard so they could embed within the course shells and interact with students.

3. They would need user accounts in the patron database for Millennium, the CMU libraries' integrated library system. Without this they would not have the ability to access library resources.

4. They would need librarian accounts in QuestionPoint, the web-based reference management service used by GCLS librarians to answer and track reference inquiries.

An overriding concern of the OIT staff and the university's Blackboard administrator was information security; neither group wanted the SJSU students having access to information not relevant to the embedded librarian project or the ability to edit content in any of the systems in which they would operate. OIT was able to use the student librarians' SJSU e-mail addresses instead of assigning CMU Global IDs. This would still provide temporary access to the systems that would be needed for the project, but limits were placed on their accounts to ensure that they would not have full access to non-project systems. It was agreed that this access would be permanently disabled once the project was completed at the end of the semester. The systems librarian profiled the SJSU students into Millennium to facilitate remote access to the library's catalog and licensed databases, and the project coordinator set up individual user accounts for QuestionPoint. Each student librarian and each GCLS mentor librarian was also profiled into their assigned Blackboard course shells, and the project coordinator created a separate Blackboard shell to serve as the project classroom, providing tutorials, documentation, and a practice area for student librarians as well as facilitating communication among all participants throughout the project. This project course shell included a discussion board where all participants could introduce themselves and practice answering questions; it also served as an archive for training materials and contact information.

Beyond facilitating access, GCLS also needed to develop training materials that would help prepare the SJSU students to be effective at providing research assistance for courses that were unfamiliar to them within the GCLS service model. To ensure consistency of service to CMU patrons, these "guest" librarians would need to have a solid understanding of the research needs for the course as well as GCLS reference practices and procedures. The group assumed that considerable effort on the part of GCLS librarians would be needed to prepare the SJSU students for their roles, with less intensive involvement—monitoring interactions and serving as mentors—once the project was underway. The GCLS librarians felt that extra effort on the front end would help the project run more smoothly once implemented.

The GCLS librarians worked together to develop an online orientation session that provided an overview of library systems and services as well as background on the MSA courses and their assignments. This session, scheduled a week before the semester began, covered CMU library resources such as research guides, article databases, and course syllabi; the various GCLS systems; and the GCLS reference procedures and practices that student librarians would be expected to follow. Lillard was invited to attend this orientation so she would have a better understanding of what her students would be expected to do. While the student librarians were encouraged to take on the responsibility of assisting the MSA students, the GCLS librarians made a point of discussing situations that might need to be referred to GCLS for resolution. It was felt that certain issues, such as database access problems, document delivery requests, and patron complaints, could be better managed by experienced CMU staff, so student librarians were encouraged to refer these to their assigned GCLS librarians.

Implementation

Each of three MSA courses was assigned three SJSU students to act as embedded librarians and a pair of GCLS librarians to serve as monitors. The mentor librarians had previously contacted the MSA faculty to explain the pilot project and discuss how an embedded librarian service would work with their Blackboard courses. Because the embedded librarians were library school students who were not affiliated with CMU, the GCLS librarians felt that faculty would be more open to participating if familiar GCLS librarians were the primary contacts for each course. This decision imposed some limits to how the student librarians interacted with the class, but GCLS librarians felt that this approach would ensure the best experience for faculty.

Once access was enabled, the orientation session was completed and the student librarians were assigned to their sections. The SJSU students were introduced virtually to their GCLS librarian partners and invited to participate as observers in the scheduled library instruction session for their assigned MSA courses. During these sessions, the student librarians were introduced to the CMU students they would be serving and to the instructor who would be teaching the courses in which they were embedded. The CMU students enrolled in the classes were encouraged to request assistance using the library discussion board available in their Blackboard course page. The SJSU student librarians in each CMU class worked out a schedule amongst themselves for monitoring their respective discussion boards, and the GCLS librarians assigned to each class set up automatic e-mail notifications that would allow them to monitor these interactions and step in as needed. As the courses progressed, GCLS librarians would occasionally supplement answers provided by the student librarians with additional helpful information or links. If direct feedback were warranted, the GCLS librarian would take on more of a mentoring role and communicate directly with the student librarian offline. GCLS librarians were not often called upon to assist as most student librarians seemed to have a patron-focused attitude and a good understanding of resources.

Unfortunately, the project participants found that not many of the CMU students requested help through the library discussion board in Blackboard. It was not clear whether the students were instead requesting help through the existing ask-a-librarian service being handled by the GCLS librarians (with which many MSA students would have already been familiar) or if the students just didn't need much help after participating in the online instruction session for their course. To encourage better participation, some student librarians used the library discussion board to proactively solicit questions or suggest useful resources based upon the assignments being given in the MSA class. These outreach efforts sometimes prompted new questions from students enrolled in the course but not in every case. The embedded service was particularly unsuccessful in the MSA 601 course. While the two MSA 600 courses received a handful of requests over the eight weeks of the pilot, there were no requests submitted for the MSA 601 class, even after student librarians sent messages offering helpful tips and a reminder to request assistance if needed. GCLS librarians suspected that the assignments for this class simply did not have a significant research component, so encouragement by the student librarians did not make a difference in the number of students who took advantage of the service. At the outset of the project, a reason to involve the MSA 601 instructor was that GCLS had worked with him for previous MSA 600 classes and believed he would be an active pilot project participant. The librarians could not have realized that there would be no library research involved in his MSA 601 class.

Midway through the project, the GCLS librarians conducted an online session with the SJSU librarians to discuss how the project was going. While the feedback from this session provided excellent guidance for future projects, suggestions for streamlining procedures and promoting higher use by CMU students came too late to benefit this pilot project. Even so, the midpoint discussion was a good opportunity for student librarians to share their experiences and the GCLS librarians gained a better sense of how the project design and student training could be improved going forward.

Evaluation

Once the project was completed, the student librarians' access was disabled and all project participants were surveyed to gather feedback on the project. Online surveys were used to gather feedback from the SJSU student librarians and the GCLS librarians who participated in the pilot. Surveys were also sent to the CMU students enrolled in the classes and the CMU faculty who taught them. The feedback would be used to evaluate the success of the embedded student librarian pilot project and to inform GCLS decisions for any future such projects.

The most positive responses came from the participating CMU faculty, with all three faculty indicating that having a librarian embedded in their Blackboard course was useful and that they would be interested in participating again. They offered very few suggestions for improving the experience, although one noted that their students would have liked to have had the service earlier in the graduate MSA program.

Only 21 CMU students responded to the survey, out of a total of 70 students enrolled in the three MSA courses. Even so, 51% of respondents indicated that they had not used the embedded librarian service. The survey asked those who responded in this manner to indicate why they had not used the service, and, as expected, several students indicated that they had requested librarian assistance through other means (e-mail, telephone, chat, etc.). Other students explained that all of their questions had been addressed through the initial instruction session while others said they simply did not need the help. Nearly all of the students said they liked the idea of having an embedded librarian in Blackboard, and one even commented, "Every online course should have this assistance if it was feasible."

Of the eight participating SJSU library science students, seven submitted survey responses. Most respondents (71%) indicated that participating in the project helped improve their professional skills, and this same percentage found the orientation and training materials to be helpful. While the overall response was fairly positive, several students offered suggestions for how the experience might be improved. The most common complaint was that there was not enough for the student librarians to do. The students seemed frustrated because of the low volume of requests in their assigned courses. In their comments, they suggested targeting classes that have more robust research needs (in an effort to avoid the situation experienced with the MSA 601 class) and embedding student librarians in more classes so that fewer would be assigned to each class. Several students suggested that the training materials, while helpful, should be streamlined and shortened. As one student noted, "The information presented was extremely useful, however there was a lot of content and it was rather difficult to manage."

Finally, a few students highlighted the need for a clearer understanding among all of the participants, suggesting earlier collaboration and group brainstorming as a possible way to ensure that future projects would meet the needs of all stakeholders. Lillard's feedback underscored this point. At the project's completion, she indicated that her students "were disappointed in their level of embedded participation in the course," although she felt partly responsible since she had "described it as more involved because that's how it was with Central Missouri" (L.L. Lillard, personal communication, February 20, 2012). In retrospect, the GCLS librarians agreed with one student's observation that the project would have been more successful with "clearer expectations and outcomes between all parties [CMU librarians, CMU instructor, SJSU students and SJSU instructor]."

Lessons Learned

After reflecting upon the experience of embedding library school students into the online classroom and reviewing the feedback collected, the GCLS librarians came up with the following list of lessons learned and will use them to guide efforts in the future:

Communication with the library school faculty partner is vital. Though the project began with the feeling that GCLS and SJSU were on the same page in terms of expectations, it eventually became clear that this was not the case. As experienced distance librarians, the GCLS staff follows a standardized GCLS workflow intended to streamline reference services to remote students. For this project, they had developed procedures and training with the intention of integrating the SJSU student librarians into their existing service model. Because the SJSU student librarians had spent several weeks receiving instruction from a professor who had had a different experience and service model embedding student librarians at other institutions, the SJSU students thought they would have much more flexibility in how they interacted with the students and faculty in the CMU courses. This difference in expectations began to surface during the midpoint discussion and was strongly reflected in the feedback received once the project was completed. In retrospect, regular two-way communication between GCLS and SJSU should have been pursued more vigorously. Ongoing discussion between GCLS and their SJSU faculty partner might have allowed the project to accomplish its goals as fully as had been hoped.

Understanding student expectations is a must. Due to the mismatch of expectations and lack of communication throughout the project, the SJSU students were frustrated because they had hoped to do things that just weren't possible within the parameters of the project. The student librarians expected to interact with CMU faculty to determine how they could best meet the needs of the students enrolled in the courses, but the GCLS librarians actually handled this interaction before the SJSU students got involved. There was also an expectation among the SJSU student librarians that they would be involved in tasks beyond being embedded in the online course shell, and they had hoped to have an opportunity to serve on a virtual reference desk and create online learning objects to support research assignments. While these were not part of the original project, the librarians agreed that this type of experience could be of real benefit to both the student librarians and CMU students; these types of activities will be considered for future projects.

Flexibility is necessary. One error the librarians made was expecting the SJSU students to conform closely to existing GCLS practices and processes. Because offering an embedded librarian service was a completely new effort, the GCLS librarians developed standard practices based on existing GCLS workflows. For example, rather than having the student librarians answer patron queries right within Blackboard, student librarians were asked to copy the question into the QuestionPoint reference management system to answer it. QuestionPoint allowed the librarians to use pre-designed scripts to provide standard text (such as contact information and links to frequently used services) in their responses to students. It was also used to track all GCLS reference transactions, regardless of how they were submitted. Not only did this require the student librarians to learn how to use another system, but it also slowed the process of getting answers to the CMU students. As one of the SJSU students pointed out, this practice also prevented the rest of the students in the class from learning from the answer, which was sent only to the student who made the request. In retrospect, GCLS librarians should have recognized that embedding in Blackboard was a completely different type of service and should have worked to develop less rigid processes to enable the novices to respond to patrons more easily.

Selection of the right classes is imperative. Delivering an embedded librarian service will be more effective if the service is matched to a research-intensive course wherein students have real information needs. In the pilot, the two MSA 600 classes were research-intensive, but the MSA 601 class was not. The student interaction with the embedded librarians in MSA 601 clearly demonstrated that students cannot be enticed to request help unless there is an assignment that requires library research. This results in an unsatisfactory experience for the mentor and student librarians. Since one of the goals of this project was to expose student librarians to real-world professional duties, in the future GCLS will make every effort to select classes that provide ample opportunity for student librarians to provide research assistance to students enrolled in the class.

Encouragement of proactive outreach is valuable. The discussion board transcripts showed that there was increased activity when the student librarians proactively promoted themselves to the CMU students they were supporting. Most of the student librarians in the project reached out on their own, but going forward, GCLS will certainly emphasize this point during training. Encouraging the embedded librarian to reach out to students and faculty right from the start should ensure better participation by the CMU students. It will also provide a more satisfactory experience for the student librarians because they will have the opportunity to tailor their interaction and identify the resources and services that would best benefit their assigned class. Actively monitoring the assignments given and the student discussion boards is a great way to discover additional ways to help.

Overall, GCLS found that partnering with library school students to provide embedded librarian service to be a good idea, but changes are needed to ensure that future projects reach the desired outcomes. In the pilot, the embedded student librarians proved to be eager partners and provided a level of service that was equivalent to what would have been offered by the GCLS librarians themselves. While reevaluating procedures and rethinking how the service is implemented will require additional effort on the part of GCLS librarians, it will be worth the effort to provide student librarians with valuable professional experience and give them hands-on familiarity with the real-world tasks they will be expected to assume upon graduation. This can be especially important to online library school students, some of who may not have the opportunity to engage patrons directly as the traditional, face-to-face student has. The benefits reaped by developing a more effective embedded librarian experience for the novice librarians will, in turn, directly benefit CMU's growing population of online students and help Global Campus Library Services fulfill the service objectives proposed by CMU's Global Campus Programs.

Future Directions

Having reflected upon both the positive and negative aspects of the embedded student librarian project, the GCLS librarians remain encouraged by the pilot effort and are convinced that embedding library school students within a professional setting is something that can be beneficial both to the embedding student librarians and the students enrolled in the online class. It also allows the library to leverage the skills of the library school students in the name of increasing its own ability to serve its online students. The relative success of the pilot project has encouraged the GCLS librarians to consider undertaking this project a second time.

In one sense, offering embedded services in online classes was not as time- and labor-intensive as the GCLS librarians thought it would be (especially once the initial set-up was completed), but the librarians also realize that one reason for this is that the CMU students did not utilize the embedded librarian service nearly as much as was hoped for. In future iterations, the GCLS librarians will have to more clearly demonstrate the value of the service provided by the embedded student librarians. In light of the feedback received from the participating student librarians and the lessons learned, there has already been discussion about how best to streamline processes used in the project as a way to decrease the learning curve of participating student librarians. There are also discussions around expanding the roles of the embedded student librarians to include building course guides and creating learning objects that could be embedded within the Blackboard course shells in addition to monitoring Blackboard activity to provide timely reference assistance.

By refining their approach, the GCLS librarians hope to make future experiences less labor-intensive and more learning-intensive for embedding student librarians. Streamlined processes and more active cooperation between student librarians and GCLS will ensure that CMU students and faculty receive the greatest possible benefit from embedded library services. Not only will online students receive prompt, thorough research assistance at their point of need, but the fresh perspectives of library school students outside of CMU will help GCLS to continually evaluate and improve services overall. The increase in capacity due to this type of partnership can go a long way towards making it possible for GCLS librarians to explore new ways to provide exemplary library services for distance students.

REFERENCES

Allen, I. E., & Seaman, J. (2011). *Going the distance: Online education in the United States, 2011*. Babson Park, MA: Babson Survey Research Group. Retrieved from http://www.babson.edu/Academics/centers/blank-center/global-research/Documents/going-the-distance.pdf

Angelino, L. M., Williams, F. K., & Natvig, D. (2007). Strategies to engage online students and reduce attrition rates. *Journal of Education Online, 4*(2), 1–14.

Bambara, C., Harbour, C., Davies, T., & Athey, S. (2009). Delicate engagement: The lived experience of community college students enrolled in high-risk online courses. *Community College Review, 36*(3), 219–238.

Lee, Y., & Choi, J. (2011). A review of online course dropout research: Implications for practice and future research. *Educational Technology Research and Development, 59*(5), 593–618.

Lillard, L., Norwood, S., Wise, K., Brooks, J., & Kitts, R. (2009). Embedded librarians: MLS students as apprentice librarians in online courses. *Journal of Library Administration, 49*(1-2), 11–22.

Merisotis, J. P., & Phipps, R. A. (1999). What's the difference?: Outcomes of distance vs. traditional classroom-based learning. *Change: The Magazine of Higher Learning, 31*(3), 12–17.

Nistor, N., & Neubauer, K. (2010). From participation to dropout: Quantitative participation patterns in online university courses. *Computers & Education, 55*(2), 663–672.

Schachar, M., & Neumann, Y. (2010). Twenty years of research on the academic performance differences between traditional and distance learning: Summative meta-analysis and trend examination. *MERLOT Journal of Online Learning and Teaching, 6*(2). Retrieved from http://jolt.merlot.org/vol6no2/shachar_0610.htm

Schaeffer, C. E., & Konetes, G. D. (2010). Impact of learner engagement on attrition rates and student success in online learning. *International Journal of Instructional Technology and Distance Learning, 7*(5). Retrieved from http://itdl.org/Journal/May_10/article01.htm

Embedding in the LMS: Faculty Evaluations of a Low-Touch Widget

Amy R. Hofer and Karen Munro

Libraries have been offering proactive, user-centered services in the campus learning management system (LMS) for many years. This practice is sometimes called "embedding," in recognition of the fact that librarians are entering user spaces, becoming more aware of and responsive to users' needs, and collaborating with users to improve the library's scope of services. As Bell and Shank wrote as early as 2004,

> While it might seem that courseware is an academic technology resource that falls outside the bounds of what the academic library contributes to the institution, failure to include the library in the courseware equation deprives faculty and students of a convenient access path to valuable library content and services. (para. 4)

Librarians and faculty alike have grasped the importance of embedding library services within the campus LMS and have experimented with many different strategies for doing so.

In this study, the authors consider the overall investment of time and effort that embedding strategies require from library staff relative to their reported usefulness to faculty. Library services within the LMS that can be automated, reused, prepared in advance, and/or transferred from one instance to another are considered to be, relatively speaking, lower-investment or "low-touch." Examples of these services include system-wide links to the library's website, reusable video tutorials, or preprogrammed "widgets" combining links to synchronous or asynchronous services. The authors recognize that these strategies may require significant initial investment but characterize them as low-touch because they can be subsequently used and reused with minimal effort. Library services that require librarians' time and attention for each instance or usage are considered to be, relatively speaking, higher-investment or "high-touch." Librarian office hours within the LMS, live video chat with a librarian, librarian-led discussion boards, and librarian assessment of student assignments are examples of this type of approach.

As of the writing of this chapter, library services within the LMS may be said to have matured to the point at which most librarians and faculty expect them to be present. But while librarians understand the importance of embedding services in the LMS, many have neglected substantive usability testing of their strategies. This study captures faculty responses to the Portland State University (PSU) Library's LMS widget-integration strategy to gauge the library's return on its investment and determine the best direction for further service developments. In other words, the present study is not about PSU's implementation of the widget (described in Flakus & Hofer, 2013[1]) but rather about user feedback on the implementation.

The authors hope this study will be useful in

1. Determining the perceived usefulness of PSU library's low-touch embedding strat-

egy and informing the redesign of the LMS widget,

2. Addressing a deficit in the literature on librarian strategies for gathering user perceptions of library services within the campus LMS,

3. Identifying themes that may inform library strategies for embedding in the LMS.

Background

PSU is Oregon's largest public university with nearly 30,000 enrolled students. Approximately 12% of generated credit (a measure that combines both headcount and credit value) comes from online and partially online courses (J. De Gruyter, personal communication, June 3, 2013). Strategic growth in online learning is an organizational priority; issues around online teaching and learning are a major part of ongoing campus conversations.

Since 2010, PSU has used Desire2Learn (D2L) as its LMS. Unlike Blackboard and some other commonly used systems, D2L does not have top-level tabs where the library can provide a page of content within the LMS. However, the PSU library was able to claim real estate on the default course homepage for a box—called a "widget"—that contains relevant library links for students. Beginning in Winter 2012, the widget appeared on the default homepage for all D2L course shells.

PSU's widget contains four elements as shown in Figure 10.1. First is a WorldCat Local catalog search box. Second is a dynamically generated link to the most relevant research guide available: a course guide if one has been created, a subject guide for the discipline, or a general library research guide if neither a course nor a subject guide is available; more than one guide can be displayed if the subject librarian determines that multiple guides are relevant. Third are "Ask Us!" buttons to contact a librarian via chat, text, e-mail, or phone, identical to the buttons that appear on

every page in the library's website. Last is a link to the PSU library homepage.

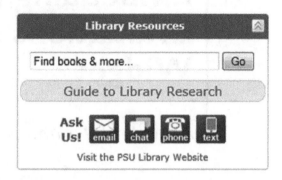

Figure 10.1. PSU's library widget in the LMS. Beginning in Winter 2012, the widget appeared on the default homepage for all D2L course shells.

This study did not seek input from faculty on whether to have a library presence in the LMS. Because PSU's D2L course homepages get more views than all of PSU library's webpages combined, integration of the widget in the LMS is strategically important to the library. The purpose of this study is to determine, having gained this essential toehold in the LMS, what could make the integration more useful and valuable to users.

Literature Review

There is considerable practical and descriptive literature on library embedding strategies within the LMS. Many articles have been published describing the role and features of different LMS systems and the ways in which libraries have embedded their services into these systems (see Bell & Shank, 2004; Gibbons, 2005a; Gibbons, 2005b; Shank & Dewald, 2003).

There is comparatively less literature substantially concerned with requesting feedback from the users of library services in the LMS to determine whether users consider these services genuinely helpful. In some cases, librarians have requested feedback from users, but it is unclear whether that feedback was incorporated into an iterative design process. In other cases, user feedback was anecdotal and informal, or librarians relied on data from the LMS to judge how much a service was used and how useful it was perceived to be. There are few studies concentrating substantially on qualitative user feedback to determine whether the investment that librarians have made in LMS integrations has been worth the cost or whether the embedding strategies effectively match user needs and preferences. Most articles with this focus have been published in recent years, perhaps indicating a maturation of the field from descriptions of implementation to analysis of performance.

Several recent articles specifically solicited student user feedback on library LMS integration strategies. Bowen (2012) used a survey to assess students' perceived value of course-level LibGuides within the Blackboard LMS, finding that students valued links that were highly visible and easy to access. Ismail's survey findings (2011) indicated that a majority of adult learners surveyed were aware of outreach strategies within the LMS and approved of them. Washburn (2008) surveyed students about the effectiveness of customized library research pages embedded in the Brigham Young University Blackboard instance, finding that students who were aware of the library presence were appreciative of it and would recommend it to their peers.

Horn and Owen (2011) took a slightly different approach, administering a large-scale survey about students' preferred information searching behaviors to inform their library's presence within the campus LMS. The discovery tools they embedded in the LMS resulted in increased usage of library subject guides as well as increased awareness of the library's services among faculty.

Other studies solicited both faculty and student feedback. Daly (2011) interviewed faculty and surveyed students about links to library resources inside 12 Blackboard courses. This study found that both groups of users perceived the library content as somewhat or very useful, and faculty reported planning to promote the tool better to their students in the future. McLure and Munro (2010) interviewed faculty and students at two universities about their opinions on

different library services within the LMS. Their findings showed that while faculty unanimously approved of a library link or tab as a default feature of online courses—one faculty interviewee "described this as a 'no-brainer'" (p. 40)—users also took multiple factors such as visual design and time savings into consideration when evaluating library services. Black (2008) conducted a survey of faculty and students during a pilot project to determine the usefulness of a library resource page within the LMS. Her findings indicated that faculty are less likely to use an embedded link than students.

Jeffryes, Peterson, Crowe, Fine, and Carrillo (2011) conducted both interviews and surveys of students and instructors at the University of Minnesota, with findings similar to those of the previous studies. They found that—

> instructors wanted a course-specific library resource that covered general information on how to search, access, and evaluate materials. They wanted a central resource that incorporated various library tools, something that would be simple for students to access and simple for instructors and staff to administer. In addition, instructors wanted resources to be customized to the individual course level, but they stated that they do not have time to do it themselves. Instructors often felt as though there were many useful library tools or services that they did not know about. (p. 25)

Ganster and Walsh (2008) conducted a focus group of undergraduate students on the usefulness of their LMS-embedded, course-specific research tutorial. In this case, user feedback was incorporated directly into the library's revision process. Hanna (2007) reported surveying faculty on the effectiveness of a metasearch tool within the LMS and receiving both concrete suggestions for improvement of the tool as well as general enthusiasm for its functionality. Leeder and Lonn (2013) surveyed both users and non-users of library tools in the LMS and found that both groups reported low awareness of available library tools and services; they recommended that promotion and outreach should be coupled with attention to visibility and user-friendliness of the tools themselves to overcome this obstacle.

The present study builds upon recent efforts to focus substantially on qualitative user feedback to inform the design of library integrations in the LMS.

Method

Faculty recruited for this study participated in the Advanced Design workshop series hosted by PSU's Center for Online Learning during Summer 2012. The workshop series included a two-hour librarian-led session about information literacy outcomes and assignment goals. All of the faculty in this workshop learned about the library widget and linked subject guides. The authors expected these faculty members to have a high level of awareness of library services and to be "power users" of D2L.

The authors sent an invitation to participate in an online survey to the 27 instructors who completed the Advanced Design workshop series (Appendix 10.A). The survey instrument (Appendix 10.B) included an invitation to participate in a face-to-face follow-up interview (Appendix 10.C). Of the seven faculty who completed the survey, all agreed to be contacted to arrange an interview. The authors were able to schedule interviews with six faculty members. The survey response of the seventh faculty member was excluded from the analysis as it became clear that the most substantial feedback surfaced in the interviews.

Four of the interviews were conducted in the faculty member's office or a convenient conference room. Using a library laptop and external microphone, the authors used Camtasia to record the screen and audio during the interviews. The other two interviews were conducted over Google Hangouts because interviewees were unable to

meet in person. Those interviews were recorded to YouTube using Hangouts On Air; immediately after the interviews, the videos were made private. For both the in-person and the online interviews, Author Hofer conducted the interviews while Author Munro typed a transcript of each interview on a second laptop.

The authors reviewed the interview transcripts independently and tagged consistent or salient themes. They then compared tags and reviewed the transcripts again to create tag clusters grouping related ideas together. The authors' goal was to draw the most relevant and useful comments from each interview, compare them, and identify tensions and insights that could productively inform the PSU Library strategy for embedding in D2L. Participants were assigned numeric codes (P1, P2, P3...) and quotations from interviews were also labeled with the corresponding interview question number (Q1, Q2, Q3...).

Additionally, the authors consulted usage data generated by the library widget, including transaction logs, chat transcripts, and catalog search terms. The authors compared these quantitative data with comments from the interviews to investigate whether faculty reports of perceived usefulness matched the behavior of students in their courses. One interviewee did not use D2L, and one interviewee did not use the library's D2L widget (instead setting up a custom box with a hard-coded link to the course guide). Therefore, the authors looked at course-specific D2L data for four courses.

Limitations of the Study

This study gathered qualitative feedback from faculty users of the PSU library widget to model substantive inquiry into user needs and determine the value of the service to users. However, the sample size of six interviews is too small to provide generalizable results. The themes and ideas reflected in this study must be considered suggestive rather than statistically significant.

The recruitment method for this study relied on invitations to faculty who participated in an advanced course design workshop, "Advanced Design," with a library component. The authors expected that many of these faculty members were "power users" of both D2L and the library. In fact, one participant did not use D2L in her course, although she had participated in the Advanced Design workshop. Other participants did not use the library widget for other reasons. In this sense, the recruitment method produced a more heterogeneous group than the authors expected, but it was still not a random or representative group of PSU faculty. Because the author (AH) was familiar with some of the participants before the study and because she made clear that she is a PSU librarian, there was an inevitable association with the library as sponsor of the study. This may have affected some participants' feedback.

Other limitations reflect data collection methods used. Quotations are pulled from transcripts made during interviews and may not be completely verbatim. Further, data on student clicks from the widget reports only that a click occurred—not whether students interacted successfully with the information they retrieved by clicking.

Results

Faculty Value Clear, Professional Wayfinding, and Design

Most faculty commented on the look and feel of the library widget as well as on the overall design and function of the LMS itself. Their comments frequently focused on the need for the PSU library widget to distinguish itself from the surrounding LMS and to brand itself clearly as originating from and connecting to the library. Design and wayfinding issues were expressed in a nutshell by the remark, "Make it clear" (P3, Q7); examples of more detailed views on this theme follow.

- "Part of the problem is that everything looks the same. It all looks like D2L. I'm not sure students understand this is from the library specifically. If there was something in the widget like 'how you search for an article, what's a peer-reviewed article,' it would still need something to differentiate it from the text and visual content of D2L." (P3, Q5)

- "The 'ask us' buttons are the thing that stands out…. What seems very backgrounded is the course guide. I don't even recognize it as a link. Part of it is the ugliness of D2L…. I think the link to the PSU [library] website should also be more prominent." (P1, Q2)

- "There's not much explanation on the buttons for [students] to know who they're talking to and about what. There's very little I like about the widget. I like that the subject guide is there, right on the face of it. But it could be made more attractive to the eye…. I think the design isn't enhancing the usability and needs to be thought about." (P6, Q4a)

- "One thing I don't think students understand is that 'ask us' is linked to the library specifically. Just because of the way everything in D2L is laid out. One would think that it's clear and makes sense, but I'm not sure they get that it's connecting to the librarians." (P3, Q4.)

- "'Find books and articles' may be clearer [wording for the widget catalog search box] than 'find books and more… ,' which implies they may find a YouTube video or whatever. That tantalizing ellipsis! What am I going to find?" (P3, Q7)

- "[The widget] was there for a term or two, and I didn't even notice it." (P4, Q1)

- "Oh my God, I never noticed I could go directly to the library website." (P5, Q2)

Faculty Value Having Multiple Library Services Bundled in One Consistent Location

Faculty commented that the core function of the widget—to provide access to a range of library services from within the context of the course page—was useful. Some saw the widget as a "portal" to the library, offering access to librarians as well as research guides and the catalog. Others commented that they specifically directed their students to use the link from the widget to access their subject-specific research guides because they knew this link would be consistent and easy for students to find and remember. PSU students and faculty alike are very busy, so the efficiency of convenient access is valuable.

- "I like that it drives them to the library portal [website]. It helps interrupt their frustration the most. Gets them through there. Another helpful thing is it's all in the same place." (P2, Q4b)
- "One less hurdle. Just look things up in the search bar—I would simplify it a bit so they don't have to go multiple places to find things. Just use this toolbar, and it will get you where you need to go." (P4, Q3)
- "Whenever I talk about [the widget], I talk about accessing it via the course homepage. Why do I do that? So they know how to get there themselves, and I don't want them to rely on that link they saw somewhere in some instruction. I want them to know where it lives so they can get there when they want it…. If they know it's on the course homepage they can find it whenever they need it." (P1, Q1)
- "How can I use [the widget] to make the class better, more educational, easier on me?" (P6, Q1)
- "My guess is that their attention is pretty short. If they can't get something in two minutes, they move on." (P2, Q1)

Faculty Value Customizable Tools That Address Specific Student Needs

Faculty interview responses emphasized the ability to customize their course page according to the specific needs of the students and curriculum—perhaps reflecting their "power-user" status. Along similar lines, faculty expressed appreciation for tools specifically designed for their courses and assignments. Sample comments in this theme group included—

- "I made my own widget because I didn't trust whoever's job it is to get [the library widget] into my courses. So I just made one and got it in there." (P1, Q1)
- "I would want to change the color of the widget…. [I would like] something that was more customizable, so that I could add stuff to it. Some kind of update-able thing… to make it less static. So that it becomes not just the library but the research/resource widget. Make it the focus of 'here's where you find stuff, search for information.' Some text box in the widget where you can change information like a news feature." (P1, Q3)
- "Students are always asking me, is the course book available at the library? I don't know. So having a link to course reserves might be useful. Having a demonstration or tutorial of the research databases would be helpful…. Tell them what they're going to find and how they can find particular types of information for specific courses. Like a 'top ten' or 'top five' FAQ. Very customized." (P6, Q3)
- "Specificity is helpful for students. Otherwise they don't see the point of clicking through in D2L. [They think] 'How can it help me?'" (P3, Q2)
- "I think the course guide is helpful because it's so specific, and they don't have to wade through other things, which they're not always good at." (P3, Q4)

Faculty Value Information Literacy

Faculty recognize the expertise of librarians in teaching research methods, information literacy, and information management skills. While students come to class with a wide range of skill levels, faculty may feel they do not have time to address this discrepancy or consider it outside the scope of the class. Comments showed awareness that information literacy skills are distinct from content mastery skills and that they require separate instruction and practice.

- "[Students] spend two hours online, archive using Zotero, and don't remember how to get there a week later when they're working. File management is still a problem. So, a refresher on file management might be good. I'm answering those questions a lot." (P2, Q3)
- "I want to encourage students to get peer-reviewed articles and investigate if they're credible and relevant." (P4, Q3)
- "My expectation is that when I send [students] to the real world, they should know how to find EBSCO and other databases. But I don't get in and demo." (P6, Q1)
- "A student put in 'Howard's End' and 'socialism' [to the widget search box] and nothing came up, and I said, you may have to be more specific. But I didn't know what to tell him." (P5, Q2)

Faculty Do Not Always Feel in Control of How Their Students Use the Widget or the Library

Some faculty commented that although they demonstrate the widget or recommend it to their students in class, they are not sure that their students actually use it (one faculty member was very interested to learn that the library can retrieve click-through data to determine whether and how students use the widget). This uncertainty about student use extended from the widget to the library and its resources. Faculty expressed mixed feelings about this: pragmatism combined with a desire to build information literacy skills, self-efficacy, and independence in their students.

- "Students bypass the course homepage… I've demonstrated and showed it to them, but I can tell they don't go there, or I'm curious to know if they go there… I don't know if they're using it or not…. I'm trying to break them of learned helplessness." (P2, Q1)
- "Students don't tend to ask librarians much. Even with the [widget] buttons, I'm not sure they'll ask." (P6, Q3)
- "Part of academic life is knowing how to do a certain amount of research, and I assume they've learned how to do some of that in previous classes. But some people remember or get it better than others. So some direct links and tutorials would be helpful, for how to get the most out of your research time." (P6, Q3)
- "I don't talk to [students] much about [research] because I think they probably know how to do it more than I do." (P5, Q2)
- "Honestly, as great as it is to have a librarian help with research, I want my students to learn how to do it themselves…. We should have students who know their way around the library and are able to do the research. We shouldn't have to rely on them going to a librarian for everything." (P6, Q6)
- "Less navigation is better. The less they have to type in on their own… typing in a website on their own is too much. I don't know why they can't find it. But even having the links to e-books in my [course guide] produces so much more compliance than having them look up e-books on their own." (P3, Q6)

Faculty Want Today's Students to Connect with the Library

Faculty commented that they consider the library an integral part of the undergraduate experience, but are not sure how or whether their students are using library services. Several faculty commented on the importance of the library as a physical location, both for browsing collections and contacting librarians, and as a social hub for students. Comments also revealed awareness of a generational or professional disjuncture between how the faculty learned and how they teach, and how students today navigate library and campus resources.

- "It's important for them to think about the library. I really want the library to be a presence for them as a resource, especially in online courses. If you can't figure it out, use the buttons to contact a librarian. I really encourage them to contact librarians. I don't know if they do it or not." (P1, Q1)
- "I often try to get people to go to the library. We talk about the difference between browsing online and in the shelves. To see what different ideas get triggered. I think they should do both. If you browse online you find different things than if you browse in the library. Because you don't have any idea what you'll find when you go over there." (P5, Q1)
- "I'm trying to use the library as much as possible. I often give extra credit (or pretend to) for students who have actually gone to the library. I ask who's gone to the library and a lot of people (even seniors) have never gone into the building. Which is no big deal if they use it in other ways. But going in, you see people and make friends. It's why people go to coffee shops. You get bored at home. And distracted." (P5, Q7)
- "I used to tell [students] 'no online sources' to get them into the library. Now, there's all this online technology, and you can do well in school without ever going into the library, which breaks my heart as a scholar and for aesthetic reasons. There's so much good stuff there that you'll never find if you don't go in and look at the shelves." (P4, Q3)
- "There are things I'd like to do [in the widget] as an instructor that would just confuse students. Like, I'd want to go straight to Philosopher's Index [from the widget search box]." (P4, Q3)
- "I love a good romp through a library." (P6, Q6)

Faculty Highly Value Librarians and Share Their Perception with Students

Faculty repeatedly expressed appreciation for the work of librarians, both within the LMS and in more traditional roles, and attempted to share their appreciation with their students. At the same time, several faculty expressed an understanding that librarian time and resources are limited. In addition, some faculty commented that they thought design considerations or lack of context would prevent students from connecting with librarians within the LMS.

- "[High-touch librarian interventions] could be really valuable. You'd want to minimize [librarian prep time] down to 15 minutes or so. Students could do group presentations to research a topic. Once they do it, maybe give it to the librarian and have them explain to a future class what was good, what they could have done better…. That would be really great." (P4, Q6)
- "I've been so impressed with all that the librarians do. I'm overwhelmed with how much is there; we just need to know about it as instructors and start incorporating it." (P4, Q7)

- "[A high-touch intervention] would be totally cool, and it would integrate librarians into instruction in a way that I don't think students have any concept of. I'm constantly telling my students that librarians have master's degrees in information. They're not just shelving books. That would change how students see librarians and would reduce my workload." (P1, Q6)
- "People don't realize what a great resource librarians are. I try to build that up a bit, saying librarians understand research, not just books." (P6, Q4a)
- "[The subject librarian came] over and did a tutorial on databases and stuff. Connecting this to the research they do, the questions they go through, ends up being help-

ful. I feel like quality of research in final projects is getting better. I think it's working." (P4, Q2)

Quantitative Data results

In addition to the qualitative data collected in the faculty interviews, the authors analyzed quantitative data generated by the widget logs for the five quarters spanning Winter 2012–Winter 2013.[2]

During this time period, there were 6,393 active courses in D2L—3,132 unique courses logged clicks in the library widget. This represents a basic usage rate of 49%.

Click-through rate measures the number of clicks in the widget per homepage views. Counting views and clicks for all users (faculty and students) shows that over the time period for which

Table 10.1. Clicks in Courses Taught by Faculty Interviewed, Faculty Perceptions of Use, and Faculty Efforts to Promote Widget

Participant	Clicks from course	[In your opinion], how useful is the widget? (Interview data)	If you direct your students to use the library widget, how do you do so? (Multiple-select survey data)
P2	3 clicks[1]	"I've demonstrated and shown it to them but I can tell they don't go there, or I'm curious to know if they go there... I don't know if they're using the widget or not." (P2, Q1)	I point it out to them in person or in my course materials; I suggest the library as a resource for their research; I demonstrate how to use the widget.
P3	64 clicks	"[Students] don't see the point of clicking through in D2L. 'How can it help me?'... They rarely use 'find books' in the library resources box. Just the way I've seen them work.... For the long term, the widget would be more helpful because it would provide direct access for the online student to find what they need within D2L.... less navigation is better." (P3, Q2)	I point it out to them in person or in my course materials; I suggest the library as a resource for their research; I state my expectation that my students will use the widget to access library content.
P4	2 clicks	"I should get student feedback but I think it's a good thing.... Connecting [librarian-led one-shot] to the research they do, the questions they go through ends up being helpful. I feel like the quality of research in final projects is getting better. I think it's working." (P4, Q2)	I point it out to them in person or in my course materials; I suggest the library as a resource for their research; I state my expectation that my students will use the widget to access library content; I demonstrate how to use the widget; this term I invited a representative from the library to provide a short tutorial.
P6	0 clicks	"I haven't used the widget. And mine is not a research class." (P6, Q1)	I don't think the widget requires explanation for students to use it.

data is available, there were 14,712 clicks on widget features out of 8,155,591 course homepage views, for an overall click-through rate of .18%.

Table 10.1 presents click data for the courses taught by the faculty interviewed. The authors compared the use data both with faculty perceptions of widget use by their students as reported in the interviews and with faculty efforts to promote or demonstrate the widget as reported in the survey.

Table 10.2 separates click data by widget feature to better understand how the widget was used beyond the basic function of providing a library presence in the LMS. Data are expressed as clicks on a specific widget feature as a percent of total clicks for that course (or as a percent of total clicks overall for the overall average). It is not possible to determine in which course a catalog search originated. As noted earlier, one limitation of transaction log analysis is that it is only possible to count views and clicks. Generally speaking, it is not possible to know whether a user viewing the course homepage looked at the library widget at all or whether a click in the widget resulted in the user being satisfied with the resulting information.

Data from chat reference and catalog searches, however, offer a deeper view into user behavior.

PSU's chat tool was configured to make this analysis possible for two quarters, Fall 2012 and Winter 2013. Out of 188 widget clicks on the chat button during this time period, there were 29 chat transcripts logged, meaning that 15% of users made the transition from a widget click to a chat reference interaction. Chat reference transcripts were analyzed to determine that eight (28%) of these interactions could be characterized as library reference questions that were successfully answered. Ten (34%) were dropped calls, and 11 (38%) were operational questions about D2L. Overall chat statistics show that 0.7% of chat reference traffic originates in the D2L widget.

Finally, Table 10.3 presents the most frequently used search terms in the widget's catalog search box.

Discussion

Design considerations were among the most-critiqued aspects of the PSU library widget, making this a highly salient finding. As one faculty

Table 10.2. Use of Specific Widget Feature as a Percent of Total Use

Participant	Course or subject guide	Catalog search	E-mail form	Library homepage	No available guide default page	Ask us!	Chat box	[In your opinion], what is the most valuable feature of the widget for your students? (Interview data)
Overall rate	44%	19%	15%	10%	4%	4%	3%	–
P2	66%	NA	–	–	–	–	33%	"They use the chat the most." (P2, Q4)
P3	94%	NA	2%	3%	–	2%	–	"Course guide." (P3, Q4a)
P4	100%	NA	–	–	-	–	—	"I think the 'ask us' button. Really good to have that browsing/ search bar there to find sources as well." (P4, Q4a)
P6	–	NA	–	–	–	–	–	"Students don't tend to ask librarians much." (P6, Q4a)

Table 10.3. Top Catalog Searches from D2L Widget

Search term	# of searches	Notes
No term entered	641	Delete default text and click "search"
Find books & more… (default text)	145	Click "search" without changing default text
Tal Como Somos: The Latino GBT Community	20	Video available through Films on Demand database
Switch: A Community in Transition	17	Video available through Films on Demand database
Galtung, J. (1969). Violence, peace, and peace research. *Journal of Peace Research, 6*(3), 167–191.	13	Entire APA citation
Conflict Resolution	8	Video available through Films on Demand database
33434	8	Item number of "Conflict Resolution" video available through Films on Demand database
Managing technological innovation, Betz	8	Title, author search

member stated, "I think the design isn't enhancing the usability and needs to be thought about" (P6, Q4a). This concern is also raised in McLure and Munro's 2010 study of faculty and student responses to LMS integration strategies, in which users commented on "design features such as color schemes, white space, headers, buttons, links, and bullet points. They even commented on the aesthetics of functional features such as help links and search boxes" (p. 52). Faculty comments in the present study focused on several components of the widget's design, including its visibility and layout. These remarks underline the importance of visual design to library services and suggest that libraries can benefit from paying more attention to design.

Quantitative usage data provide an additional dimension to these findings. For example, several faculty wondered if students were confused by the function of the widget's chat button based on its design. The usage data show that this concern is valid. Analysis of chat statistics and transcripts revealed serious problems with user experience after clicking on the chat button. A review of the chat transcripts shows that many librarians did not know how to answer or appropriately refer questions about D2L, suggesting that improved staff training might be in order. Overall, very clear labeling is needed to provide context for the chat feature, particularly as users might not expect to gain direct access to a librarian via course homepages.

Faculty concerns about students' understanding of the catalog search box were also borne out by analysis of the search terms used. Over 25% of searches conducted from the widget were on a blank search box or the default box text. Other common search strings indicate misunderstanding of the purpose and functionality of the search box. Repeated searches for content available through the Films on Demand database suggests that more outreach to faculty about how to embed library content in courses would be productive. Faculty made specific suggestions about changes that could clarify the purpose of the search box in addition to pointing out that the catalog may not be the best place to initiate a search in every course.

Several participants emphasized their desire for customizable library services in the LMS. Nearly half of all widget clicks were on links to course or subject guides, indicating that links to contextually relevant course or subject guides are perceived as highly useful by students as well. This echoes the findings of Casden, Duckett, Sierra, and Ryan (2009) who reported that dynamically generated content relevant to the user's context had significantly higher use than static content.

All of these facts suggest that library services in the LMS should be designed with flexibility in mind.

Other themes that emerged from the interviews seemed to suggest tension or conflict within faculty perspectives. For instance, a number of participants praised the convenience of providing direct links to library resources within the course site. These comments were not surprising and are reflected in other studies. Bowen (2012) found that "a significant part of the value of the [library course guide] is its placement within the environment students use to access their coursework" (p. 461). However, while faculty emphasized the importance of making library resources easy for students to find, they were also concerned with building students' information literacy skills and their ability to do research independently after completing the class. This mix of comments suggests that faculty must balance pragmatism—students are most likely to use convenient resources—with the aspiration of increasing students' information literacy competencies. Time constraints, class sizes, and prioritizing disciplinary learning objectives all likely play into the decisions that faculty make in deciding whether to include information literacy objectives.

Another interesting tension emerged in comparing faculty perceptions of the widget's usefulness to actual student use of the widget's features as reflected in click-through data. Only one faculty member accurately predicted which feature (the course guide) would be most useful for her students. The data do not indicate which types of faculty commitment might correlate with increased widget use. It was clear, however, that the faculty member who promoted the widget and built an expectation of use into her course had the most widget use.

Faculty also remarked several times on how differently students use the library today compared to how they used (or use) the library themselves. At times, these comments seemed to hint at tensions in the faculty-student relationship. Faculty and students face a wide range of pres-

sures, which in turn make it more important to design user-friendly library services. There is an opportunity for the library to offer consistent services both in person and within the LMS, helping to smooth potential sources of disconnect between faculty and students.

Finally, although faculty expressed enthusiasm for many of the high- and low-touch integration strategies mentioned during the interviews, there are other lower-threshold issues that warrant attention first. For example, one faculty member commented that she created her own library widget because she did not trust that the default widget would function correctly. Others were not aware of the widget's features or believed that their students would not understand them. On the most basic level, the view and click data collected for the widget suggest room for improvement. Design changes to the widget overall and to individual features may well increase traffic to the widget since more than one faculty member commented that the widget is currently easy to overlook on the course homepage. This kind of feedback suggests that there is still work to be done at a fundamental level—raising awareness, building trust, and ensuring that the widget is a reliable element of the faculty toolkit—to ensure that the library's initial investment will be returned.

Conclusion

Participant feedback indicated that PSU faculty consider the library widget a useful tool with some qualifications. Faculty expressed preferences for LMS embedding strategies that use good visual design, are customizable, save faculty and student time and energy, and collocate course- and discipline-specific library resources. Several faculty members emphasized the importance of librarians to their teaching and recognized the unique skills of librarians in information literacy instruction. However, the feedback also suggested that some library services are not well advertised or represented in the courseware and that students may not understand how to use them. Quantitative usage data from the PSU library widget supports this conclusion as do the findings of Leeder and Lonn (2013). Low-threshold library interventions to redesign or raise awareness of the widget and its uses may be warranted before high-cost strategies to develop new tools are explored.

While the results of this study are not generalizable to all PSU faculty, there are many benefits to this study. It is helpful for librarians to practice gathering and analyzing qualitative data directly from users. This research method produces rich results that can make the library's overall strategies more efficient. In addition to its local benefits to the PSU library widget redesign, this study contributes to the literature evaluating user satisfaction with library LMS integrations.

An additional benefit of conducting in-person interviews is the increased contact time between librarians and users. In the course of conducting this study, the authors had social and professional conversations with study participants and other faculty and staff nearby. Some of these conversations led to on-site trouble-shooting sessions or to users knowing more about the library's services overall. All increased the visibility of the librarians and the library. Daly (2011) reports a similar benefit to her faculty interviews: "Several faculty members confessed that they wished they had done more to make their students aware of the [library] resources and hoped to be able to do so the following semester" (p. 83). The exact value of these informal face-to-face interactions is hard to quantify, but the authors believe it is significant.

Finally, while studies of this scale do not produce generalizable results, the library may choose to use some of the findings to pilot small "seedling" projects or experiment with changes to existing ones. In the case of this study, PSU library staff will use the feedback to inform an ongoing redesign of the library widget. The same findings could be used to inform broader surveys about user perceptions and needs or to steer new projects.

To expand on the findings of this study, further interviews could be conducted with faculty after a redesign of the PSU library widget, a promotion campaign could be designed to raise awareness of the widget, or another intervention could be organized to address the issues raised by this study. At a broader level, more library research could be done with a substantial emphasis on soliciting and analyzing user feedback. Washburn (2008) says that "further research should investigate whether faculty think student papers/projects are better as a result of the [library LMS integration]" (p.313). A study such as this would tie user feedback on library LMS integrations directly into learning outcomes.

The authors would like to thank Mike Flakus, lead web programmer at Portland State University, for his help with the quantitative data for PSU's D2L widget.

Appendix 10.A
Invitation to Participate in Study

Dear Advanced Design Faculty,

You are invited to complete a short survey about the library widget in D2L. This survey has a total of eight questions and should take about 5–10 minutes to complete depending on your responses.

Your participation is voluntary; there are no foreseen risks in volunteering for this study, and your responses will be anonymized. You may withdraw from this study at any time. You may not receive any direct benefit from taking part in this study, but the study may help librarians plan future strategies for embedding a library presence in D2L or another online course system.

By clicking on the "continue" button, you indicate your consent to participate in the study.

Thank you for your participation!

Amy Hofer
Distance Learning Librarian, Portland State University

Karen Munro
Head, University of Oregon Portland Library & Learning Commons

If you have any questions about the study, please contact—
    [Redacted]

Appendix 10.B
Survey Instrument

1. Please tell us the course number(s) of your Advanced Design course(s).
2. Does your class have a research component?
   In this context, research means that your students must use the library's print or digital collection to complete at least one of their assignments.
   Yes/No
3. Do you have the library widget on your D2L course homepage?
   The library widget is a box that contains a catalog search box, a link to the most relevant course or subject guide and buttons to chat, call, or e-mail a librarian.
   Yes/No/I don't know
4. Do you direct students to use the library widget?
   Yes/No
5. If you direct your students to use the library widget, how do you do so? Please check all that apply.
   a. I point it out to them in person or in my course materials.
   b. I suggest the library as a resource for their research.
   c. I state my expectation that my students will use the widget to access library content.
   d. I demonstrate how to use the widget.
   e. I do something else or want to explain further (please use "other" below).
6. If you don't direct your students to use the library widget, why not? Please check all that apply.
   a. I removed the widget from my course homepage.
   b. I didn't notice the widget was on my course homepage.
   c. I don't think the widget requires explanation for students to use it.
   d. There is no research component to my course, or the library's collections are not relevant to my course.
   e. I have another reason or want to explain further (please use "other" below).
7. The library widget is designed to help students and faculty access library content and services in their online courses. If you are familiar with the widget, please tell us how well you think it achieves this goal. We are interested in any specific details and examples that you can provide.
8. Is there anything else you would like to say about the library's widget in D2L?
9. Are you willing to be contacted for a possible follow-up interview on the library's presence in D2L? The interview should take no more than 20 minutes.
   Yes/No
10. If you would like to be contacted by a librarian who can work with you on any problems you have had with the library's presence in D2L, please indicate here.
    Yes/No

Appendix 10.C
Semi-Structured Interview Questions

1. How do you use the library's D2L widget in your class?
2. Overall, how useful is the widget?
3. More specifically, what would you like to be able to do with the library's D2L widget that you currently can't?
4. More specifically, what features do you like as they are?
    a. What do you see as the most valuable feature of the widget for your students?
    b. What do you see as its most valuable feature for you as the instructor?
5. Some libraries offer reusable online tutorials or automatically graded quizzes for online courses. How useful do you think these things would be compared to the widget?
6. Some librarians individually assess student work or hold real-time online office hours for online courses. How useful do you think these things would be compared to the widget?
7. Is there anything else you would like to tell us about the library widget in D2L?

NOTES

1. The open-source code for this widget—written by Mike Flakus, PSU's lead web programmer—is available from http://code.google.com/p/pdx-contextually-aware-library-widget/

2. The library's technology team inadvertently changed file permissions to "read only" while moving content to a new server during a power outage. The server access logs are unavailable from 11/6/12–11/8/12 and 11/18/12–12/8/12. This means that the data for Fall 2012 is missing 23 out of 77 days (30%). All catalog search data from this time period is available.

REFERENCES

Bell, S. J., & Shank, J. D. (2004). Linking the library to courseware: A strategic alliance to improve learning outcomes. *Library Issues, 25*(2), 1–4.

Black, E. L. (2008). Toolkit approach to integrating library resources into the learning management system. *Journal of Academic Librarianship, 34*(6), 496–501.

Bowen, A. (2012). A LibGuides presence in a Blackboard environment. *Reference Services Review, 40*(3), 449–468. Casden, J., Duckett, K., Sierra, T., & Ryan, J. (2009). Course views: A scalable approach to providing course-based access to library resources. *Code{4}lib Journal, 6.* Retrieved from http://journal.code4lib.org/articles/1218

Daly, E. (2011). Instruction where and when students need it: Embedding library resources into learning management systems. In C. Kvenild & K. Calkins (Eds.), *Embedded librarians: Moving beyond one-shot instruction* (pp. 79–94). Chicago, IL: American Library Association Press.

Flakus, M., & Hofer, A. (2013). Library widget for the LMS (with a dash of contextual relevance). In C. Kvenild & K. Calkins (Eds.), *The embedded librarians' cookbook: Recipes for making long-term connections* (pp. _____). Chicago, IL: Association of College and Research Libraries Press.

Ganster, L.A., & Walsh, T. R. (2008). Enhancing library instruction to undergraduates: Incorporating online tutorials into the curriculum. *College & Undergraduate Libraries, 15*(3), 314–333.

Gibbons, S. (2005a). Chapter 2: Course-management systems. *Library Technology Reports, 41*(3), 7–11.

Gibbons, S. (2005b). Chapter 3: Integration of libraries and course-management systems. *Library Technology Reports, 41*(3), 12–20.

Hanna, K. A., Minick, M. B., & Eiszner, J. W. (2007). A Nontraditional Application of MetaSearch: Using Ex Libris' MetaLib to Enhance Delivery of Full-Text Articles in a University Campus Course Management System. *Internet Reference Services Quarterly, 12*(3/4), 297–308.

Horn, A., & Owen, S. (2011). Deakin University Library: An active partner in the implementation of the new generation e-learning platform, Desire2learn. *IATUL Annual Conference Proceedings, 21,* 1–11. Retrieved from http://docs.lib.purdue.edu/cgi/viewcontent.cgi?article=1923&context=iatul

Ismail, L. (2011). Getting personal: Reaching out to adult learners through a course management system. *Reference Librarian, 52*(3), 244–262.

Jeffryes, J., Peterson, K., Crowe, S., Fine, E., & Carrillo, E. (2011). Integration innovation: Launching the library into a course management system. *Journal of Library Innovation, 2*(1), 20–34.

Leeder, C., & Lonn, S. (2013). Faculty usage of library tools in a Learning Management System. *College & Research Libraries.* Advance online publications. Retrieved from http://crl.acrl.org/content/early/2013/05/13/crl13-459.full.pdf+html

McLure, M., & Munro, K. (2010). Research for design. *Communications in Information Literacy, 4*(1), 29–60.

Shank, J. D., & Dewald, N. H. (2003). Establishing our presence in courseware: Adding library services to the virtual classroom. *Information Technology and Libraries, 22*(1), 38–43.

Washburn, A. (2008). Finding the library in Blackboard: An assessment of library integration. *MERLOT Journal of Online Learning and Teaching, 4*(2), 301–316.

Linking to Course-Specific and Subject-Specific LibGuides from Blackboard

Pru Morris and Deirdre R. McDonald

You know the feeling. You have a great new service; you've tried everything you can to market it, but you just can't get your faculty on board. What's a librarian to do? At Texas A&M University-San Antonio, the authors had this problem with their LibGuides. They had created a number of useful, relevant, and even course-specific guides and marketed them through outreach, faculty meetings, e-mail, and the library newsletter. The faculty loved them, but this did not translate into them linking the guides in their Blackboard, A&M-San Antonio's learning management system (LMS), courses, or syllabi. The authors needed a solution: a way to get the LibGuides into Blackboard automatically—without depending on the professors or the instructional designer to include them.

Over the past few years, there has been some discussion about ways to integrate LibGuides directly into a LMS (Bowen, 2012). Duke University integrated their LibGuides and LMS in 2008. Using a combination of JavaScript and a Django middleware database, they were able to pull information from each course's content to link it to the appropriate LibGuide. While this system was very robust and allowed for mid-semester changes, it needed programmers to make it work. Additionally, the system only directed students to a general subject area LibGuide. Course-specific guides had to be added manually to each Blackboard course (Daly, 2010). The (Third-)Party Librarian website offered a simple, JavaScript solution that could be implemented by technologically savvy librarians (Frierson, 2011). The only outside help needed was from the Blackboard administrator, who would have to embed the code in the LMS shell. The authors decided to test it out and see how it would work at their institution.

The authors must disclose that this was their first JavaScript; meaning, they are not expert code writers. However, they attacked this project with a "can-do" attitude, constantly bouncing ideas off of each other, and, eventually, they came up with a script that makes it easy for students to find course- and subject-specific research support. You don't have to be a techie to implement this for your institution—some of these instructions will sound complicated, but in practice they are much easier to accomplish than you will initially think. The instructions will take you through four easy to follow steps and, in the end, you too will be able to institute this at your library. One of the authors (PM) presented an earlier version of this project during Springshare's November 2012 SpringyCamp (http://help.springshare.com/springycamp-nov12/recordings). This version has been updated to be even simpler!

This chapter will outline the steps you need to take to link to course- and subject-specific LibGuides from Blackboard (the authors are currently using Blackboard 9.1, Service Pack 11). First, you'll need to make sure the course names and numbers show up in Blackboard. Second, you will edit the JavaScript for your institution. Third, you will test the script functionality. Finally, you will add the JavaScript to your Blackboard shell. In addition, the authors will review the advantages and disadvantages of using this particular script for your institution as well as discuss some key troubleshooting tips.[1]

Step 1: Display Course Name and Number

First things first. Work with your Blackboard administrator to ensure the course names and numbers are being displayed in the course menu (the left sidebar menu that displays when you are in a course) for each Blackboard course at your institution. The script reads the course name and number off the screen a student is actively viewing to know which LibGuide to bring up when the student clicks on *Library Research Guide*. The Blackboard administrator at your institution will need to do the following six steps in the administrative module of Blackboard to display the course names and numbers in the course menu:

1. Login to Blackboard as an administrator.
2. Go to *System Admin > Communities > Brands and Themes*. Figure 11.1 shows the left-hand side of the *Administrator Panel* in Blackboard, where the *Communities* section is located.

Figure 11.1. Blackboard administrator panel. This figure illustrates where to find Brands and Themes in the Administrator Panel.

3. Choose *Customize Default Brand*. Figure 11.2 shows the left-hand side of the *Brands and Themes* menu where *Customize Default Brand* is located.

Brands and Themes

Customize Login Page
Define the login page to meet the needs of your institution, or integrate with remote systems for authentication.

Customize Default Brand
Choose themes, color palettes, and navigation settings for the interface for your users.

Figure 11.2. Brands and themes menu. This figure illustrates where to find Customize Default Brand in the Brands and Themes menu.

4. Choose *Navigation Settings*. Figure 11.3 shows the *Default Brand* menu, where *Navigation Settings* is located.

Customize: Default Brand

Changes made here will be reflected in the Preview panel only. Click Apply all Changes to update the brand with these changes for all users.

Indicates a required field. Indicates unsaved changes.

| Themes and Colors | Customize Colors | **Navigation Settings** |

1. Tabs

Figure 11.3. Default brand menu. This figure illustrates where to find Navigation Settings in the Default Brand menu.

5. Under *Course Name Usage*, choose *Show Course ID followed by Course Name*. Figure 11.4 shows the *Course Name Usage* menu, where you can select *Show Course ID followed by Course Name*.

5. **Course Name Usage**

Choose how you would like course name to be displayed in the orientation bar and course menu.

Select
- Show Course Name
- Show Course ID
- Show Course Name followed by Course ID
- ⦿ Show Course ID followed by Course Name

You can reset the navigation settings to the defaults specified by the selected theme.

Reset Navigation Settings

Figure 11.4. Navigation settings menu. This figure illustrates the Course Name Usage menu, where you can select Show Course ID followed by Course Name.

6. Click *Apply All Changes*.

The course name and number will now be displayed on each course page. Figure 11.5 illustrates how the course name and number will be displayed in the course menu in a Blackboard course. They will be displayed at the top of the left-hand side navigation bar. The first step is complete!

Figure 11.5. Course name and number. This figure illustrates how the course name and number will be displayed in the course menu in a Blackboard course.

Step 2: Edit JavaScript

Before you start editing, here are a few things you need to know. You will now be working with a text file. You can either type the code yourself from Appendix 11.A, or you can get a copy of the authors' code from their Linking to LibGuides from Blackboard guide, located at http://libguides. tamusa.tamus.edu/linkinglibguides. You should use Notepad or another plain text editor to edit the code because a more complex word processing program may autocorrect or add formatting that would prevent the code from running properly. It is also important to note that you will need to copy and paste the finished code into a Word document if you plan to e-mail the code. Typically, the code will not pass through e-mail in a Notepad document or embedded in the body of an e-mail.

Now the fun begins—editing the script! First, open Notepad. Type in the code from Appendix 11.A, or copy and paste the code from the document on the authors' LibGuide (http://libguides. tamusa.tamus.edu/linkinglibguides). Save your text file (.txt). If you close your file and want to continue to edit it, you will need to open Notepad, and then, from Notepad, open the text file. If you double click on the text file, the file will open in a browser, and you will not be able to edit the code from there.

The first part of the script (shown below) tells the program where to look for the course name and number in your browser. You do not need to edit this part. This section of the code was simplified between Fall 2012 and Spring 2013 to reduce problems with different versions of various browsers. The authors have not had any issues with browsers reading the code since they simplified it.

```
<script type="text/javascript"
language="JavaScript">
var browserName=navigator.app-
Name;
{
var breadcrumbs = document.
getElementById('breadcrumbs').
innerHTML;
var courseIDstartin-
dex = breadcrumbs.
indexOf("courseId")+10;
var courseIDendindex =
breadcrumbs.indexOf("<\/
span>",courseIDstartindex);
var courseID = breadcrumbs.sub
string(courseIDstartindex,cour
seIDendindex);
var destName; var destURL;
coursePrefix = courseID.sub-
string(0,20);
}
```

Next, you will edit the script for your specific courses. You want to keep your courses in a specific order for a couple of reasons. First, a librarian's nature is to have things organized, right? Second, the code will be read through from top to bottom, and, once a match is found, a result will be returned, so you need your code to follow some sort of logical order. The authors listed their course-specific information (i.e., the information for an EDCG 5316 course) first, in alphabetical order, and then followed that with their subject-specific information (i.e., the information for all other EDCG courses). This way, a student in an EDCG 5316 course will be taken directly to the EDCG 5316 guide, and students in all other EDCG courses will be directed to the basic counseling guide (see Appendix 11.A).

Your first statement in the script will use an *if statement*. *If statements* tell the program that if a condition is met, do an action; if the condition is not met, continue to the next line of code. If you happened to see the SpringyCamp presentation, you will find that this part of the code has changed. The authors now use *coursePrefix.match* for both course- and subject-specific statements, a change that was made to simplify the code. The first line of this code is shown below. To edit this for your institution, you will need to change three things:

1. the course prefix (LIB101_0),
2. the name of the page you are pointing to (Get S.M.A.R.T. \@ Your Library: Surefire Methods and Research Techniques),
3. destination URL (http://libguides. tamusa.tamus.edu/getsmart).

Make sure that you do not remove the punctuation surroundings these items. (Items that need to be changed are in bold type below.)

```
if (coursePrefix.
match("LIB101_0")) {dest-
Name = "Get S.M.A.R.T. \@ Your
Library: Surefire Methods and
Research Techniques"; destURL
= "http://libguides.tamusa.
tamus.edu/getsmart"; }
```

You can continue editing the script for course-specific entries using *else if statements*. After the initial *if statement*, the program will read each *else if statement* in order until a condition is met. Again, you need to change the course prefix, name of the page, and destination URL for each entry.

```
else if (coursePrefix.
match("CRIM4340")) {destName
= "CRIM 4340: Special Top-
ics Research Guide"; destURL =
"http://libguides.tamusa.tamus.
edu/CRIM4340"; }
else if (coursePrefix.
match("EDCG5316")) {destName
= "School Counseling Research
Guide"; destURL = "http://lib-
```

```
guides.tamusa.tamus.edu/school-
counseling"; }
else if (coursePrefix.
match("EDCG5351")) {destName
= "School Counseling Research
Guide"; destURL = "http://lib-
guides.tamusa.tamus.edu/school-
counseling"; }
```

Next, continue editing the script for your subject-specific entries using *else if statements*. As before, change the course prefix, name of the page, and destination URL for each entry.

```
else if (coursePrefix.
match("LIB")) {destName =
"TAMU-SA Library Research
Guides"; destURL = "http://lib-
guides.tamusa.tamus.edu"; }
else if (coursePrefix.
match("CRIM")) {destName =
"Criminology Research Guide";
destURL = "http://libguides.
tamusa.tamus.edu/crim"; }
else if (coursePrefix.
match("EDAD")) {destName =
"Educational Leadership and
Administration Research Guide";
destURL = "http://libguides.
tamusa.tamus.edu/leadership"; }
```

If you have an ampersand (&), apostrophe ('), or at symbol (@) in the name of a guide, place a backslash (\) before it.

```
else if (coursePrefix.
match("EDBL")) {destName =
"English as a Second Language
\& Bilingual Education Research
Guide"; destURL = "http://lib-
guides.tamusa.tamus.edu/esl"; }
else if (coursePrefix.
match("WMST")) {destName =
"Women\'s Studies Research
Guide"; destURL = "http://lib-
guides.tamusa.tamus.edu/wom-
ensstudies"; }
```

For the last statement, you will use an *else statement*. In a nutshell, this statement means if all else fails, send the user here. Of course, change the name of the page and destination URL. In the script below, the authors sent the student to their LibGuides homepage.

```
else { destName = "TAMU-SA
Library Research Guides";
destURL = "http://libguides.
tamusa.tamus.edu"; }
```

The end of the script (shown below) tells Blackboard what to display in the Blackboard window when a user clicks on the *Library Research Guide* link. This part of the script also serves as a redirect screen. If a user has a pop-up blocker turned on, the user will be able to click a link that will open the guide in a new window. You do not need to edit this portion of the script.

```
document.write('<p>You are
being redirected to the
<strong><a href="' + destURL
+ '" target="_blank">' + dest-
Name + '</a></strong>. If you
are not redirected within 5
seconds, please <a href="'
+ destURL + '" target="_
blank">click here</a>.</p>');
window.open(destURL,"_blank");
</script>
```

After all of the course- and subject-specific entries have been altered, your script is complete! The entire code used at Texas A&M University-San Antonio for the Fall 2013 semester is available for your reference in Appendix 11.A as well as at our LibGuide (http://libguides.tamusa.tamus.edu/linkinglibguides).

Step 3: Test the Script

Step three requires you to have administrator access to a course on your Blackboard test server. If you do not have access to the test server, you will need to work with your Blackboard administrator to complete this step. First, login to your Blackboard test server, go to a course, and complete the following eight steps:

1. Turn off the pop-up blocker in your browser.
2. Enable Edit Mode. Look in the top, right

corner for *Edit Mode is:*. If the button is set to *OFF*, click it once to turn it *ON*. Figure 11.6 shows where *Edit Mode is:* is located.

Figure 11.6. Edit mode. This figure illustrates where the edit mode can be changed.

3. Click the plus sign (+) at the top of the left navigation bar and choose *Blank Page*. Figure 11.7 shows the + menu.

Figure 11.7. The + menu. This figure illustrates the + menu, where you can add a blank page.

4. Type in a name for the page. This name will display on a button in the left-hand navigation bar. Click *Submit*. Figure 11.8 illustrates naming the blank page.

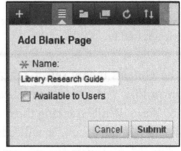

Figure 11.8. Naming a blank page. This figure illustrates how to name a blank page.

5. In the *Content* section, click the *HTML button* in the text editor. Figure 11.9 shows the content editor. The *HTML button* is located in the bottom right-hand corner.

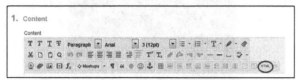

Figure 11.9. HTML button. This figure illustrates where the HTML button is located in the content editor.

6. Copy and paste your JavaScript into the *HTML code view* box and click *Update*. Figure 11.10 shows an example of how the code looks when it is pasted in the *HTML code view* box. Note that once you click update, you will no longer see the code as it will not be displayed in the content editor. The content editor will remain blank.

Figure 11.10. HTML code view box. This figure illustrates what the HTML code view box looks like with the script pasted in.

7. In the *Options* menu, select *Yes* by *Permit Users to View this Content* and *Track Number of Views*. While tracking the number of views is not necessary, it will allow your Blackboard administrator and each course instructor to access statistics at any time.

You will also have access to additional statistics through LibGuides. Figure 11.11 illustrates how to make these changes in the *Options* menu.

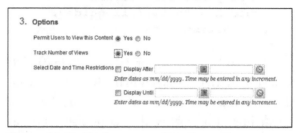

Figure 11.11. Options menu. This figure illustrates the Options menu, where Permit Users to View this Content and Track Number of Views can be changed.

8. In the *Submit* section, click *Submit*.

The script should run, and you should be redirected to the LibGuide for the course you are in. You should test your script in all four major browsers: Microsoft Internet Explorer, Google Chrome, Mozilla Firefox, and Apple Safari.

Step 4: Add JavaScript to Your Blackboard Shell

Once you are happy with your testing, work with your Blackboard Administrator to add the script to the Blackboard shell for the upcoming semester. Your Blackboard administrator can follow these same steps to add the script to the shell, and it will be applied to all courses.

Advantages and Disadvantages

Adding the script to your Blackboard shell provides several benefits. First, students can go from a Blackboard course to the best research guide available for a particular course or discipline with a single mouse click! Taking this a step further, even if a student has multiple courses in Blackboard, the student will be redirected to the Lib-Guide appropriate for whichever course the student is actively viewing. You don't have to include every course in the code. You can tell the code to send the students to course-specific LibGuides for some courses, for example, EDED 3303: Child and Adolescent Development, and then to send them to general subject LibGuides for all other EDED classes. And it's simple! One easy-to-implement script is all that is needed.

On the down side, the JavaScript must be prepared before the semester begins so it can be included in the Blackboard shell. Once the script is in the shell, you can make changes, but you will have to do so on an individual course basis, trying your best not to bug your Blackboard administrator too much. Also, if a student is using a pop-up blocker, the LibGuide will be blocked. However, a redirect link is available in Blackboard to account for this.

Workaround for a LibGuide in Progress

If you plan to work on a new LibGuide but need to get the code in the shell before the semester starts, you can use the following workaround. Yes, in this case, you can have your cake and eat it too! First, set a placeholder for the LibGuide in progress by creating the guide and giving it a title and a friendly URL. This guide will serve as a "dummy guide." Now, redirect the dummy guide to a working guide so your link will take students to a useful guide while you flush out your new guide. Add the title and URL to your script. Adding the title and URL to your script now will keep you from having to bug your Blackboard administrator mid-semester—do this now, so you don't have to mess with the code later. (Remember, you can't edit a LibGuide while it is being redirected, so you can't add content to the dummy guide.) Next create another LibGuide with the same title as your dummy guide and put your content in this one. When your LibGuide is complete, delete the dummy guide and give the second guide the same friendly URL you set the dummy guide up with. Voila!

If you happen to make a new LibGuide during the semester, you can always work with your Blackboard administrator to edit the code for those courses on the production server. Just remember that they are usually busy people, so they probably aren't going to want to make a bunch of changes mid-semester.

Care and Maintenance

The authors believe that the changes they made to the code between Fall 2012 and Spring 2013 simplified the code for working in various browsers and that those changes will alleviate the need to make lots of changes in the future. However, you may occasionally need to make small adjustments to your code as new versions of and updates for browsers and Blackboard are released. The authors will keep up with these on their Linking to LibGuides from Blackboard guide, located at http://libguides.tamusa.tamus.edu/linkinglibguides.

Conclusion

Embedding LibGuides into the Blackboard shell has been extremely successful in terms of use despite faculty unresponsiveness. The authors have seen the use of the guides increase every semester, especially course-specific guides. Table 11.1 illustrates the number of hits and percentage increase on the welcome pages of various research guides for the Spring 2012 and Spring 2013 semesters.

Table 11.1. LibGuides Welcome Page Comparison for Spring 2012 and Spring 2013

Guide	Welcome page hits Spring 2012	Welcome page hits Spring 2013	Percentage increase
EDED 3303	106	490	362%
HIST 4346	12	69	475%
Counseling	186	610	228%
English as a Second Language	130	148	14%
School Counseling	37	136	268%
Special Education	106	228	115%

None of the course- and subject-specific LibGuides were linked from Blackboard in Spring 2012, except for English as a Second Language, which included a link from the course to the subject-specific LibGuide within the Blackboard *Course Content* section. While the number of hits on the welcome page of this guide increased from Spring 2012 to Spring 2013, the percentage increase was not as dramatic. The authors believe this to be a result of how well embedded links to course- and sub-ject-specific research guides serve students in those courses.

By using the JavaScript to link to course- and subject-specific LibGuides, the authors are no longer dependent on faculty members or the instructional design team adding individual links to the guides within the Blackboard *Course Content* section. They are able to guarantee that students have access to the most appropriate guide for their course and provide a standardized access point to LibGuides across courses and disciplines.

Appendix 11.A
Texas A&M University-San Antonio's Script for Linking to Course-Specific and Subject-Specific LibGuides from Blackboard for Fall 2013

```
<script type="text/javascript" language="JavaScript">

/*First part of the script. This part tells the code how to read the
course name and number in Blackboard.*/

var browserName=navigator.appName;

{

var breadcrumbs = document.getElementById('breadcrumbs').innerHTML;
var courseIDstartindex = breadcrumbs.indexOf("courseId")+10;
var courseIDendindex = breadcrumbs.indexOf("<\/
span>",courseIDstartindex);
var courseID = breadcrumbs.substring(courseIDstartindex,courseIDendin
dex);
var destName; var destURL; coursePrefix = courseID.substring(0,20);

}
/*End of the first part of the script.*/


/*First statement. This will be an if statement.*/

if (coursePrefix.match("LIB101_0")) {destName = "Get S.M.A.R.T. \@ Your
Library: Surefire Methods and Research Techniques"; destURL = "http://
libguides.tamusa.tamus.edu/getsmart"; }

/*End of the first statement. */

/*Course-specific statements. These will be else if statements. */

else if (coursePrefix.match("CISA4321")) {destName = "Cybersecurity and
Information Assurance Research Guide"; destURL = "http://libguides.
```

```
tamusa.tamus.edu/cybersecurity"; }
else if (coursePrefix.match("CISA4322")) {destName = "Cybersecurity and
Information Assurance Research Guide"; destURL = "http://libguides.
tamusa.tamus.edu/cybersecurity"; }
else if (coursePrefix.match("CISA4325")) {destName = "Cybersecurity and
Information Assurance Research Guide"; destURL = "http://libguides.
tamusa.tamus.edu/cybersecurity"; }
else if (coursePrefix.match("CISA5321")) {destName = "Cybersecurity and
Information Assurance Research Guide"; destURL = "http://libguides.
tamusa.tamus.edu/cybersecurity"; }
else if (coursePrefix.match("CISA5322")) {destName = "Cybersecurity and
Information Assurance Research Guide"; destURL = "http://libguides.
tamusa.tamus.edu/cybersecurity"; }
else if (coursePrefix.match("CISA5359")) {destName = "Cybersecurity and
Information Assurance Research Guide"; destURL = "http://libguides.
tamusa.tamus.edu/cybersecurity"; }
else if (coursePrefix.match("CRIM4340")) {destName = "CRIM 4340: Special
Topics Research Guide"; destURL = "http://libguides.tamusa.tamus.edu/
CRIM4340"; }
else if (coursePrefix.match("EDAD5383")) {destName = "Public School Law
Research Guide"; destURL = "http://libguides.tamusa.tamus.edu/educa-
tionlaw"; }
else if (coursePrefix.match("EDCG5316")) {destName = "School Counseling
Research Guide"; destURL = "http://libguides.tamusa.tamus.edu/school-
counseling"; }
else if (coursePrefix.match("EDCG5351")) {destName = "School Counseling
Research Guide"; destURL = "http://libguides.tamusa.tamus.edu/school-
counseling"; }
else if (coursePrefix.match("EDED3301")) {destName = "EDED 3301: Prin-
ciples of Learning Research Guide"; destURL = "http://libguides.tamusa.
tamus.edu/learning"; }
else if (coursePrefix.match("EDED3303")) {destName = "EDED 3303: Devel-
opment and Behavior of Children and Adolescents Research Guide"; des-
tURL = "http://libguides.tamusa.tamus.edu/EDED3303"; }
else if (coursePrefix.match("EDED3349")) {destName = "Social Studies
Methods PreK-12 Research Guide"; destURL = "http://libguides.tamusa.
tamus.edu/socialstudies"; }
else if (coursePrefix.match("EDED3359")) {destName = "Social Studies
Methods PreK-12 Research Guide"; destURL = "http://libguides.tamusa.
tamus.edu/socialstudies"; }
else if (coursePrefix.match("EDED3380")) {destName = "Special Education
Research Guide"; destURL = "http://libguides.tamusa.tamus.edu/edse"; }
else if (coursePrefix.match("EDED5354")) {destName = "Social Studies
Methods PreK-12 Research Guide"; destURL = "http://libguides.tamusa.
tamus.edu/socialstudies"; }
else if (coursePrefix.match("HIST4319")) {destName = "HIST 4319 \& HIST
4370: The Holocaust Research Guide"; destURL = "http://libguides.
tamusa.tamus.edu/hist4319"; }
else if (coursePrefix.match("HIST4334")) {destName = "HIST 4334: Civil
War and Reconstruction Research Guide"; destURL = "http://libguides.
tamusa.tamus.edu/civilwar"; }
else if (coursePrefix.match("HIST4346")) {destName = "HIST 4346: Texas
History Research Guide"; destURL = "http://libguides.tamusa.tamus.edu/
txhist"; }
```

```
else if (coursePrefix.match("HIST4356")) {destName = "HIST 4356: Mex-
ico Research Guide"; destURL = "http://libguides.tamusa.tamus.edu/
HIST4356"; }
else if (coursePrefix.match("HIST4358")) {destName = "HIST 4358 \& HIST
4396: Asian History Research Guide"; destURL = "http://libguides.
tamusa.tamus.edu/HIST4358"; }
else if (coursePrefix.match("HIST4370")) {destName = "HIST 4319 \& HIST
4370: The Holocaust Research Guide"; destURL = "http://libguides.
tamusa.tamus.edu/hist4319"; }
else if (coursePrefix.match("HIST4380")) {destName = "HIST 4380: Special
Topics Research Guide"; destURL = "http://libguides.tamusa.tamus.edu/
HIST4380"; }
else if (coursePrefix.match("HIST4396")) {destName = "HIST 4358 \& HIST
4396: Asian History Research Guide"; destURL = "http://libguides.
tamusa.tamus.edu/HIST4358"; }
else if (coursePrefix.match("MKTG4363")) {destName = "International Mar-
keting Research Guide"; destURL = "http://libguides.tamusa.tamus.edu/
internationalmarketing"; }
else if (coursePrefix.match("MKTG5363")) {destName = "International Mar-
keting Research Guide"; destURL = "http://libguides.tamusa.tamus.edu/
internationalmarketing"; }
else if (coursePrefix.match("MKTG5369")) {destName = "MKTG 5369: Brand
Management Research Guide"; destURL = "http://libguides.tamusa.tamus.
edu/brandmarketing"; }
else if (coursePrefix.match("PSYC3381")) {destName = "Data for the
Social Sciences Research Guide"; destURL = "http://libguides.tamusa.
tamus.edu/SSData"; }
else if (coursePrefix.match("SOCI3381")) {destName = "Data for the
Social Sciences Research Guide"; destURL = "http://libguides.tamusa.
tamus.edu/SSData"; }

/*End of course-specific statements. */


/*Subject-specific statements. These will be else if statements. */

else if (coursePrefix.match("LIB")) {destName = "TAMU-SA Library
Research Guides"; destURL = "http://libguides.tamusa.tamus.edu"; }
else if (coursePrefix.match("ACCT")) {destName = "Accounting Research
Guide"; destURL = "http://libguides.tamusa.tamus.edu/accounting"; }
else if (coursePrefix.match("BCOM")) {destName = "Business Research
Guide"; destURL = "http://libguides.tamusa.tamus.edu/business"; }
else if (coursePrefix.match("BIOL")) {destName = "Biology Research
Guide"; destURL = "http://libguides.tamusa.tamus.edu/bio"; }
else if (coursePrefix.match("BLAW")) {destName = "Business Research
Guide"; destURL = "http://libguides.tamusa.tamus.edu/business"; }
else if (coursePrefix.match("BUAD")) {destName = "Business Research
Guide"; destURL = "http://libguides.tamusa.tamus.edu/business"; }
else if (coursePrefix.match("CHEM")) {destName = "Databases by Subject:
Science/Technology"; destURL = "http://libguides.tamusa.tamus.edu/con-
tent.php?pid=295802&sid=2428694"; }
else if (coursePrefix.match("CISA")) {destName = "Computer Information
Systems Research Guide"; destURL = "http://libguides.tamusa.tamus.edu/
cis"; }
```

```
else if (coursePrefix.match("COMM")) {destName = "Communications
Research Guide"; destURL = "http://libguides.tamusa.tamus.edu/comm"; }
else if (coursePrefix.match("COMJ")) {destName = "Communications
Research Guide"; destURL = "http://libguides.tamusa.tamus.edu/comm"; }
else if (coursePrefix.match("CRIM")) {destName = "Criminology Research
Guide"; destURL = "http://libguides.tamusa.tamus.edu/crim"; }
else if (coursePrefix.match("CSCI")) {destName = "Computer Information
Systems Research Guide"; destURL = "http://libguides.tamusa.tamus.edu/
cis"; }
else if (coursePrefix.match("ECON")) {destName = "Economics Research
Guide"; destURL = "http://libguides.tamusa.tamus.edu/economics"; }
else if (coursePrefix.match("EDAD")) {destName = "Educational Leadership
and Administration Research Guide"; destURL = "http://libguides.tamusa.
tamus.edu/leadership"; }
else if (coursePrefix.match("EDBL")) {destName = "English as a Second
Language \& Bilingual Education Research Guide"; destURL = "http://lib-
guides.tamusa.tamus.edu/esl"; }
else if (coursePrefix.match("EDCG")) {destName = "Counseling Research
Guide"; destURL = "http://libguides.tamusa.tamus.edu/counseling"; }
else if (coursePrefix.match("EDEC")) {destName = "Early Childhood Edu-
cation Research Guide"; destURL = "http://libguides.tamusa.tamus.edu/
ece"; }
else if (coursePrefix.match("EDED")) {destName = "Education Research
Guide"; destURL = "http://libguides.tamusa.tamus.edu/eduresearch"; }
else if (coursePrefix.match("EDFR")) {destName = "Education Research
Guide"; destURL = "http://libguides.tamusa.tamus.edu/edfr"; }
else if (coursePrefix.match("EDHL")) {destName = "Education Research
Guide"; destURL = "http://libguides.tamusa.tamus.edu/health"; }
else if (coursePrefix.match("EDKN")) {destName = "Kinesiology Research
Guide"; destURL = "http://libguides.tamusa.tamus.edu/kinesiology"; }
else if (coursePrefix.match("EDRG")) {destName = "Reading Research
Guide"; destURL = "http://libguides.tamusa.tamus.edu/reading"; }
else if (coursePrefix.match("EDSE")) {destName = "Special Education
Research Guide"; destURL = "http://libguides.tamusa.tamus.edu/edse"; }
else if (coursePrefix.match("EDSL")) {destName = "English as a Second
Language \& Bilingual Education Research Guide"; destURL = "http://lib-
guides.tamusa.tamus.edu/esl"; }
else if (coursePrefix.match("ENGL")) {destName = "Databases by Subject:
Humanities"; destURL = "http://libguides.tamusa.tamus.edu/content.
php?pid=295802&sid=2428689"; }
else if (coursePrefix.match("FINC")) {destName = "Finance Research
Guide"; destURL = "http://libguides.tamusa.tamus.edu/finance"; }
else if (coursePrefix.match("GEOG")) {destName = "Databases by Subject:
Science/Technology"; destURL = "http://libguides.tamusa.tamus.edu/con-
tent.php?pid=295802&sid=2428694"; }
else if (coursePrefix.match("HIST")) {destName = "Databases by Sub-
ject: History"; destURL = "http://libguides.tamusa.tamus.edu/content.
php?pid=295802&sid=2428688"; }
else if (coursePrefix.match("MATH")) {destName = "Databases by Subject:
Science/Technology"; destURL = "http://libguides.tamusa.tamus.edu/con-
tent.php?pid=295802&sid=2428694"; }
else if (coursePrefix.match("MGMT")) {destName = "Management Research
Guide"; destURL = "http://libguides.tamusa.tamus.edu/management"; }
else if (coursePrefix.match("MKTG")) {destName = "Marketing Research
```

```
Guide"; destURL = "http://libguides.tamusa.tamus.edu/marketing"; }
else if (coursePrefix.match("MSCI")) {destName = "Databases by Subject:
Government Resources"; destURL = "http://libguides.tamusa.tamus.edu/
content.php?pid=295802&sid=2428686"; }
else if (coursePrefix.match("POLS")) {destName = "Political Science
Research Guide"; destURL = "http://libguides.tamusa.tamus.edu/polisci";
}
else if (coursePrefix.match("PSYC")) {destName = "Psychology Research
Guide"; destURL = "http://libguides.tamusa.tamus.edu/psych"; }
else if (coursePrefix.match("SOCI")) {destName = "Sociology Research
Guide"; destURL = "http://libguides.tamusa.tamus.edu/soc"; }
else if (coursePrefix.match("WMST")) {destName = "Women\'s Studies
Research Guide"; destURL = "http://libguides.tamusa.tamus.edu/wom-
ensstudies"; }

/*End of subject-specific statements. */

/*Last statement. This will be an else statement. */

else { destName = "TAMU-SA Library Research Guides"; destURL = "http://
libguides.tamusa.tamus.edu"; }

/*End of the last statement. */

/*Last part of the script. This part tells the code how to display the
guide to the student. */

document.write('<p>You are being redirected to the <strong><a href="' +
destURL + '" target="_blank">' + destName + '</a></strong>. If you are
not redirected within 5 seconds, please <a href="' + destURL + '" tar-
get="_blank">click here</a>.</p>');

window.open(destURL,"_blank");

/*End of the last part of the script. */

</script>
```

NOTES

1. The authors would like to thank Eric Frierson, the (Third-)Party Librarian, who provided the initial code that got them started. A special thank you also goes out to Sherita Love, the Blackboard administrator at TAMU-SA, who helped test their code, gave them access to their Blackboard playing ground, and embedded their code in the shell for the first time for the Fall 2012 semester. And their gratitude goes out to Cesar Garcia-Hernandez, a senior systems analyst, who looked over their JavaScript and helped them work out the kinks in time to get it in the shell before the semester started.

REFERENCES

Bowen, A. (2012). A LibGuides presence in a Blackboard environment. *Reference Services Review, 40*(3), 449–468.

Daly, E. (2010). Embedding library resources into learning management systems: A way to reach Duke undergrads at their point of need. *College and Research Libraries News, 71*(4), 208–212.

Frierson, E. (2011). *The (third-)party librarian: Laughing in the face of impossible interfaces* [Blog]. Retrieved from http://thirdpartylibrarian.wordpress.com/2011/07/08/librarylinksinlms/

MOOCs: Getting Involved

Elizabeth Leonard and Erin McCaffrey

No book on librarianship and embedding into online learning would be complete without a discussion of the massive open online course (MOOC). The chapters presented in this work have provided examples of integrating library services into online learning environments. Can these same strategies for embedding apply to MOOCs, where students number in the thousands and their only common denominator is an Internet connection?

Wu (2013) notes that there is not much examination of the connections between academic libraries and MOOCs in the current literature. While the literature on academic library support for MOOCs is growing, most articles "are expository rather than analytical" (Pritchard, 2013, p.128). Here, the authors review the current literature on library involvement with MOOCs and explore avenues for collaboration. MOOCs create new opportunities for collaboration at a number of levels: between faculty and librarians, between students and librarians, between academic libraries at different institutions, and between public and academic libraries.

History of MOOCs

Many writers agree that MOOCs began in the mid 2000s, although Calter (2013) states that the first MOOC was the iTunes pilot program via Stanford, while Creed-Dikeogu and Clark (2013) suggest that the first "proto-MOOC" occurred at Utah State University in 2007. Most academics (Association of College and Research Libraries [ACRL] Virtual World Interest Group, 2013; Creed-Dikeogu & Clark, 2013; EDUCAUSE, 2011; Mahraj, 2012) agree that the first MOOC,

which was designed by George Siemens and Stephen Downes, occurred at the University of Manitoba in 2008. It was coined a "MOOC" by Dave Cormier of the University of Prince Edward Island (Creed-Dikeogu & Clark, 2013). Stanford professor and Google fellow Sebastian Thrun and Google Director of Research Peter Norvig developed the first MOOC to spark mainstream interest in 2011 (ACRL Virtual World Interest Group, 2013; Mahraj, 2012); it had an initial enrollment of over 100,000 students (EDUCAUSE, 2011). The popularity and diversity of the enrolled students garnered as much national attention as the notion of free education from such a well-regarded institution.

Currently, the major providers of MOOCs are the for-profits Coursera and Udacity and the non-profit edX. Coursera, a consortium of more than 80 colleges and universities, offers over 400 courses across a wide range of disciplines, partnering with academic institutions across the globe. Udacity, founded by the faculty of the first Artificial Intelligence MOOC at Stanford University, offers a smaller number of courses, primarily in computer science, business, mathematics, and science. EdX is a consortium of almost 30 colleges and universities worldwide. Non-U.S. based MOOC initiatives include FutureLearn, an initiative led by the Open University in the United Kingdom; OpenupEd, an Europe-wide initiative announced by the European Association of Distance Teaching Universities; and Open2Study, the MOOC platform of the Open Universities Australia consortium (Barnes, 2013).

Those institutions involved in MOOCs have provided a variety of reasons for their involvement in the modality. Smith (2013) writes that Duke University's involvement in Coursera's platform is based on fostering innovation, giving a global impact, and providing teaching experiences beyond the traditional reach of Duke's borders. Other institutions are using their MOOC experiences to leverage new endeavors. For example, Calter (2013) discusses Stanford University's early partnership with iTunesU, their experimentation with a variety of online learning endeavors, and the newly created position of a vice provost for online learning. The Stanford Libraries manage CourseWork, the university's implementation of the open source learning management system Sakai. While CourseWork is well utilized, the Stanford Libraries will be upgrading the system "and that work is informed by developments in MOOCs" (Calter, 2013, p.7). Pennsylvania State University expects their participation in MOOCs will generate additional interest in their online World Campus as well as provide an opportunity to examine teaching strategies and highlight expert knowledge of their faculty (Pennsylvania State University, 2013).

What Is a MOOC?

The definition of a MOOC is by necessity an amorphous one. With the MOOC landscape changing on a near constant basis, it would be inappropriate to define it in certain terms. Librarians and information professionals who have attempted this definition may end up disagreeing. For example, Calter (2013) notes that peer grading is "integral to the MOOC platform" (p. 4), while Creed-Dikeogu & Clark (2013) note the frequent use of digital auto-graders in MOOCs.

Several general trends seem to be consistent. The number of students in a MOOC is far higher than a traditional in-person or online class, numbering in the thousands. Enrollment is free. Fees are rarely charged for participation, although some platforms, like Coursera and edX, are starting to offer transcripts, credits, and identity verifi-

cation for minimal fees. Massis (2013) notes that, while the original MOOC model was one of free access, steps are already being taken to monetize and profitize the model. As a result, MOOCs experience huge dropout rates over the duration of the learning experience, again in the thousands. Since there are no admissions requirements, students may find that they have neither the time nor the interest or background to be able to complete the required work. "Course load is entirely up to the individual. The degree of freedom offered to learners is unprecedented" (Wu, 2013, p. 578). This freedom can lead to a lack of commitment. When both authors attempted to take MOOCs, they forgot to log in to the courses. E-mails from the course instructors got lost in their too-full inboxes. One's life can get in the way, and the lack of financial cost lowered the perceived penalty of missing the coursework.

Specialized pedagogies are also often seen in a MOOC. Like other online coursework, the MOOC frequently utilizes a flipped classroom approach (Calter, 2013), which emphasizes lecture learning experiences via learning objects and recorded video lectures outside of the "classroom" and utilizes classroom "time" as practice. Also, Masters (2013) notes that active learning is crucial to the success of the course. Without the participation of the students, there is no active knowledge transfer. Additionally, connectivist pedagogy, the development of knowledge through networking, is another important part of the MOOC paradigm (ACRL Virtual World Interest Group, 2013; Creed-Dikeogu & Clark, 2013; Mahraj, 2012). As the faculty cannot possibly have more than minimal contact with the thousands of students in the course, the majority of active learning will occur as students share and discuss knowledge among themselves. Peer grading may also serve as a valuable tool in evaluating the work of large numbers of students (Calter, 2013). Students can provide feedback on each other's work, generating another avenue for peer interaction and collaboration in the course.

Getting Involved: Intra-Library

Librarians interested in the MOOC phenomenon should increase their understanding of the modality by enrolling in a MOOC. This involvement will provide a wealth of insight into course structure and the pedagogies employed in the course, a first-hand understanding of student-student and student-faculty relationships, and an opportunity to examine the availability and use of external resources. This experiential assessment can help engender ideas for how the librarian can enrich the learning experience and support the faculty or sponsoring institution of a MOOC. Additionally, the experience of taking a MOOC will provide direct access to other students, which can engender anecdotal data on the needs of MOOC students. It may also help to take more than one MOOC across various MOOC platforms (e.g. edX, Coursera) as suggested at the Online Computer Library Center (OCLC) MOOC March 2013 event, "MOOCs and Libraries: Massive Opportunity or Overwhelming Challenge?" There is great value in comparing the experience from provider to provider and institutional sponsor. It is likely that these experiences will vary widely.

In each library, librarians can to organize MOOC-related activities within the library. Some examples include designating a librarian to act as point person for MOOC activities at your institution; capitalizing on the library's existing strengths in working with stakeholders across campus to hold strategic stakeholder meetings; and keeping your ear to the ground for institutional developments (OCLC, 2013). Networking with other departments that may be evaluating MOOCs, such as centers for technology in teaching and learning, distance/online learning, instructional design teams, and prior learning assessment, can foster communication and collaboration around MOOC issues and institutional decisions.

Getting Involved: Librarian-Student

Due to open enrollment, students in a MOOC represent an unusual cross section of higher education students; it is very likely that they will not represent any traditional college student population. As such, they will need extra support in many ways at many levels. Wright (2013) noted that the sheer size of MOOCs make it difficult to offer traditional library services. Additionally, traditional models of embedded online librarianship that involve students interacting with librarians may not be possible because MOOCs are hosted primarily by third-party companies (Wright, 2013); direct access to courses may not be readily available. Massis (2013) questions who will provide research assistance and library instruction to these large student populations taking courses through a provider rather than directly through the academic institution affiliated with the provider.

Indeed, enterprising academic and public libraries can develop learning and support communities for local pockets of students. Udacity provides learning communities on the popular site Meetup (http://www.meetup.com/udacity/), offering their students a voluntary opportunity to connect, get together to study, and share ideas. Libraries can serve as the physical meeting space for these communities. As participants of the OCLC MOOC event suggested (Proffitt, 2013b), librarians can create opportunities for students to discuss course materials in face-to-face groups or provide study and tutoring opportunities. Learning communities such as these can leverage the materials provided to a new level and may also encourage student retention in MOOCs through greater cohesion between individual students and between course materials and students.

White (2013) noted that, after taking three MOOCs, she felt it would take an "exceptionally motivated student to take full advantage of this type of course" (p. 281). MOOCs tend to last between four to 15 weeks, and White's

(2013) suspicion is that it is the expert or more experienced learner, not the typical undergraduate, is better able to keep up with the accelerated MOOC format. Librarians can help students by presenting synthesized course materials and open-access resources that support course activities to simplify the MOOC educational process. Supplemental wikis or LibGuides can be used to provide extra or alternative materials as needed. Sometimes, a list of frequently asked questions (FAQs) developed from prior students' inquiries can be of great use to students currently enrolled in the same course. These alternative modes of support will be necessary for librarians who may not have access to the course itself.

Information Literacy and Critical Thinking

In addition to copyright, one tool of the library's arsenal that has been ignored thus far in MOOCs may be vital to student success. Information literacy is a key part of the 21st century education experience. At the ACRL Virtual World Interest Group's "MOOCs and Librarians" event in February 2013, Valerie Hill of Texas Woman's University's School of Information Literacy and Studies noted the importance of information literacy in a digital age. Creed-Dikeogu and Clark (2013) suggest that a connectivist course structure requires strong information literacy skills because it is the students' responsibility for gathering and evaluating information. Because students provide so much of the learning experience in a MOOC, it is incumbent on them to be able to develop arguments and provide conclusions based on authoritative (or at least not spurious) sources. The student in the MOOC must be able to discern the quality of the information sources shared by the thousands of other students in the course. Since MOOCs are open to all, librarians cannot assume a baseline level of information literacy knowledge in students that they might ascertain from admissions standards at their own institutions. Therefore, it can be helpful to assume no skills with or

knowledge of information literacy concepts and create very basic lessons.

The University Library at the University of Illinois at Urbana-Champaign (2013) suggests that a way for libraries to get involved with MOOCs is to "create a sequenced information literacy course using screencasts, LibGuides, videos, exercises, quizzes, discussion forums" ("Libraries and MOOCs" page, "How Can I Get Involved?" section). Modifying an existing for-credit or required information literacy course into a MOOC allows a library to focus on transferable skills, such as critical thinking, and fundamental concepts around information organization (Wu, 2013).

Wright (2013) suggests that it may be too difficult for librarians to create information literacy tutorials for a MOOC due to the time needed to create such objects. However, the creation and implementation of low-touch learning objects could be highly effective in this medium. While it is true that online learning objects take time to develop, the front loading of this effort will lead to long-term positive outcomes. Such objects can be made for any MOOC in which information literacy is necessary. If the librarians have little time to create learning objects, there are many excellent open source alternatives such as those found at the Cooperative Library Instruction Project (http://www.clipinfolit.org). Librarians with access to the necessary software and possessing some technical skills can also add the MOOC's brand or make other changes to the object content. Other sources, such as the PRIMO database (http://www.ala.org/CFApps/Primo/public/search.cfm), ANTS (http://ants.wikifoundry.com/), or MERLOT (http://www.merlot.org/merlot/index.htm), are also worth reviewing for open source library and information literacy tutorials. The popularity of YouTube suggests that a MOOC Help channel could provide great value to students.

The OCLC MOOC event (2013) resulted in a suggestion that librarians could offer a course on "Introduction to Disciplinary Thinking," which would incorporate library research skills but also include knowledge specific to the academic area of the MOOC. The authors suggest that this idea may be better, not as a course, but as a series of low-touch learning objects that could serve students at a variety of academic levels and information literacy needs. These learning objects could be repurposed across courses, reaching large numbers of students with a single development effort.

Getting Involved: Librarian-Institution and Faculty

Librarians can reach out to local institutions to join their discussions around on-campus and online learning (OCLC, 2013). Mahraj (2013) contends the best use of librarians' skills in the MOOC environment is in taking on diverse, collaborative roles such as consultant, instructional designer, tutor, and collection developer (p. 365). Librarians can develop partnerships that align with institutional initiatives and volunteer to be on the MOOC support team (OCLC, 2013). Librarians can also create repositories of information related to MOOCs (OCLC, 2013) such as FAQs. These FAQs can be provided to both faculty and fellow librarians to help them with MOOC support and development. Information for these FAQs could come from a number of sources: copyright and fair use information, students' questions or feedback, product licensing, and open-access information.

Copyright and Permissions

Wright (2013) suggests that the librarian's first offer of support should be to the faculty member teaching the course, which may avoid technical and other proprietary issues related to the third-party MOOC provider. The traditional locale of copyright management has been the library, and many faculty continue to look to librarians to help navigate this area for MOOCs. It is also a far more complex area as there are few legal guidelines that were written specifically for the MOOC modality (Creed-Dikeogu & Clark, 2013).

It is not the intention of the authors to review MOOC and copyright issues in this chapter. For that, they suggest reviewing several excellent works on the topic, particularly the appendices of Fowler and Smith (2013) and Association of Research Libraries' issue brief, "Massive Open Online Courses" (2012). Rather, they do emphasize the necessity of offering copyright and permissions services to support MOOC development. The research from the OCLC event suggests that one MOOC can require hundreds of hours of copyright clearance work (Calter, 2013; OCLC, 2013; Proffitt, 2013a). Duke University's Center for Copyright and Permissions calculated managing copyright and permissions issues took the office an average of 27.5 hours per MOOC (Fowler & Smith, 2013).

Fowler and Smith (2013) wrote that faculty found value in the library's work (as part of the Office of Copyright and Scholarly Communications) with "permissions requests, consultations on fair use, and assistance locating open access alternatives" ("Feedback from Faculty," para. 4). It would behoove the library of every institution venturing into MOOCs to provide these services. The University of Pennsylvania Libraries (2013) have a "Copyright Resources to Support Publishing and Teaching" guide that includes copyright issues, fair use considerations, and resources for faculty participating in the university's MOOCs offered on Coursera. Smith (2013) contends that MOOC use is likely to fall under fair use because "fair use follows mission." The paradigm, he asserts, allows us to reexamine traditional models of copyright.

The Stanford Intellectual Property Exchange (SIPX) developed from research projects at Stanford University examining copyright issues, digital documents, and Internet law. SIPX (www.sipx.com) provides web-based digital copyright management and works with the Copyright Clearance Center and has partnerships with many publishing platforms. Calter (2013) points out that both users of the Stanford libraries' course management system and users of MOOC platforms can access content the library has licensed through SIPX. The University of Texas at Austin partnered with SIPX this fall to provide course readings to students enrolled in their MOOCs on the edX platform. The service is unique because it provides access to open access and public domain content along with copyrighted and licensed materials (Schwartz, 2013b).

Libraries need to continue to be strong proponents of new licensing models. As Wu (2013) points out, academic libraries and MOOCs appear to be on opposing sides of access. Academic library license agreements outline specific boundaries for access, typically only for current students, faculty, and staff of the institution. MOOCs, on the other hand, currently provide free access to all aspects of the course experience, from course content to many supplemental materials. It is vital to read any licensing agreement thoroughly to ensure the item is licensed for MOOC use; few actually are (Creed-Dikeogu & Clark, 2013; Fowler & Smith, 2013). MOOCs present a large potential market for publishers. The attendees at the OCLC MOOC event (2013) suggest working with platform providers and resource vendors to establish a basis for content licensing. Indeed, librarians can be integral to creating new models for MOOC licensing (Wu, 2013). Wu (2013) speculates as to whether the "iTunization of information" (p. 582) will occur, where publishers align with MOOC providers and faculty to offer information on a per view basis. The limitations placed by agreements with traditional publishers can serve as opportunity for libraries to advocate for open access.

Media and Accessibility

Since the selection of educational materials can be fraught with copyright issues, librarians can support the MOOC by helping to find and select open-access materials. Academic librarians understand licensing and the costs associated with access better than most in their institutions and are more aware of open access initiatives (Almeida, 2013). Additionally, they can support the classroom by providing media expertise in the area of filming and video editing (Calter, 2013). Since some countries employ geoblocking, preventing certain types of material from being viewed by its denizens (Fowler & Smith, 2013), Becker (2013) suggests that librarians can help ensure media can be viewed by global student participants by testing worldwide access to online media with sites like just-ping.com.

By obtaining the syllabus or course outline of the MOOC, librarians can identify open source, creative commons, or other appropriate resources for use in the course space and "synthesize public domain and free access archives" (OCLC, 2013). Librarians can employ lessons learned from the development of blended, flipped, and distance learning models and utilize existing tools such as social media, online chat, blogs, and LibGuides to extend assistance in the MOOC environment.

Materials for students with disabilities will be another area in which the librarian may provide expertise (Association of Research Libraries, 2012; Fowler & Smith, 2013). Educational institutions have a legal responsibility to provide equal access to all students, and faculty need to confirm that course materials are accessible to all students including those with disabilities. Librarians can assist in faculty in ensuring materials are accessible and examine current licenses for permission to modify content for those students using assistive technologies. MOOC providers and their partner institutions in all likelihood will share the obligation to guarantee content is accessible (Association of Research Libraries, 2012).

Instructional Design

Librarians may be able to help with both the instructional design of MOOCs and the incorporation of instructional technology in these courses. At Duke University, "the relationship between the professors and the online Coursera platform has largely been bridged by the Center for Instructional Technology," (Tuchler, 2013, para. 2) a department within the Duke libraries that helps faculty incorporate technology into their courses. The Stanford University Libraries have an Academic Technology Specialist program, where staff are embedded within a department to provide technical support for academic programs (Calter, 2013).

Archives and Preservation

Librarians should consider ways to archive MOOC course materials and user-generated course content (Wu, 2013). Librarians have an opportunity to serve as the architects in outlining preservation guidelines and utilizing institutional repositories in preserving content created by faculty for MOOCs. The role that librarians might have in developing recommendations for creating, preserving, and managing digital content for MOOCs is largely missing from the literature on libraries and MOOCs (Almeida, 2013).

Getting Involved: Librarian-Librarian

As librarians are generally excellent collaborators and team builders, another opportunity to get involved will be via library MOOC consortia. Participants at the OCLC MOOC event (2013) suggested creating different types of communication forms such as list-servs, MOOC communities, and consortium for librarians involved in MOOCS.

Several groups exist to bring together librarians on this topic. Eleni Zazani has set up MOOCs & Librarians on Mendeley (http://www.mendeley.com/groups/3599501/moocs-librarians/). Another community created by Jennifer Dorner of the University of California-Berkeley Library, MOOCs and Librarianship, has since been decommissioned (https://groups.google.com/forum/#!topic/moocs-and-librarianship/HH-

-IGymLYQ) now that the Library Support for Massive Open Online Courses (MOOCs) discussion group (http://www.ala.org/acrl/aboutacrl/directoryofleadership/discussiongroups/acrdgmoocs) was formally established by the ACRL. Working together at an early stage of MOOC development can ensure our continued relevance.

New Collaborations

MOOCs will lead to new types of collaborations; one in particular is that between academic and public libraries. The vast numbers of students taking a MOOC are beyond any academic library's ability to support. As mentioned earlier, enrolled students in a single MOOC can number over 100,000 individuals. Academic libraries simply cannot provide individual support for this many students. For this reason, students will likely turn to public libraries for support. Academic librarians can form partnerships with public librarians who are often already providing support to distance learners and MOOC participants in their communities (OCLC, 2013). Author EL has noted that students who need extra academic support in the online environment have turned to local public libraries for that support. Indeed, she found that providing information on local libraries was an important part of these students' needs. For some students, in-person support is necessary and desirous.

Mahraj (2012) further suggests that librarians themselves start a MOOC. Developing a MOOC focused on information literacy may be one way to dive into the MOOC waters. Library and information science faculty are also beginning to offer MOOCs. Dr. Jeffrey Pomerantz, associate professor and director of undergraduate studies in the School of Information and Library Science at the University of North Carolina at Chapel Hill, teaches Metadata: Organizing and Discovering Information on Coursera. While not directly targeted to librarians and library students (Schwartz, 2013a), it seems likely that library staff would be one segment of the student population. The Hyperlinked Library MOOC (http://slisweb.sjsu.edu/programs/moocs/hyperlinked-library-mooc) is focused on librarianship and was adapted from a San Jose State University School of Library and Information Science course into a MOOC for professional development. The New Librarianship Master Class MOOC (http://ischool.syr.edu/future/grad/newlibopencourse.aspx), offered through the iSchool at Syracuse University, was centered on new librarianship based on knowledge and learning.

Conclusion

MOOCs are still unfolding, and, as quickly as questions about this educational trend are answered, more arise. One of the biggest impacts of the MOOC phenomenon so far is that it has jump-started conversation about new technologies and new pedagogies as well as the importance of open access and repositories. MOOCs provide libraries the opportunity to collaborate and also reevaluate current library assumptions and practices (OCLC, 2013). MOOCs afford academic librarians the chance to think outside the box in providing services to a truly global population; to collaborate across institutions and across library types to partner in MOOC development and support; and to showcase their expertise in matters of copyright and open access, the preservation and organization of content, instructional design, and emerging technologies. No matter how we struggle to define ourselves, whether in the face of Google or in the face of a MOOC (Bohle, 2013), we will find a way to keep ourselves relevant. It is the nature of the information professional to be nimble and ever changing.

REFERENCES

Almeida, N. (2013, August 21). A new polemic: Libraries, MOOCs, and the pedagogical landscape. *In the library with the lead pipe*. Retrieved from http://inthelibrarywiththeleadpipe.org/2013/a-new-polemic-libraries-moocs-and-the-pedagogical-landscape/?format=pdf

Association of Research Libraries. (2012, October). *Massive open online courses: Legal and policy issues for research libraries* (Issue Brief). Washington, DC: B. Butler. Retrieved from http://www.arl.org/storage/documents/publications/issuebrief-mooc-22oct12.pdf

Association of College and Research Libraries Virtual World Interest Group. (2013). *MOOCs and librarians* [Slideshow]. Retrieved from http://www.slideshare.net/valibrarian/acr-lmooc-panelsildeshare

Barnes, C. (2013). MOOCs: The Challenges for Academic Librarians. *Australian Academic & Research Libraries, 44*(3), 163-175. Retrieved from http://dx.doi.org/10.1080/00048623.2013.821048

Becker, B.W. (2013). Connecting MOOCs and library services. *Behavioral & Social Sciences Librarian, 32,* 135–138. doi:10.1080/01639269.2013.787383

Bohle, S. (2013, May 9). Librarians and the era of the MOOC. Retrieved from the SciLogs website: http://www.scilogs.com/scientific_and_medical_libraries/librarians-and-the-era-of-the-mooc/

Calter, M. (2013, August) *MOOCs and the library: Engaging with evolving pedagogy.* Paper presented at IFLA World Library and Information Congress, Singapore. Retrieved from http://library.ifla.org/160/1/098-calter-en.pdf

Creed-Dikeogu, G., & Clark, C. (2013). Are you MOOC-ing yet? A review for academic libraries. *CULS Proceedings, 3,* 9–13. Retrieved from http://newprairiepress.org/journals/index.php/CULS/article/view/1830_

EDUCAUSE. (2011, November). 7 things you should know about MOOCs. Retrieved from http://net.educause.edu/ir/library/pdf/ELI7078.pdf

Fowler, L., & Smith, K. (2013). Drawing the blueprint as we build: Setting up a library-based copyright and permissions service for MOOCs. *D-Lib Magazine, 19*(7-8). doi:10.1045/july2013-fowler

Mahraj, K. (2012). Using information expertise to enhance massive open online courses. *Public Services Quarterly, 8,* 359–368. doi:10.1080/15228959.2012.730415

Massis, B.E. (2013). MOOCs and the library. *New Library World, 114*(5-6), 267–270. doi:10.1008/0307480311326894

Masters, K. (2011). A brief guide to understanding MOOCs. *The Internet Journal of Medical Education, 1*(2). Retrieved from http://ispub.com/IJME/1/2/10995

Online Computer Library Center. (2013, March). Next steps. *MOOCs and libraries: Massive oppor-*

tunity or overwhelming challenge? Retrieved from http://www.oclc.org/content/dam/research/events/2013/03-18moocs-next-steps.pdf

Pennsylvania State University. (2013, October 2). Penn State's early MOOC faculty share lessons from their classes. *Penn State News.* Retrieved from http://news.psu.edu/story/289952/2013/10/02/academics/penn-state%E2%80%99s-early-mooc-faculty-share-lessons-their-classes

Pritchard, S. (2013). MOOCs: An opportunity for innovation and research. *portal: Libraries and the Academy, 13*(2), 127–120. doi:10.1353/pla.2013.0015

Proffitt, M. (2013a, April 11). MOOCs and libraries: Copyright, licensing, open access. Retrieved from HangingTogether website: http://hangingtogether.org/?p=2677

Proffitt, M. (2013b, April 19). MOOCs and libraries: Next steps? Retrieved from HangingTogether website: http://hangingtogether.org/?p=2809

Schwartz, M. (2013a, May 10). Massive open opportunity: Supporting MOOCs in public and academic libraries. Retrieved from Library Journal website: http://lj.libraryjournal.com/2013/05/library-services/massive-open-opportunity-supporting-moocs/

Schwartz, M. (2013b, May 30). SIPX launches content, copyright service. Retrieved from Library Journal website: http://lj.libraryjournal.com/2013/05/technology/sipx-launches-content-copyright-service/

Smith, K. (2013, January 24). Peer to peer review: Making MOOCs easier [Blog post]. Retrieved from Library Journal website: http://lj.libraryjournal.com/2013/01/opinion/peer-to-peer-review/making-moocs-easier-peer-to-peer-review/

Tuchler, M. (2013, April 4). Duke librarians aid MOOCs with technology, research. *The Chronicle.* Retrieved from http://www.dukechronicle.com/articles/2013/04/04/duke-librarians-aid-moocs-technology-research

University of Illinois at Urbana-Champaign University Library. (2013, April 8). Libraries and MOOCs. *MOOCs at Illinois.* Retrieved from http://uiuc.libguides.com/content.php?pid=453057&sid=3712692

University of Pennsylvania Libraries. (2013, September 27). *Copyright resources to support publishing and teaching.* Retrieved from http://guides.library.upenn.edu/copyright

White, S. (2013). Reflections on MOOCs after taking three classes: Strengths and weaknesses. *Biochemistry and Molecular Biology Education, 41*(4), 280–1. doi:10.1002/bmb.20703

Wright, F. (2013). What do librarians need to know about MOOCs? *D-Lib Magazine, 19*(3-4). Retrieved from http://dlib.org/dlib/march13/wright/03wright.html

Wu, K. (2013). Academic libraries in the age of MOOCs. *Reference Services Review, 41*(3), 576–587. doi:10.1108/RSR-03-2013-0015

About the Authors

Chanitra Bishop

Chanitra Bishop is a digital scholarship and emerging technologies librarian at Indiana University Bloomington. Her responsibilities include exploring and recommending new technology to incorporate into the delivery of library reference and instructional services. Chanitra, a technology enthusiast, promotes the use of technology by libraries and librarians and has done presentations on online technology tools for librarians. In addition to exploring new technologies, her professional interests include accessibility and usability issues with libraries and exploring new ways to market library services to users.

Philip Clarke

Philip (Phil) Clarke is library manager at the Open Polytechnic of New Zealand. Since completing his postgraduate qualification in 1992, he has worked as an information specialist in government departments and the private sector, both in New Zealand and the United Kingdom. Phil's interests include measuring the impact of academic libraries on student success and developing strategies to incorporate library and information literacies into university courses.

Audrey Donaldson

Audrey Donaldson is an academic librarian at Montgomery County Community College, providing instruction to students in the classroom, reference support from within the library setting, and embedded library services from within virtual learning environments. Audrey's educational background includes a BA in computer science from LaSalle University; a MIS from Drexel University, with a Pennsylvania certification for K–12 instruction of library skills from Arcadia University; and a doctorate in educational leadership with a specialization in curriculum and instruction from the University of Phoenix. Pre-

vious experience includes 15 years as a school librarian for the School District of Philadelphia. In her current role, embedded librarianship highlights Audrey's strong belief in equitable learning opportunities. Audrey aims to address diverse learning preferences by providing pertinent tools within the learning environment while offering research support at the point of need.

Alison Fields

Alison Fields is a senior lecturer in information and library studies at the Open Polytechnic of New Zealand. She received her MLS from Victoria University of Wellington and is currently completing a doctorate in education by distance from Otago University. Before lecturing, Alison worked in public and academic libraries across New Zealand, from Dunedin to Auckland. She was awarded a Fellowship of the Library and Information Association of New Zealand Aotearoa in 2008 and currently serves on the association's Professional Registration Board. Alison's research interests include learner support in distance education, student support and success in the online environment, and continuing professional development.

Linda Frederiksen

Linda Frederiksen is the head of Access Services at Washington State University Vancouver. Before receiving her MLS from Emporia State University, Linda worked in both public and academic libraries. She is active in local, regional, and national interlibrary loan; document delivery; and resource sharing projects and initiatives. Current research interests include e-content copyright and licensing, international borrowing and lending, and improving library access to distance and virtual students.

Kristin Heathcock

Kristin Heathcock is a librarian at Hillsborough

Community College in Plant City, Florida. She received a MLIS from the University of South Florida and an EdD in curriculum and instruction with an emphasis in educational technology from the University of Florida. Her research interests include information literacy instruction for distance learning students, assessment of information literacy skills, and the role of the library in student success.

Amy R. Hofer
Amy R. Hofer has been a distance learning librarian at Portland State University since 2010. Her research interests include embedded librarianship and threshold concepts for information literacy instruction. By night she is a fiddler and square dance caller.

Swapna Kumar
Swapna Kumar is a clinical assistant professor of educational technology at University of Florida's School of Teaching and Learning. She coordinates the online doctoral program in educational technology and teaches courses on distance learning, blended learning, the design and development of online environments, technology integration, and media ecologies. Her research interests include online education (design, development, facilitation, and assessment); blended learning; online communities; doctoral education; and the integration of new technologies in higher education. Dr. Kumar's successful collaboration with information literacy experts at the University of Florida has resulted in an outstanding paper award at the World Conference on E-Learning in Corporate, Government, Healthcare, and Higher Education in 2011 and in publications in the *Journal of Information Literacy, Journal of Library and Information Services in Distance Learning*, and *Communications in Information Literacy*.

Julie LaDell-Thomas
Julie LaDell-Thomas is a distance librarian for Central Michigan University, providing user-centered reference and instruction and integrat-

ing web-based instructional tools to support the research needs of CMU's Global Campus students and faculty. She received her MLIS degree through the distance learning program at the University of South Carolina and earned a MA in educational technology online through Central Michigan University. She began her library career as a reference librarian for Dekalb County (GA) Public Library and then held various positions at the Southeastern Library Network (SOLINET)—now known as LYRASIS—a non-profit membership organization that provides support and training for academic, public, and special libraries. Julie has taught online classes as adjunct instructor for LYRASIS and served as the keynote speaker for the Tennessee Board of Regents ROCC 2012 Library Summer Academy.

Kathleen A. Langan
Kathleen (Kate) A. Langan joined Western Michigan University in 2009 and serves as the humanities librarian. She holds two master's degrees, a MLIS from the University of Wisconsin-Madison and a MA in French literature from the University of Oklahoma. In addition to serving as liaison to the English and world languages and literatures departments and developing collections for those areas of study, she is involved in other activities that include providing reference service, teaching information literacy, and implementing a digital humanities initiative. She is heavily involved in developing a library curriculum for the college-level writing course and is researching students' high school experience with the research process. Past research includes redesigning online tutorials for Millennials, the impact of background music on the retention of information literacy, and politeness theory and HCI in chat reference. Currently, research includes projects on threshold concepts and the academic dialog and the emotional and professional responsibilities of supervisors of student employees.

Elizabeth Leonard
Elizabeth Leonard is the Assistant Dean of

University Libraries for Information Technologies, Resources Acquisition and Description at Seton Hall University. She holds a MLIS from Rutgers University, a Masters in Urban Planning from NYU's Wagner School of Public Service, and doctoral work in Clinical Psychology. Additionally she has over 12 years of experience in Information Technology Management, specializing in project management, systems development and administration. Elizabeth is Chair of the Assessment, Evaluation, and Statistics Committee for the Virtual Academic Library Environment (VALE) of New Jersey, on the Board of the 2014 Distance Library Services Conference, and a co-founder, along with Naomi House, of the Facebook group, I Need a Library Job. She has published and presented on the subject of Online Libraries, marketing of online library services, and the value of academic libraries.

Erin McCaffrey

Erin McCaffrey is an electronic services librarian at Regis University in Denver, Colorado. Previously, she was a distance learning librarian at Regis University and an assistant instruction coordinator at DePaul University. Her research interests are in human-computer interaction and interactive media. She has experience in web-based library services, system administration, distance learning, and reference and instruction. Erin received her BA from DePaul University with a major in psychology and earned her MLIS degree from Dominican University.

Deirdre R. McDonald

Deirdre R. McDonald is an education librarian and instruction coordinator at Texas A&M University-San Antonio and a doctoral student at Texas Woman's University. She is embedded in a number of graduate and undergraduate courses each semester. Her research interests include ways to expand library outreach in virtual environments and Texas library history.

Pru Morris

Pru Morris graduated from Texas A&M University in 2001 with a BS in recreation, park, and tourism sciences. After graduating, she landed a job as a part-time library technical assistant at the Blinn College Library in Bryan, Texas. She quickly learned that working in libraries rocks (!) and pursued her MLS degree online from Texas Woman's University. She began her first professional position as a reference librarian and bibliographer at the University of Texas at San Antonio in 2005, and, during her four years there, she also held the position of interim instruction coordinator. In 2010, she began working at Texas A&M University-San Antonio, a new institution serving the south side of San Antonio, as a Library Specialist II and became a digital resources librarian a year later. She absolutely loves the digital resources career path and is now the digital resource manager at this up-and-coming institution.

Alex Mudd

Alex Mudd is a reference and instruction librarian at Emporia State University in Emporia, Kansas. He is a graduate of the School of Information Science and Learning Technologies at the University of Missouri. He has presented nationally on information literacy, and his research focuses on incorporating new technologies into instruction, distance learning service and e-learning, and instruction for students in the social sciences and humanities.

Karen Munro

Karen Munro is head of the University of Oregon Portland Library and Learning Commons. She is interested in transformative user services in academic libraries, outreach to users, and services to graduate students. She currently serves as a member at large for the Association of College and Research Libraries Instruction Section and as a member of the planning committee for Online Northwest, a conference focused on instruction and technology in libraries.

Gail Nicula

Gail Nicula graduated from the University of Michigan with a BA in geography and a MALS. She is a 2001 PhD graduate of Old Dominion University (ODU), with a public administration management focus. She was the chief of Joint Forces Staff College's Library Division from June 1991 to January 2013 and is now JFSC librarian emerita. Gail is an adjunct assistant professor in the College of Business and Public Administration at ODU. She has been an active member of the Special Libraries Association since 1975 as well as a member and DOD director of the Military Libraries Division of SLA. She is currently president of the Friends of the Old Dominion University Libraries, a member of the ODU Department of Urban Studies and Public Administration Advisory Board, and a member of the board of the ODU planning council. Her research and teaching area of interest is civic engagement.

Marilyn N. Ochoa

Marilyn N. Ochoa is the associate library director for Reference, Instruction, and Special Collections at the State University of New York at Oswego Penfield Library. Previously, she was at the University of Florida George A. Smathers' Libraries for 12 years, serving as both the interim head and assistant head education librarian and also as a digital services librarian. She currently serves on the Association of College and Research Libraries Board of Directors and is the chair for the Society for Information Technology and Teacher Education's Information Literacy Education Special Interest Group. Her research has focused on topics such as digital libraries, collaboration and teaching tools, learning spaces, usability, and embedded librarianship.

Timothy Peters

Timothy Peters is the director of Information Services in the Central Michigan University Libraries. His responsibilities include overseeing and facilitating the delivery of library resources and services to on-campus, off-campus, and online students and faculty. Timothy is active in state and national professional organizations, including the Distance Learning Section of the Association of College and Research Libraries, for which he currently serves as chair. He participates in several library and university committees, and he serves as the chairperson of the Central Michigan University Copyright Committee. Previously, he worked at North Hennepin Community College, Southwestern Michigan College, and Southern University. He received his BS from the University of Wisconsin-Stevens Point in 1986 and his MLIS from Louisiana State University in 1989.

Sue F. Phelps

Sue F. Phelps is a reference librarian at Washington State University Vancouver and has been providing reference and teaching services there since graduating from Emporia State University School of Library and Information Management in 2006. She teaches an online credit-bearing information literacy class and has increasingly promoted embedded services within her liaison departments. Her research interests include assessment of student learning, research methodologies as they apply to the library and library services, accessible information services to students with disabilities, and library anxiety.

Bridget A. Powell

Bridget A. Powell, Lt Col, USAF (ret.) has a MA in national security studies from California State University, San Bernardino and an online MA in distance education from University of Maryland University College; she is ABD for EdD in distance education from Regent University. She retired from the United States Air Force after more than 20 years. From January 2001 until she retired in December 2013, Bridget developed and then taught a blended-learning program to deliver an advanced level of joint professional military education to members of the National Guard and Reserve. She led more than 20 seminars through the demanding 40-week curriculum, which included periods of in-residence in addition to distance learning portions. Currently, Bridget works at University of Wisconsin-Madison in the Distance Education Professional Development unit of the Division of Continuing Studies.

Christina Sheley

Christina Sheley is the head of the Business/SPEA Information Commons at the Indiana University Bloomington Libraries, where she manages the library facility and staff, provides business information literacy instruction and research consultation, and oversees and manages the business and public policy collections. Her research interests include information literacy in the workplace and career, business reference sources and strategies, and virtual reference environments. Previously, Christina served as a reference and instruction librarian at Ivy Tech Community College in Indianapolis, Indiana and visiting librarian for anthropology, folklore, social work, and sociology at the Indiana University Bloomington Libraries. Her degrees include a BS in psychology and an MLS from Indiana University Bloomington.

Terri Pedersen Summey

Terri Pedersen Summey is a tenured faculty member at the rank of professor and the head of Public Services at Emporia State University Libraries. She received her MLIS from North Texas State University in 1987 and is currently working on a PhD in library and information management from Emporia State University. Since 1987, she has been a librarian at Emporia State University in a variety of roles. Throughout her career, Terri has been an active researcher, publishing variety of articles and presenting on various topics of interest at conferences. Her research interests include information seeking, distant library services, embedded librarianship, marketing library services, and library instruction.

Matt Upson

Matt Upson is a reference and instruction librarian at Emporia State University. He has earned a BS in secondary education from Oklahoma State University and an MLS from Emporia State University, and he is currently working toward an MA in instructional design and technology from Emporia State. He has taught courses on information literacy and library instruction for undergraduates and graduate students and enjoys collaborating with ESU's School of Library and Information Management, First Year Experience Program, and Intensive English Program. Matt is also the co-author of a series of comic book guides to research and information literacy skills. You can view some of his work at his website, Matt Upson—Librarian (http://upsonlibrarian. weebly.com/).

Alyssa M. Valenti

Alyssa M. Valenti is an electronic resources and web services librarian at Raritan Valley Community College located in Branchburg, New Jersey. She holds a BA in music from Slippery Rock University of Pennsylvania and an MLIS from The Catholic University of America. She is working towards a second master's degree in web design and development from the University of Denver. Alyssa first began work as an embedded librarian several years ago and has found online teaching to be one of her main areas of professional interest. Alyssa is involved in the New Jersey Library Association College and University Section Technology Committee, where she currently serves as co-chair. She is also involved in the Virtual Academic Library Environment of New Jersey (VALE) as a member of the Open Library Environment project committee. She presents at local conferences on topics such as connecting with students in person and online and hybrid and online information literacy.

Catrina Whited

Catrina Whited is a librarian at the Joint Forces Staff College (JFSC), National Defense University. Catrina provides reference services and instruction for the distance and in-residence students, staff, and faculty. She is the embedded librarian for the Advanced Joint Professional

Military Education (AJPME) distance program. Catrina has a BS in psychology from Ball State University and a MLS from Indiana University. Before coming to JFSC in January 2010, she was a clinical librarian at Eastern Virginia Medical School in Norfolk. Catrina co-presented at Blackboard World on the topic of embedded librarianship. While at JFSC, she has been recognized for distance library services, receiving the Commandant's Unsung Hero Award (2013) and the Outstanding Service Award (2012).